Cyber Security and Cyber Law

CYBER SECURITY AND CYBER LAW

Capt. S.L. Soni

Col. C.P. Bhargav

PRASHANT PUBLISHING HOUSE
DELHI-110094

Published by :
Prashant Publishing House
C-34, 28 Foota Road, Gali-3,
West Karwal Nagar, Delhi-110094
Phone : 011-22963970, Mob. : 9810396373
e-mail.: prashantpublishinghouse@gmail.com

Cyber Security and Cyber Law

First Published 2016

ISBN 978-93-80565-72-9

PRINTED IN INDIA
Published by Mr. R.K. Jha M/s Prashant Publishing House and Published at H.S. Offset House Press, Delhi.

Contents

Preface

Cyber security is a distributed problem partly because of the distributed nature of the underlying infrastructure and partly because industries, government and individuals all come at it with different perspectives. Under these circumstances regulation is best attempted from the bottom up, and legalisation, especially in the area of criminal law, should be sharply focused.

Cyber security is vital in the modern age of computers. Modern society, economy and critical industrial infrastructures are greatly dependent on computer networks and other IT solutions. Mounting cyber attacks on them is both cheaper and less risky than attacks with armies and bombs. Military forces of the advanced nations and their computer wizards have turned the internet into the battle arena of the future.

A well-balanced cyber security policy framework is highly complex. Such a policy framework has no bounds or limits—geographical or jurisdictional. It necessarily encompasses a full spectrum of business, societal, and governmental interests. Although cyber security policy will inevitably address grave concerns about national and global security, as well as well-organized criminal activity, it is fundamentally about creating the very underpinnings of stable economic growth and open, transparent, just, and vibrant societies.

A "network model"—essentially, a communications network—illustrates how actors in the public and private sectors can work together to manage future cyber risks. Rather than focus on institutions and functions, the focus is on processes, procedures, and information flows within these sectors. In other words, the framework promotes thinking in terms of functions, rather than titles or national or international institutions.

Cyber law gained popularity with the growth of the Internet and increased e-commerce. In India the course gained some momentum in early 2000, especially when the .com enterprise sprang up. Going into details, one realize that the scope of the subject is vast and deals with jurisdiction issues in internet related cases, contractual issues in cyber operations, e-commerce issues such as net banking.

The Internet came into existence, when a computer was first connected to a switch or routes and later to another computer. Many years elapsed before the concept took oil in academic circles and more time still before the general public grasped the potential of a worldwide computer network. Internet has revolutionized society to enable users to search for material, retrieve it, store it on their computers and open it with a single command.

This book fully introduces the theory and practice of cyber security. Comprehensive in scope, it covers applied and practical elements, theory, and the reasons for the design of applications and security techniques.

—*Editor*

1

Introduction

In a networked world, there are no real safe harbours—if you are on the network, you are available to everyone else on the network. As economies become more dependent on information and communications technology (ICT), they are becoming more vulnerable to network attacks (*e.g.*, threats to the Internet, as well as other private and public networks). The most serious cyber security risks are those that threaten the functioning of critical information infrastructures, such as those dedicated to financial services, control systems for power, gas, drinking water, and other utilities; airport and air traffic control systems; logistics systems; and government services.

Although the prevailing rationale for cyber security is to ensure a favourable climate for ICT investment, national and international security concerns are becoming equally important rationales. In the developing world, foreign direct investment as a whole may eventually be affected by the safety and integrity of data networks available to investors in host countries. In advanced industrial nations, basic public trust in modern economies and the electronic networks on which they depend is eroded when electronic data is stolen, becomes corrupted, or can no longer be authenticated.

Cyber security is thus a collective concern that is comprehensive in scope—the Internet has no national boundaries. Whereas security is typically regulated at the government level, cyber security is at once national, international, public and private in character. In fact, the capacity for cyber risk management and security lies largely in the hands of private entities that manage and operate most ICT infrastructure. Such security cannot be adequately assured by market forces or regulation; rather, it requires a novel mix of solutions involving a range of stakeholders working both in their own domains and in concert.

No single strategy, set of governance arrangements, or operational practices will be right for every country. However, it is imperative that countries develop improved lines of communication based on trust to discuss cyber security both within and among themselves.

SECURITY CHALLENGING

Efforts to identify intruders are critical both to the assessment of the challenge and the nature of the response. Potential intruders run the gamut from young hobbyists engaged in the equivalent of joy riding to terrorist organizations and nations that are intent on maximizing damage to the target.

The problem of identification is particularly difficult in a domain where maintaining anonymity is easy and there are sometimes time lapses between the intruder action, the intrusion itself, and the actual disruptive effects. Moreover, the consequences are not always commensurate with the objectives, in some cases falling short of what the intruders hoped to achieve, and in others going well beyond what they had envisaged.

There is a broad spectrum of potential intruders on the Internet and an almost equal number of motives for intrusions against organizations. Not surprisingly, this includes perpetrators conducting operations against other perpetrators.

As enticing as this prospect is, it does not mitigate the effects of such internecine rivalry. New and more sophisticated tools are often the result of such interplay. This sort of jousting can also provide valuable insights to analysts once it is recognized, but does not simplify the analytic task and puts an incredible strain on limited analytic/warning resources. With the continuing proliferation of sophisticated computer technologies into the mainstream population, attribution for an intrusion becomes more difficult by the day. The dynamism of the intruder population is itself a problem. On the one hand, success breeds imitation and the sophistication of readily available tools means that even those with limited skills can become intruders.

On the one hand, there is a certain degree of attrition in the intruder community. Indeed, there are many reasons why intruders might cease their activity, including increased maturity, a need to find gainful employment, and a perception of the rewards of working to increase network security rather than attack it. The implication, of course, is that the mix of agents threatening network security is changing as the nature of the Internet changes.

The vast majority of the intrusions are probably being conducted by nuisance hackers or "ankle-biters" who have limited objectives and are usually satisfied with the actual penetration of the system or conduct relatively harmless cyber-vandalism such as the defacement or alteration of web-sites. While aggravating to the target, no significant or lasting damage occurs. The more serious problem occurs when an intrusion is carried out by a more sophisticated intruder (either an individual or a group) whose objective is better defined and involves malicious intent. Motives for these sorts of intrusions are also as varied as the persons carrying them out. They range from greed to defined military strategy and doctrine, and all that falls in between.

Four of the more dangerous, and less well defined categories of intruder are governments conducting operations against other sovereign states, the organized terrorist group, insurgency or revolutionary groups, and organized crime. All these entities are beginning to appreciate the potential power, anonymity, and effectiveness of the Internet. There are myriad examples of governments instituting programmes for Computer Network Warfare. In the case of Russia, policy-makers consider the security of their information infrastructure so critical that–rhetorically at least-they equate an attack against it with a strategic nuclear strike (and have promised an appropriate response). As a result of the realization of the criticality of information infrastructures, computer warfare is now a part of the formal Russian Military Strategy and Doctrine. The same is true of organized terrorist groups. In fact, "most of the 30 top terrorist organizations identified by the U.S. government have web pages and use e-mail, and are "fairly well developed" at using the Internet."[Casciano] In many cases, dependence on technology is viewed as an Achilles Heel to be exploited by terrorist organizations.

Within the U.S., many of the more militant indigenous groups have discovered the power of the Internet and have well designed and effective Web sites. Indeed, militia and supremacist groups have had significant increases in membership since developing their Web pages. It is a natural progression from using the Internet for propaganda and recruiting to exploiting its potential as a weapon. There is also growing evidence that some of the active insurgency groups around the world are discovering the potential of the computer. It is just a matter of time until they discover the effect of a computer-generated attack against the infrastructure of the government they are fighting. Once that realization is made, cyber-attacks will likely become a weapon of choice for organizations intent on overthrowing an existing government. Disturbingly, Aum Shinrikyo, the group responsible for the Sarin gas attack on the Japanese subway, has increasingly been involved in the Japanese software industry!

Organized crime probably was the first of the sophisticated intruder threats to realize the power and value of the computer. In 1995, it was discovered that the Cali cartel had sophisticated state-of-the-art equipment for electronic eavesdropping, while smaller drug trafficking organizations in Colombia are using the Internet to pressure the Colombian government to change the policy of extraditing traffickers to the United States. Furthermore, the use of computers by organized crime organizations to garner illicit profits is well documented. However, some criminal efforts have gone beyond simple siphoning of funds and money laundering. Extortion of money from financial institutions by threatening to destroy or modify their computer databases is also evident. It is probable that at least some of these extortion operations are conducted by transnational criminal groups. Some of the extortion efforts go wrong–as did the effort to extort Bloomberg. In other cases, however, large payoffs are almost certainly made to the extortionist. It seems likely, therefore, that larger and potentially more dangerous operations should be anticipated.

The obvious challenge is to develop a capacity to identify and track the activities of these potential intruders with the goal of being able to provide predictive analysis and warning of intrusions. Some of the traditional intelligence techniques should apply to these threats, but new methodologies and the ability to contemplate new and complex concepts have to be developed concurrently. This will become even more important (and difficult) as perpetrators of increasing sophistication operate on the Internet. As motivations vary, so will the efforts of the individuals behind malicious operations to either conceal or reveal their responsibility. All of this complicates efforts to track responsible parties determine attribution. Nations and transnational criminal organizations, by their nature, will be diligent in their efforts to maintain anonymity. In some of these cases, identifying the intended victim may give valuable insight into tracking the intruder. Sometimes the target of an intrusion allows the analyst to rule out certain possible perpetrators. A multi-million dollar extortion plot against a major financial institution is probably not the work of a 13-year-old hacker working out of his bedroom. At the same time, however, many victims, especially within government or sensitive industries such as banking or insurance, often complicate the effort to track intruders because of their reluctance to report the incident. In other cases, such as politically motivated attacks, the perpetrators may want their identity known, but not their location. As such operations become more sophisticated, tracking the attack back to its point of origin will be a major challenge to the intelligence analysts involved. What is clear from all of this is that tracking intruders and gaining attribution is much more than just a technical challenge.

One difficulty, of course, is that there are legal constraints on intelligence collection, especially by the military and the national security establishment. Traditionally the focus of intelligence has been on foreign threats, and there are restrictions on intelligence activities directed against individuals or groups that are domestic in nature. Insofar as these groups are the focus of government attention, it is from the law enforcement community. This points to yet another problem: that of coordination and information sharing between the traditional national security agencies and the law enforcement community. Generally law enforcement focuses on individual cases and wants evidence that stands up in court;

intelligence agencies in contrast are concerned with protecting the sources of their information so that they can continue to use them. The problem with cyber-threats is that they fall in the gray area where crime and national security merge into one another.

Forms of Intrusion are Occurring

It is tempting to see intrusions in terms of a pyramid that goes from transient vulnerability probing and defacing web-sites at the base to large scale efforts to undermine the critical missions of an organization or the critical functions of a nation at the top-and to suggest that there is an inverse relationship between frequency and significance, with many trivial incidents and comparatively few of the more serious incidents. There are several difficulties with this however. The first is that probes that appear relatively insignificant could be a harbinger of more serious intrusions. The second is that there is sometimes a gap between intent and consequences–the effects and impact of an incident can either fall far short of what was intended, or far exceed what the perpetrator initially envisaged. This lack of congruence between limited intent and far-reaching consequences stems from the capacity of worms and viruses for infinite replication and multiplication combined with the seamless inter-connectivity of systems. Incidents such as the Love Bug cross the public-private divide and have an indiscriminate impact on corporations, governments, and private individuals irrespective of the initial target. In cases such as this, the consequences have less to do with targeting than with the ubiquity of a particular programme such as Microsoft Outlook that is used as the vector of transmission. In effect, the incident takes on its own momentum.

When the consequences are widespread, of course, the incident becomes very public and is the subject of much media and official commentary. In many other cases, however, there is far greater reticence about the scale, type and targets of attack. The analytic effort must successfully build a trust relationship for the collection of data across a broad variety of organizations. This trust relationship allows for observation of incidents from early probing and experimentation through widespread deployment of automated forms of intrusion. For example, in recent months

(June and July 2000) CERTÒ/CC has received reports of intrusions involving a wide variety of automated tools, ranging from simple viruses and system corruption toolkits through complex viruses designed to attack relatively hardened sites with low probability of detection and distributed tools designed to crash network infrastructure. Roughly 10%-25% of the CERT/CC reports involve viruses. Roughly 20%-40% are intrusions where the victim site cannot discern the type of the intrusion from available data. The remaining intrusions are a large number of other forms of intrusion, including compromise of system administration accounts, web defacements, reconnaissance attempts and misuse of computing resources.

Being Intruded Upon

Determining who are the victims of intrusions is, in some respects, an enormously significant part of the intelligence process. It is important-at least in those cases where attacks are not indiscriminate-to differentiate between public and private targets, to distinguish infrastructure targets from individual targets, to distinguish between intrusions that focus on targets of convenience and those that are much more precise and calculated. For example, existing analysis has shown a link between port scanning and certain types of later intrusions, but this needs to be more fully explored to provide for effective warnings. Profiling victims can sometimes play a critical role in determining the nature of the intrusion and the nature of the intruders. For this to be done, understanding is needed of the level of "background noise", probes and intrusion attempts occurring across the Internet. Once understood, it may be possible to isolate this activity from the more significant activity directed at a particular victim.

Victim profiles will be just as important, in terms of strategic intelligence analysis of the Internet, as profiling potential intruders. The more serious the intrusion, the more critical this sort of profiling will be. One of the potential hurdles to this effort, however, will be the natural tendency of the victim, whether private or public, to withhold sensitive or proprietary information. A few examples of this kind of reticence would be financial institutions withholding information about loses due to intrusions; companies failing to divulge the nature of an intrusion due to proprietary corporate data; or a government agency protecting information that is sensitive or even classified. Beyond simply protecting proprietary or sensitive data, there are also serious legal questions that have not yet been resolved in the courts or in the legislature. These include constitutional guarantees of privacy; contradictory national laws (or lack of laws) as perpetrators use the global network; laws limiting various governmental agency's efforts to track down the source of an intrusion, and the need to determine what is domestic and what is foreign.

If these barriers can be overcome, critical information will become available. Details of the victim's infrastructure, the nature of the intrusion, identity clues left by the intruder, network traffic flow as observed by the victim site, and intrusion tools left as artifacts on the victim hosts can all provide indispensable clues. Without such information, motivation becomes more difficult to define and profiling efforts will be seriously flawed. Some work has already been accomplished in this area by organizations involved in incident monitoring, including the members of the Forum of Incident Response and Security Teams (FIRST) community. Much more remains to be accomplished, however, as new cooperative agreements are forged and additional analytic efforts and methodologies are developed. Furthermore, while it is true that some of the legal restrictions are avoided by the voluntary nature of the cooperative relationships, they are by no means completely overcome. The keys to success seem to be twofold. First, the analytic organization has to prove itself to be a highly secure confidant, never disclosing victim identities while working to assist victims in recovering from intrusions. Second, it must return information that is of value to the victims, including information that might place the intrusion in a larger context as well as providing assistance in dealing with vendors or other sites. More simply put, the exchange of information must be in both directions. Experience with other organizations has shown that neither trustworthiness nor returned value alone is sufficient, but both appear to be required for effective information gathering with victims.

Beyond their reticence, victim organizations are often unaware of critical parts of their security stance. Available data suggests that victims are often not aware that their networks have been intruded upon. The effectiveness of installed security measures is often overestimated. Levels of trust given to users by computing practices are often unwarranted. All of this hampers both analysis and defence. One of the reasons that profiling the victims is so critical is that it provides insights in to motivations that can greatly assist analysts in predicting future intrusions under similar circumstances. This insight will need to incorporate identification of circumstances that facilitate or hamper intrusion. For example, K-12 educational institutions might offer a significant opportunity for intruders to stage their attacks, since many such institutions lack knowledgeable system administrators. However, such hosts may be removed from the network during summer break and other times when school is not in session. During the Year 2000 rollover, conditions for system intrusion were relatively poor not only because of the active presence of a large number of system administrators, carefully monitoring their systems, but also the significant number of alternative activities available to potential intruders. These examples serve to identify that there exist time-varying circumstances; further analysis is required to delineate these factors more fully.

CYBER-SECURITY RISKS

New risk factors and challenges to data and communications networks seem to be evolving as rapidly as the spread of high-speed Internet infrastructure. Among these compelling risks are: Computer worms and viruses. Debilitating worms and computer viruses have demonstrated destructive capabilities for a number of years, as evidenced by the damage caused by such programmes as Sasser, Blaster, Netsky, Welchia and Code Red. Organized criminal activity. The booming growth of ICT-services has spawned new gray-and black-market opportunities that organized criminal elements are exploiting for huge financial advantage. Financial institutions, for example, have already experienced significant losses through "phishing" and "pharming" operations.

The more significant the volume of revenues that flow over ICT-based networks, the greater will be the incentive for organized criminal elements to corrupt or economically exploit high-value data resources.

A global "black economy" can, for example, generate financing for terrorism, as well as "off-budget" funding for military, police, or national security agencies of nation states.

A NETWORK MODEL FOR CYBER SECURITY

A well-balanced cyber security policy framework is highly complex. Such a policy framework has no bounds or limits—geographical or jurisdictional. It necessarily encompasses a full spectrum of business, societal, and governmental interests. Although cyber security policy will inevitably address grave concerns about national and global security, as well as well-organized criminal activity, it is fundamentally about creating the very underpinnings of stable economic growth and open, transparent, just, and vibrant societies.

A "network model"—essentially, a communications network—illustrates how actors in the public and private sectors can work together to manage future cyber risks. Rather than focus on institutions and functions, the focus is on processes, procedures, and information flows within these sectors. In other words, the framework promotes thinking in terms of functions, rather than titles or national or international institutions.

The focus on information flows is intended to help policymakers and other stakeholders visualize the systemic, inter-related nature of cyber security and how the actions of individual entities are likely to impact the decisions and responses of other participants in the network. It should be noted that such a model may require significant changes in traditional roles of intelligence and (inter)national security agencies, requiring them to operate on a more collaborative, interinstitutional basis.

The network model is based on three types of nodes or groups of stakeholders (policymakers, policy implementers, and operational personnel), which exchange three types of information on cyber-security: assessments, responses, and policy. Information exchange occurs both among the nodes, as well as between individual nodes and their peers in outside organizations at all levels. The model operates in the same way at four different levels, as risk management generally has the same components, regardless of whether it is conducted at the level of a firm, industrial sector, nation, or international organization. First, it requires communications across "organizational" boundaries. Second, it requires information exchange between stakeholders at different levels in the same organization and with other organizations regarding threats that have been encountered and handled. Third, procedures for handling such incidents are required and, fourth, legal or law enforcement sanctions may need to be applied.

At the national level, the major network "nodes" are central coordinating bodies, telecommunications regulators and e-economy ministries, intelligence agencies, law enforcement bodies, and national and governmental Computer Emergency Response Teams (CERTs) and Information Sharing and Analysis Centres (ISACs).

The model works at the international level, where the top-level node is comprised of multinational firms, political and military alliances, which coordinate with such international bodies as the ITU, G8, and the United Nations and its specialized agencies. The implementation node in the international model is comprised of individual national ministries (telecommunications, intelligence, e-economy, and defence ministries, together with law enforcement bodies) and the operational level of national firms (including software and hardware vendors), CERTs, and national defence organizations.

The drivers of various information exchanges—the factors that shape and influence critical flows of information—include regulatory requirements, liability obligations, and market signals (*e.g.*, risk-related information through which the performance of a network may be influenced). Each national networked relationship may operate with its own unique set of additional drivers. Policymakers may further shape certain drivers to influence node behaviour and performance. It may be possible, for example, to strengthen the influence of market-related drivers by using government procurement policies. Insurance and rating companies may use liability strategies to influence the cost of capital and the incentives for security-related investments.

PROMOTING AUTOMATION OF SECURITY

Several commenters to the NOI discussed how they use automated methods to detect potentially dangerous web behaviour in order to prevent users from exposing themselves to risk suggesting that others could be doing the same. These entities said that they also were providing incentives to the owners of bad websites to reform.

By some accounts, approximately 80 percent of successful online attacks are attributable to known vulnerabilities that can be addressed with implementation of widely agreed upon industry standards, proper configurations and patches. As more computing services are based in the cloud and move further away from centralized enterprises, automating security will likely become even more important than it is today. Enterprise and service delivery will need to address vulnerabilities easily and quickly in order to assure customers of security. In particular, the automated sharing of threats and related signature information among government agencies, among the private sector, and between public and private entities is becoming more commonplace.

With leadership from NIST, the National Security Agency (NSA), DHS and the U.S. CIO Council, the U.S. government leads efforts to automate configuration and vulnerability management. The private sector has also begun to adopt automation protocols such as Security Content Automation Protocol (SCAP) and Continuous Monitoring. These efforts offer enterprises of all sizes the ability to better update security compliance at potentially lower costs and pave the way for future automated protocols.

The security automation initiative is a public/private collaboration that spans multiple government agencies, more than 30 security tool vendors, and a host of end user organizations. The goal of the project is to enable the efficient and accurate collection, correlation, and sharing of security relevant information including software vulnerabilities, system configurations and network events across disparate systems in the enterprise. Security automation work currently supports reference data such as the National Vulnerability Database (NVD), which provides software vulnerability information to users worldwide, and system configurations such as the U.S. government Configuration Baseline (USGCB) through the Technology Infrastructure Sub-committee of the CIO Council. Standardization of security information has created opportunities for innovation in the private sector and research into new information domains like network events and asset management is expected to foster additional innovation in those markets. Through procurement strategies, the U.S. government can continue to provide tools for leveraging security automation technologies, leveraging existing vendor investment while encouraging additional investment in support of new specifications and standards.

BASIC PRINCIPLES OF THE CYBER SECURITY STRATEGY

The Federal Government aims at making a substantial contribution to a secure cyberspace, thus maintaining and promoting economic and social prosperity in Germany. Cyber security in Germany must be ensured at a level commensurate with the importance and protection required by interlinked information infrastructures, without hampering the opportunities and the utilization of the cyberspace. In this context the level of cyber security reached is the sum of all national and international measures taken to protect the availability of information and communications technology and the integrity, authenticity and confidentiality of data in cyberspace.

Cyber security must be based on a comprehensive approach. This requires even more intensive information sharing and coordination. The Cyber Security Strategy mainly focuses on civilian approaches and measures. They are complemented by measures taken by the Bundeswehr to protect its capabilities and measures based on mandates to make cyber security a part of Germany's preventive security strategy. Given the global nature of information and communications technology, international coordination and appropriate networks focusing on foreign and security policy aspects are indispensable. This includes cooperation not only in the United Nations, but also in the EU, the Council of Europe, NATO, the G8, the OSCE and other multinational organizations. The aim is to ensure the coherence and capabilities of the international community to protect cyberspace.

CYBER-SECURITY AS SCIENCE

A science of cyber-security has to deal with a combination of peculiar features that are shared by no other area of study. First, the background on which events occur is almost completely created by humans and is digital. That is, people built all the pieces. One might have thought that computers, their software, and networks were therefore completely understandable. The truth is that the cyber-universe is complex well beyond anyone's understanding and exhibits behaviour that no one predicted, and sometimes can't even be explained well. On the positive side, the cyber-universe can be thought of as reduced to the 0s and 1s of binary data. Actions in this universe consist of sequences of changes to binary data, interleaved in time, and having some sort of locations in space. One can speculate as to why mathematics is so effective in explaining physics, but the cyber-world is inherently mathematical. Mathematics is a natural way for reasoning about it and this point of view is a theme that appears repeatedly in this report. Second, cyber-security has good guys and bad guys. It is a field that has developed because people have discovered how to do things that other people disapprove of, and that break what is thought to be an agreed-upon social contract in the material world. That is, in cyber-security there are adversaries, and the adversaries are purposeful and intelligent.

Thus, the reasoning in cyber-security has to be both about the constructed universe and the actions and reactions of the adversaries. Definitions and concepts will shift over time in cyber-security, as in all sciences. A successfully chosen name is a bridge between scientific knowledge and common sense, between new experience and old habits. The conceptual foundation of any science consists of a complicated network of names of things, names of ideas, and names of names. It evolves itself, and its projections on reality changes.

This quote echoes the observations of a presentation to JASON by Peter Gallison of Harvard in which he compared the type of science encountered in cyber security to a "Manichaean science" or science in the presence of adversaries. Particularly important for this type of science (and indeed any branch of science) was the development of a common language so that precise arguments could be formulated that addressed directly the problems of interest. We emphasize this point because the deninition of cyber-security itself is imprecise. The subject includes correctness properties like condentiality and integrity, and liveness properties such as are associated with denial-of-service attacks, together with a growing set of unpleasant surprises.

Security Degrades Over Time

We observed earlier that success in cyber-security requires constant attention. Not only do the threats and attacks change, but the old techniques tend to become less effective. Technology advances, and the properties of the security system become better understood.

Unix Passwords

The original UNIX passwords were up to 8 ASCII non-control characters. The passwords aren't stored directly. Rather hashes (some one-way function) are stored. In modern systems these hashes aren't easily read, but if a machine is compromised, then the hashes can be taken away, and one can attempt to break passwords by making up likely candidates, applying the one-way function, and seeing if the result matches any of the hashes. There are about 2 original UNIX passwords, which seemed like quite a lot at the time. Nowadays, one could imagine trying about 32 million guesses (2) per second on a single CPU core, so testing the entire space would only take about 3 days on 1,000 cores. That's not a particularly large computer, but the calculation is also embarrassingly parallel, so the 1,000 cores could be 1,000 machines in a (small) botnet. Or one could use 9,000 machines, still not a large botnet, and do the whole calculation in one night. For completeness we note that there has been a lot of work on making it harder to guess passwords; for instance, by using much slower one-way functions and much larger spaces. Another approach is to force people to use more complex passwords, but that has other sociological ramications which are unfortunately very difcult to deal with in terms of any science. An extreme version turned up in the recent Russian spy case, where "Ricci said the steganographic programme was activated by pressing controlalt-E and then typing in a 27-character password, which the FBI found written down on a piece of paper during one of its searches."

Lock Bumping

A second example of security decreasing over time comes from the common locks people use on doors. A simple technique called "lock bumping" makes all these locks quite easy to open with just a little practice. The locks were, of course, vulnerable, but it didn't much matter until the technique was popularized starting about 2005. There are plenty of explanatory videos online. The implication for cyber-security is that the nature of the attack can change over time. It will not in general be possible to anticipate all attacks. For this reason it becomes necessary to constantly survey the extant modes of attack to understand the nature of current technology as well as continually attack one's own systems in the hopes of finding heretofore undiscovered attacks.

The Role of Secrecy

All security regimes include some secrets. The TSA doesn't explain everything it is looking for; the credit card processors don't fully explain their criteria, and so on. In the computer science community, security by obscurity is generally considered bad, probably based on examples of awed cryptography. There seems to be little theoretical work on this subject. We mention a few examples of keeping (and not keeping) secrets.

Commercial anti-virus programmes, of the sort that run on your home computer, reveal some of the weaknesses of totally public defences. In principal, a malware author could just buy these, and adjust the malware until none of them detect it. The market has made this easier; there are online services that for a fee will run uploaded malware through a large number of commercial programmes, and report the result.

Game theory and economics teach us that keeping our private valuations secret sometimes adds value. Much effort has gone into auction mechanisms that get bidders to reveal their private valuations. On the other hand, under various circum stances, this "asymmetric information" can lead to lemon markets, where either no market exists, or only people who are forced to will trade in the market. Secrecy might also be required by the rules. For instance, the DoD might use logs of network trafc to tune its network defences. These logs might easily contain material that should not be made public. For these reasons, there may be some benefit in exploring the role an enhanced role for secrecy and obfuscation, particularly for DOD systems.

Finally, one might ask if keeping the source code secret adds much to security. First, there may be other reasons for keeping source code secret, such as the trade secrets incorporated in it. Certainly attackers with source code are likely to proceed differently, as they have a better chance of finding attacks based on logical errors, and this would be especially valuable for targeted attacks. On the other hand, there seems to be no particular shortage of effective attacks when source code is unavailable. But the code owner may have no realistic alternatives to making the source available. As an example consider the following announcement: "The agreement that we signed with the FSB is an extension of Microsoft's Government Security Programme (GSP)," Microsoft said in a statement on Friday. "The purpose of the GSP is to increase trust with national governments.

In the case of the Russian agreement, GSP participation will facilitate the development of the next generation of secured solutions for Russian government agencies based on the latest Microsoft technologies and Russian cryptography."

REGIONAL SECURITY SCENARIO, 2020

The regional situation is uncertain. Relations with China and Pakistan have not seen any major change. The J&K dispute and the boundary issue with China have not been resolved and tension prevails. Pakistan continues to flounder, with an unsettled situation in Afghanistan. India's continued growth in the region of 7 to 9% has generated an increased demand for water, energy resources and raw materials. Competition for resources and global business has grown. Global warming has had adverse environmental and demographic effects.

Back To The Future: 1997 To 2012

How bad will it be? An indicative answer emerges if we look back 15 years ago, i.e. 1996-97. Vast changes have taken place in this period. The rate and pace has been exponential in every field, whether it is the economy, the telephone revolution, industrial growth, standard of living, left- wing extremism, threat of terrorism, regional instability or the very way in which the government functions. In retrospect, despite the political instability of that period, India in a manner was much safer and insulated. Applying the same escalatory model, the security situation in 2020 is bound to be far more complex and dangerous. The standard of living will go up, however, it will be a more wired society with the e-governance, communication, power and transportation NWs, financial transactions, health and medicine, all dependent on the cyber domain. Alongside will be the aspect of increased transparency and instant dissemination or democratisation of information. All this will also create vulnerabilities and impact on security with disastrous consequences.

Events Of 30 June 2020

It has been a long hot day in a summer of internal and regional tension. At 1900 hours, when everyone is likely to call it a day, Internet traffic has broken down all over. CERT-In sends a message to the National Security Council Secretariat (NSCS) and the National Command Post that "Large-scale movement of several different zero day malware programs on Internet affecting critical infrastructure." Copies are sent globally. Soon thereafter come in reports from different ministries, state governments, establishments and institutions all over the country. Ascenario of what could happen in isolation, or in combination, in the next few hours, follows.

- Telephone NWs Collapse: BSNL exchanges hang and switching centres of mobile NWs (hardware mostly of Chinese origin) shut down or behave erratically. Defence NW routers are failing and rebooting. Close to 1000 million telephones are functioning erratically, Setting the Scene affecting every aspect of life. Worrisome messages abound. There is panic and uncertainty.
- Satellites out of Control: Communication, remote sensing and surveillance satellites are thrown out of gear. TV and other transmissions are disrupted, spreading alarm. The Indian GPS system, operationalised in 2016, malfunctions, affecting traffic and security systems.
- SCADA Systems Controlling Power Grids Collapse: The whole of North and Western India and some other regions suffer a power blackout. This affects all services, including rail and road traffic. There is chaos on the roads as traffic lights and systems are not working and the police are unable to cope with the rush-hour flow. Reports of accidents and traffic jams come in from all over the country. It also results in looting and police are unable to control the mobs.
- ATC Management Collapses: The international air traffic control (ATC) system, based on communication NWs and the Internet, is malfunctioning. Manual backup systems cannot meet the requirements. There is chaos at airports like Delhi and Mumbai which handle 2000 to 3000 flights a day. There are reports of at least three mid-air collisions from different parts of India. Rumours abound and there is widespread alarm and hysteria.
- Railway Traffic Control Collapses: The complex Indian Railway management and traffic system is clogged. Rail traffic on a number of routes is suspended due to power failure. There are reports of derailments and accidents. The metro and local train systems in major cities are also suffering from chaos.
- Oil Refineries: There are messages of explosions and devastating fires in major refineries with extensive damage

and loss of life. Pipelines are ruptured and oil flow is disrupted.

- Collapse of Financial Services: Dedicated denial of service (DDOS) attacks paralyse the financial systems. There is data theft, destruction and clogging. Millions of transactions are distorted. Banks cut off the systems from the Internet. ATM machines across the country hang. There is talk that money has run out with resultant panic.
- Collapse of Health and Civic Services: Health and civic services, dependent heavily on the Internet, collapse. Data in respect of emergency facilities are not available. Coupled with power and communication failures, the situation in hospitals is close to breaking point.
- Chemical Plants: The safety systems of chemical plants, governed by computer systems, fail. Lethal clouds of noxious gases billow, creating panic and deaths.
- Defence Forces: A large tri-service exercise, that has been underway, is in a crucial phase. There is complete dislocation due to failure of communication and GPS systems as also large-scale DDOS attacks. Amongst others:
  - Avionics on the latest MMCR aircraft blank out.
  - Computer-controlled systems in the C-17 not responding.
  - The ANTPQ-37 WLRs go into seizure.
  - The newly developed tri-service logistic management system is affected by virus and fails.

Damage and Loss

Millions of Indians have been affected. The loss of lives has been in thousands. Given the reach of the media as also the visibility that any such event would invite, it could, in a few hours constitute a disaster for the country far greater than all the wars and natural catastrophes put together. It would expose India as weak and unprepared, unsafe to live in, an unreliable business partner and vulnerable in every sense of the word. India's credibility as a country would be affected without a shot having been fired in anger. It is difficult to imagine a greater national humiliation.

The other aspect is that there would be no attributability. When investigated, these attacks will appear to have come from all over the globe as also servers within the country. Much as India would like to retaliate, there would be nobody who could be definitely identified. Even if identified, it could be denied. The foregoing scenario, which is only partial of what could happen, must serve as a wake-up call for urgent measures in this regard.

THE FUTURE OF CYBER SECURITY

The product of human ingenuity and innovation, cyberspace now delivers a range of critical services to more citizens around the world than ever before. Yet, the online world as we know it stands at the threshold of unprecedented change.

Being invited to speak at the EastWest Institute's Worldwide Security Conference in Brussels this week provided an opportunity to examine the needs faced by the global security community as we prepare to meet the needs of the Internet's next billion users. The International Telecommunication Union (ITU) reported that the number of Internet users reached the two billion threshold in March of this year and according to a Boston Consulting Group report, another billion are expected to come online in the next four years, bringing the total number of Internet users worldwide to about three billion by 2015.

Planning to ensure that our online world—cyberspace—is trustworthy, resilient and secure as we move into this uncertain future, policy leaders need to consider the fundamental changes that are occurring in cyberspace, and the policy issues that these changes will likely present and that will need to be addressed. Looking towards the future of three billion users, four factors will fundamentally change the future of cyberspace security: people, devices, data, and cloud services.

The Global Online Population Expands

The emergence of the next billion Internet users will impact security in two ways. Most important will be the impact of the demographic characteristics of these users. Consider that the next billion users will (1) be younger, (2) spend more time online,

(3) be more mobile, (4) see the world through social media and apps, and (5) make greater use of natural interfaces. These five factors could hasten the onset of totally digital lifestyles making connectivity seemingly as essential as oxygen. The next billion could also help foster new innovation in the development and application of technology.

Separately, however, this emerging user population also represents a greatly expanded "target rich" environment for cybercriminals that want to exploit their data, social networks, and devices via botnets or other means.

Internet of Things to Immersive Computing

These new users will require new devices. According to The Boston Consulting Group, the number of Internet-connected devices is predicted to exceed 15 billion—twice the world's population–by 2015, and to soar to 50 billion devices by 2020. "Devices" of course refers to more than smart phones, netbooks and tablets. It also systems such as smart grids, intelligent transportation, healthcare monitoring, smart manufacturing, and environmental sensors.

The advent of powerful wireless devices that both run infrastructure and deliver infrastructure services, including providing access to cloud services, means that cybercriminals and other threat actors need not merely target traditional, and increasingly protected, commercial software and consumer applications to execute attacks with significant consequences. Attackers may well target the embedded software, firmware and hardware in these devices to attack the infrastructure or seize control of the devices and turn them into sensors that can report status, collect personally identifiable information, or conduct other espionage.

Data: Rapid increases in Understanding

The striking growth in the number of users and devices will also produce an exponential growth in the amount of data that is being generated, stored, analysed and transformed into innovation and knowledge. Analysing large data sets—so-called big data—will become a key basis of competition, underpinning new waves of productivity growth, innovation, and consumer surplus, according to research by MGI and McKinsey's Business Technology Office. However, such data sets also represent attractive targets for organized cyber criminals and other threat actors. From a security standpoint, safeguarding these huge data sets, protecting privacy and integrity, will require concerted global effort requiring collaboration among governments, the private sector, and users.

Cloud Computing: The Information Society Enabler

With an exponentially growing community of increasingly mobile users, cloud computing will commensurately grow in importance. It will fundamentally change how businesses operate, how every manner of services are delivered, and even how lives are lived. On the positive side, the security best practices implemented by an effective cloud provider may rival or surpass the measures that cloud customers might themselves be able to provide, resulting in enhanced security. Yet there are global issues that will need to be addressed in terms of transparency and jurisdiction to enable cloud services that are both secure and scalable to service the needs of this expanded user community across multiple countries.

Reducing the Cyber-attack Surface

Reducing the cyber-attack surface can be achieved by industry and government working inpartnership to make the ICT infrastructure less susceptible to attack and compromise. One important way to achieve this is through concerted action to address risks in the supply chain for information and communications technology products and services. Vendors and service providers need to build and maintain world-class approaches to secure software and hardware development methodologies. Microsoft began this journey over 10 years ago and has openly shared its Security Development Lifecycle. The nonprofit alliance SAFECode provides a platform for companies to share, both within the software development community and more broadly, information on secure software development techniques that have proven to be effective as well as those that have not. Industry needs to do more.

For their part, governments need to understand the nature of ICT supply chain risk more clearly and work collaboratively with one another and with vendors to develop a common risk management framework rooted in core principles that both address supply chain integrity concerns and preserve the fruits of global free trade. Such a system should be risk-based,transparent, flexible, and should recognize the realities of reciprocal treatment in the global economic environment.

Improving Internet Health

Improving Internet health requires a global, collaborative approach to protecting people from the potential dangers of the Internet. Despite the best efforts at education and protection, many consumer computers host malware and may be part of a "botnet," unbeknownst to their legitimate owners. There is currently no concerted mechanism to shield users from or help them mitigate these risks. Such infected computers do not simply expose their owners' valuable information and data; they place others at risk too. This threat to greater society makes it is essential that the technology ecosystem take collective action to combat it.

Work has been underway in industry circles to build cooperation among various stakeholder groups including ISPs, software vendors, and others; to leverage investments made in key regions of the world; and to create a future roadmap for an Internet health system. The active discussions of cyber security policy and legislation now underway in many nations afford a ripe opportunity to promote this Internet health model. As part of this discussion, it is important to focus on building a socially acceptable model. While the security benefits may be clear, it is important to achieve those benefits in a way that does not erode privacy or otherwise raise concern.

2

Cyber Crime and Law

Information Technology solutions have paved a way to a new world of internet, business networking and e-banking, budding as a solution to reduce costs, change the sophisticated economic affairs to more easier, speedy, efficient, and time saving method of transactions. Internet has emerged as a blessing for the present pace of life but at the same time also resulted in various threats to the consumers and other institutions for which it's proved to be most beneficial. Various criminals like hackers, crackers have been able to pave their way to interfere with the internet accounts through various techniques like hacking the Domain Name Server (DNS), Internet Provider's (IP) address, spoofing, phishing, internet phishing etc. and have been successful in gaining "unauthorised access" to the user's computer system and stolen useful data to gain huge profits from customer's accounts.

Intentional use of information technology by cyber terrorists for producing destructive and harmful effects to tangible and intangible property of others is called "cyber crime". Cyber crime is clearly an international problem with no national boundaries. Hacking attacks can be launched from any corner of the world without any fear of being traced or prosecuted easily. Cyber terrorist can collapse the economic structure of a country from a place where that country might not have any arrangements like "extradition treaty" to deal with that criminal. The only safeguard would be better technology to combat such technology already evolved and known to the Hackers. But that still has threat of being taken over by the intellect computer criminals.

This paper contributes an understanding of the effects of negative use of Information technology, and how far the present law in India is successful in dealing with the issue, and what way is the legal structure lagging to curb the crime. Possible changes needed in the system and the ways to combat cyber terrorism having safe and trustworthy transactions.

Though there are many techniques evolved to curb the criminal activities by cyber terrorists but still the problem persists in legal structure and has failed to produce a deterring effect on the criminals.

If the suggestions are undertaken in light of conclusion there can be a better co-ordination among various national and international agencies to make the system more efficient, and Information Technology Act 2000 more secured and trustworthy.

It can still be held good for the objects it had existed to provide the benefits to the society. This paper is contributive of the fact that the till the crime rate is not curbed technology cannot produce adequate benefits for which it's been created.

Cyber terrorists usually use the computer as a tool, target, or both for their unlawful act either to gain information which can result in heavy loss/damage to the owner of that intangible sensitive information.

Internet is one of the means by which the offenders can gain such price sensitive information of companies, firms, individuals, banks, intellectual property crimes (such as stealing new product plans, its description, market programme plans, list of customers etc.), selling illegal articles, pornography etc. this is done through many methods such as phishing, spoofing, pharming, internet phising, wire transfer etc. and use it to their own advantage without the consent of the individual.

Many banks, financial institutions, investment houses, brokering firms etc. are being victimised and threatened by the cyber terrorists to pay extortion money to keep their sensitive information intact to avoid huge damages. And it's been reported that many institutions in US, Britain and Europe have secretly paid them to prevent huge meltdown or collapse of confidence among their consumers.

MEASURES TO CURB THE CRIME

Though by passage of time and improvement in technology to provide easier and user friendly methods to the consumer for make up their daily activities, it has lead to harsh world of security threats at the same time by agencies like hackers, crackers etc. various Information technology methods have been introduced to curb such destructive activities to achieve the main objects of the technology to provide some sense of security to the users. Few basic prominent measures used to curb cyber crimes are as follows:

Encryption: This is considered as an important tool for protecting data in transit. Plain text (readable) can be converted to cipher text (coded language) by this method and the recipient of the data can decrypt it by converting it into plain text again by using private key. This way except for the recipient whose possessor of private key to decrypt the data, no one can gain access to the sensitive information.

Not only the information in transit but also the information stored on computer can be protected by using Conventional cryptography method. Usual problem lies during the distribution of keys as anyone if overhears it or intercept it can make the whole object of encryption to standstill. Public key encryptograpy was one solution to this where the public key could be known to the whole world but the private key was only known to receiver, its very difficult to derive private key from public key.

Syncronised Passwords: These passwords are schemes used to change the password at user's and host token. The password on synchronised card changes every 30-60 seconds which only makes it valid for one time log-on session. Other useful methods introduced are signature, voice, fingerprint identification or retinal and biometric recognition etc. to impute passwords and pass phrases

Firewalls: It creates wall between the system and possible intruders to protect the classified documents from being leaked or accessed. It would only let the data to flow in computer which is recognised and verified by one's system. It only permits access to the system to ones already registered with the computer.

Digital Signature: Are created by using means of cryptography by applying algorithms. This has its prominent use in the business of banking where customer's signature is identified by using this method before banks enter into huge transactions.

Investigations and Search Procedures

Section 75 of Information Technology Act, 2000 takes care of jurisdictional aspect of cyber crimes, and one would be punished irrespective of his nationality and place of commission of offence. Power of investigation is been given to police officer not below the rank of Deputy Superintendent of police or any officer of the Central Government or a State Government authorised by Central Government. He may enter any public place, conduct a search and arrest without warrant person who is reasonably expected to have committed an offence or about to commit computer related crime. Accused has to be produced before magistrate within 24 hours of arrest. Provisions of Criminal Procedure Code, 1973 regulate the procedure of entry, search and arrest of the accused.

Problems Underlying Tracking of Offence

Most of the times the offenders commit crime and their identity is hard to be identified. Tracking cyber criminals requires a proper law enforcing agency through cyber border co-operation of governments, businesses and institutions of other countries. Most of the countries lack skilled law enforcement personnel to deal with computer and even broader Information technology related crimes. Usually law enforcement agencies also don't take crimes serious, they have no importance of enforcement of cyber crimes, and even if they undertake to investigate they are posed with limitation of extraterritorial nature of crimes.

How Efficient Is Information Technology Act 2000?

It can't be disputed that Information Technology Act, 2000 though provides certain kinds of protections but doesn't cover all the spheres of the I.T where the protection must be provided. Copyright and trade mark violations do occur on the net but Copy Right Act 1976, or Trade Mark Act 1994 are silent on that which specifically deals with the issue. Therefore have no enforcement machinery to ensure the protection of domain names on net. Transmission of e-cash and transactions online are not given protection under Negotiable Instrument Act, 1881. Online privacy is not protected only Section 43 (penalty for damage to computer or computer system) and 72 (Breach of confidentiality or privacy) talks about it in some extent but doesn't hinder the violations caused in the cyberspace.

Even the Internet Service Providers (ISP) who transmits some third party information without human intervention is not made liable under the Information Technology Act, 2000. One can easily take shelter under the exemption clause, if he proves that it was committed without his knowledge or he exercised due diligence to prevent the offence. It's hard to prove the commission of offence as the terms "due diligence" and "lack of knowledge" have not been defined anywhere in the Act. And unfortunately the Act doesn't mention how the extra territoriality would be enforced. This aspect is completely ignored by the Act, where it had come into existence to look into cyber crime which is on the face of it an international problem with no territorial boundaries.

Data Protection

Information stored on the owner of the computer would be his property and must be protected there are many ways such information can be misused by ways like 'unauthorized access, computer viruses, data typing, modification erasures etc. Legislators had been constantly confronted with problem in balancing the right of the individuals on the computer information and other people's claim to be allowed access to information under Human Rights. The first enactment in this regard was Data Protection Act by Germany in the year 1970. This was widely accepted by the world and also contributed to the Information Technology Act.

The origin of laws on date protection dates back to 1972 when United Kingdom formed a committee on privacy which came up with ten principles, on the bases of which data protection committee was set up. Data Protection Act, 1984 (DPA) was United Kingdom's response to the Council of Europe Convention 1981, this Act lacked proper enforcement mechanism and has done little to enforce individual's rights and freedoms. European Union directive in 1995, European Convention of Human Rights (ECHR), Human Rights Acts, and further introduction of Data Protection Act, 1998 have done much in the field of Data protection in today's date. Data Protection Act has following aims and objectives:

Personal information shall only be obtained for lawful purpose, it shall only be used for that purpose, mustn't be disclosed or used to effectuate any unlawful activity, and must be disposed off when the purpose is fulfilled.

Though Data Protection Act aims at protecting privacy issues related to the information but still we find no mention of the word "privacy" in the Act, nor is it defined, further the protection comes with various exemptions, including compulsory notification from the Commissioner in certain cases of the personal data. Due to the change in the regime of information technology for the date European Convention came, on which the Act is based amendments in the Act is advised for matching the present situation and curbing the crime in efficient way.

There is no Data Protection Act in India, the only provisions which talks about data protection are Section 72 and Section 43 of Information Technology Act, 2000. There must be a new Law to deal with the situation for a person to know that the Controller is processing his data concerning him and also that he must know the purpose for which it has been processed. It is a fundamental right of the Individual to retain private information concerning him provided under Article 21 of the Indian Constitution, which says: "No person shall be deprived of his life or personal liberty except according to procedure established by law". And due to the increasing trend of the Crime rate in the field separate legislation is required in this context for better protection of individuals.

No one can deny the positive role of the cyber space in today's world either it be political, economic, or social sphere of life. But everything has its pro's and corns, cyber terrorists have taken over the technology to their advantage. To curb their activities, the Information Technology Act 2000 came into existence which is based on UNICITRAL model of Law on e-commerce. It has many advantages as it gave legal recognition to electronic records, transactions, authentication and certification of digital signatures, prevention of computer crimes etc. but at the same time is inflicted with various drawbacks also like it doesn't refer to the protection of Intellectual Property rights, domain name, cyber squatting etc. This inhibits the corporate bodies to invest in the Information technology infrastructure. Cases like Dawood and Quattrochi clearly reveals the problem of enforceability machinery in India. Cryptography is new phenomenon to secure sensitive information. There are very few companies in present date which have this technology. Other millions of them are still posed to the risk of cyber crimes. There is an urgent need for unification of internet laws to reduce the confusion in their application. For e.g. for publication of harmful contents or such sites, we have Indian Penal Code (IPC), Obscenity Law, Communication Decency law, self regulation, Information Technology Act 2000, Data Protection Act, Indian Penal Code, Criminal Procedure Code etc but as they deal with the subject vaguely therefore lacks efficient enforceability mechanism. Due to numerous Laws dealing with the subject there lays confusion as to their applicability, and none of the Law deals with the subject specifically in toto.

To end the confusion in applicability of Legislation picking from various laws to tackle the problem, i would suggest unification of laws by taking all the internet laws to arrive at Code which is efficient enough to deal with all the problems related to internet crimes. Although these legislations talk about the problem but they don't provide an end to it. There's need for a one Cyber legislation which is co-ordinated to look after cyber crimes in all respects. With passage of time and betterment of technology in the present date, has also resulted in numerous number of Information technology related crimes therefore changes are suggested to combat the problem equally fast.

Crucial aspect of problem faced in combating crime is that, most of the countries lack enforcement agencies to combat crime relating to internet and bring some level of confidence in users. Present law lacks teeth to deter the terrorist groups for committing cyber crimes if you see the punishment provides by the Act it's almost ineffective, inefficient and only provides punishment of 3 years at the maximum.

Harsher laws are required at this alarming situation to deal with criminals posing threat to security of funds, information, destruction of computer systems etc. Data protection, by promotion of general principles of good information practice with an independent supervisory regime, would enable the law to maintain sufficient flexibility to achieve an appropriate balance between the need to protect the rights of the individuals and to have a control over the way their personal information have been used would be helpful in this increasingly networked economy. Just having two provisions in the Information Technology Act, 2000 for protection of data without any proper mechanism for to tackle the crime makes their mention in the Act redundant.

Information Technology Act is applicable to all the persons irrespective of their nationalities (i.e. to non-citizens also) who commits offence under the Information Technology Act outside India, provided the act or conduct constituting the offence or contravention involves computer, computer systems, or computer networks located in India under Section 1 and Section 75 of the Information Technology Act, but this provision lacks practical value until and unless the person can be extradited to India. Therefore it's advised that we should have Extradition treaties among countries. To make such provisions workable.

It's like 'eye for an eye' kind of situation where the technology can be curbed only by an understanding of the technology taken over by cyber terrorists. Even if the technology is made better enough to curb the computer related crime there is no guarantee if that would stay out of reach of cyber terrorists. Therefore Nations need to update the Law whether by amendments or by adopting sui generic system. Though Judiciary continues to comprehend the nature of computer related crimes there is a strong need to have better law enforcement mechanism to make the system workable.

THE EVOLUTION OF CYBER CRIME

Cyber crime has been an artifact of computer systems for a number of decades. However, the phenomenon of cyber crime did not truly come into being until the advent of the computer network.

Information moving from across physical distances was much easier to intercept than that on a standalone system. Moreover, attaching a system to a network provided would-be criminals an access point into other vulnerable systems attached to the same network. But even in the early days of networked computing, cyber crime was rare.

The relative rarity of computers, combined with the highly specialised knowledge needed to use them prevented widespread abuse. The cyber crime problem emerged and grew as computing became easier and less expensive. Cyber crime evolved from hacking of another system, the public switched telephone network. These phone "phreakers" developed methods of breaking into phone systems to make long distance calls for free. Perhaps, the most famous of these phreakers was John Draper, who discovered that toy whistles given away with Cap'n Crunch cereals generate a 2600- hertz sound, which can be used to access AT&T's long-distance switching system. Draper proceeded onto build a "blue box" which, when used together with the whistle, allowed phreakers to make free calls. Shortly after, wire fraud in the United States escalates. Draper was arrested on toll fraud charges in 1972 and sentenced to five years' probation. In the 1970's, the first affordable personal computers became available on the market, and it was shortly thereafter that the first bulletin board service, or BBS, was established.

Early hackers and phreakers seized on the BBS idea as a way to communicate with one another and share their tricks and techniques. Still, even as the Internet grew, getting online was far from easy. Designers of operating systems at the time had no idea how important the Internet would be. They didn't design software with built-in functionality to connect to an Internet service provider. ISPs were few and far between, and very pricey. For a user to connect to the Internet, they would have to obtain, install and configure a number of settings that could be tricky for the casual user. Online services such as CompuServe, AOL, and Prodigy helped to solve this problem. They provided their subscribers with software that would enable them to connect to their service with relative ease. In 1986, alarmed by the larger numbers of computer break-ins, the US government passes the Computer Fraud and Abuse Act.

This made it a crime to illegally break into computer networks. The law did not apply to juveniles. Robert Morris became the first person to be convicted under the new Computer Fraud and Abuse Act of 1986. Morris was punished for his Internet worm, which crashed 6,000 Net-linked government and university computers. Price was still an issue, though, but in the early 1990's, costs for the user dropped to around $3 an hour, and eventually, to less than $20 a month for unlimited usage, allowing not only the Internet to grow exponentially, but also for criminals to learn how to effectively exploit the system. Computers are now ubiquitous and many tasks performed in the daily lives of users depend on computers and computer networks.

The Internet has become a mission-critical infrastructure for governments, companies, and financial institutions. Computers and networks are used for controlling and managing manufacturing processes, water supplies, the electric power grid, air traffic control systems, and stock market systems, to mention a few. A benefit of online services that attracts criminals is the anonymity they offer, making it easier for criminals to change identities and cover their tracks. The rapid growth of the Internet in the mid 1990's gave rise to cyber crime as we know it today.

Evolution of Motivation

Ten years ago, hackers were dabbling on other systems to only see how they were configured and operated. Most of the time they did not cause any damage. Unfortunately, the circumstances have changed and become incredibly malicious. Instead of being driven by curiosity, hackers today are driven mostly by financial motives. The value of Internet activities and the wealth stored on computers is the source of the attraction. While e-commerce represents only a fraction of total commerce, it reached almost $70 billion in the U.S. at the end of 2004, an increase of 24 per cent over 2003. A third of the U.S. workforce is online, roughly 50 million people, an important consideration since more than half of e-commerce transactions are made from work. Sixty million residents of North America, almost half of the Internet user population in Canada and the U.S., have online bank accounts. The combination of banking and commerce draws criminals more than anything else.

EVOLUTION AND PROFILE OF THE ATTACKER

There is a growing convergence of technically savvy computer crackers with financially motivated criminals. Historically, most computer crime on the Internet has not been financially motivated: it was the result of either curious or malicious technical attackers, called crackers. This changed as the Internet became more commercialised. Financially motivated actors, spammers and fraudsters, soon joined crackers to exploit this new potential goldmine. Criminals have fully adopted the techniques of crackers and malicious code authors. These are financially motivated people, who pursue their goals considerably more aggressively than an average cracker. They have the monetary means to buy the required expertise to develop very sophisticated tools to accomplish their goals of spamming and scamming the public.

The perpetrators of these attacks vary considerably. At the low end are script kiddies, who are usually unsophisticated users that download malicious software from hacker web sites and follow the posted instructions to execute an attack on some target. These attacks are often only annoyance attacks, but they can be more severe. At the next level are hackers who are trying to prove to their peers or to the world that they can compromise a specific system, such as a government web site. Next are insiders, who are legitimate users of a system that either access information that they should not have access to or damage the system or data because they are disgruntled. Insiders are often less knowledgeable then hackers, but they are often more dangerous because they have legal access to resources that the hackers need to access illegally.

Next are organisational level attacks. In this case, the organisation's resources are used to get information illegally or to cause damage or deny access to other organisations to further the attacking organisation's gain. These can be legitimate organisations, such as two companies bidding on the same contract where one wants to know the other's bid in order to make a better offer. They could also be criminal organisations that are committing fraud or some other illegal activity. At the highest level is the nation state that is trying to spy on or cause damage to another state. This level used to be called "national lab" attackers, because the attackers have a substantial amount of resources at their disposal, comparable to those that are available to researchers at a national lab, such as Los Alamos Laboratory or Lawrence Livermore Laboratory. After the September 11, 2001 terrorist attacks on the World Trade Center, the idea of nation state level cyber attacks being carried out by terrorists became a big concern.

Malware and Threat Evolution

Viruses started appearing on dedicated networks such as the ARPANET in the 1970s. The boom in personal computers, initiated by Apple in the early 1980s, led to a corresponding boom in viruses. In1981 the first virus in the wild came into being even before the experimental work that defines viruses of today. Founded on the Apple II operating system, it was spread on Apple II floppy disks containing the operating system. While the viruses of the 1980s targeted a variety of operating systems and networks, most viruses today are written to exploit vulnerabilities in the most commonly used software: Microsoft Windows. The increasing number of vulnerable users is now being actively exploited by virus writers.

The first malicious programmes may have shocked users, by causing computers to behave in unexpected ways. However, the viruses which started appearing in the 1990s present much more of a threat: they are often used to steal confidential information such as bank account details and passwords. Classic file viruses reigned supreme in the 90s; however they have almost totally disappeared today. There are currently about 10 file viruses that are still active.

They experience peaks of activity when they infect the executable files of worms: the file virus will then travel as far as the infected worm file. For instance, samples of MyDoom, Netsky and Bagle that are infected by file viruses such as Funlove, Xorala, Parite or Spaces. On the whole, there is very little danger that classic file viruses will cause any major epidemics. The trends in epidemiology that are observed today have their primary roots in the second half of 2003. Internet worms Lovescan, Sobig, Blaster, Slammer and Sobre all not only caused global epidemics, but also profoundly changed the malware landscape. Each of these malicious programmes set new standards for virus writers. In 2003, we witnessed the emergence of an attack type that combines exploitation of server and workstation vulnerabilities with the characteristics of virus and Trojan horses.

By using more efficient attack vectors and, therefore, minimizing the human effort required to deliver attacks and use the compromised systems, the risks related to newly discovered vulnerabilities moved up in the risk measurement scale. Optimising costs, achieving greater efficiency, and applying the minimum necessary effort to accomplish goal are central concepts to modern day life. Therefore, it is not difficult to identify the same approach in the vulnerability exploitation techniques and attack trends. The appearance of many efficient worms as a result of attackers' attempts to maximize their bang for the "bug" are examples. They compromise a very large number of systems with minimal effort. The steadily increasing amount of cross-site scripting and SQL injection vulnerabilities discovered and disclosed during 2003 point to another path of less resistance into vulnerable networks. These vulnerabilities have rather simple ways of exploitation and they provide casual attackers with a high yield, direct access to internal networks, compromise of database servers and their content, and indirect ways of attacking unsuspecting users of third-party systems.

The level of sophistication in worms seen in 2003 and the installation of backdoors and tools with elaborate communication protocols and auto update capabilities indicate that attackers are trying to optimise the management of large amounts of newly acquired assets. Classic e-mail worms are on the decline, with network and instant messaging worms exploiting relatively lax security to take their place in early 2005. IM worms were at the peak of their development in spring and summer 2005, and showed the highest growth rate among all classes of network worms. In the first six months of this year, an average of 28 new IM worms were detected every month. It should be stressed here that when

P2P worms were at the peak of their evolution in 2003, approximately 10 new variants were detected every week. However, the situation changed afterwards and the flood of IM worms suddenly dried up. AOL and MSN, both of which have proprietary IM clients, were the main targets for such worms. Both companies took measures to protect their users. Firstly, by blocking the transmission of files with names and extensions which were known to be used by IM worms. In spite of the fact that IM worms rarely use file transmission as a propagation method, the move did have a noticeable effect.

The next step was to block the worms' main method of propagation, hyperlinks leading to files containing the body of the worm. These actions closed the majority of security loopholes being exploited by virus writers. And most importantly, they closed the loopholes which IM worms based on source code circulating in the computer underground used. Most of the code used in IM worms is of fairly low quality. The majority of these worms are created by script kiddies who have no significant programming skills. When the off the shelf code was no longer effective, these self styled virus writers were unable to create new propagation methods on their own, and this led to a sharp drop in the number of new worms.

Improved antivirus technologies, and increased user awareness of security issues are clearly forcing virus writers and hackers to use new approaches to access users' information and systems, mostly in the form of phishing attacks. Malicious users are starting to use viruses which propagate by exploiting vulnerabilities within web applications, particularly Internet Explorer, rather than network and e-mail worms. One consequence of this is an increase in the number of compromised sites. Exploits for IE are placed on compromised sites, which means that users who visit these sites will have trojan programmes downloaded to their machines.

To date Linux-based platforms have mainly been the victims of rootkit attacks and simple file viruses. However, the growing number of publicised vulnerabilities means that the increased number of users switching to Linux will not remain untouched by new malware. Handheld devices, such as PDAs and cell phones are almost household appliances for many people. Virus writers have been quick to take advantage of their growing popularity. The first trojan for Palm OS appeared in September 2000. And finally, the increasing interest in on-line games, with the potential profits to be made in this area, make it more than likely that malicious code designed to steal such information will continue to evolve rapidly. The first Trojan for gaming consoles had also been discovered. Sony PlayStationPortable was the first victim - the Trojan targeting this device deleted system files causing the console to cease functioning correctly. This behaviour is very similar to Trojans for mobile phones. It may be that these new Trojans for gaming consoles signal the start of a new interest among virus writers.

Evolution of Exploit Frameworks

Cyber criminals increasingly rely on powerful exploitation frameworks to launch their attacks. Free tools like Metasploit and commercial tools like CORE IMPACT and Immunity CANVAS have revolutionised the attackers' methodology. Previously, upon finding a vulnerability, the attacker either had to create custom exploit code from scratch or scour the Internet to find such code to exploit the hole. Today, instead of scraping together a bunch of individual exploits, these integrated exploit frameworks include around one hundred or more exploits to compromise target systems. One property of the exploit tools is the separation of the exploit from the payload.

An exploit is the software that takes advantage of a flaw, letting the attacker load and execute a programme of the attacker's choosing. The code triggered by the exploit is known as the payload. Old-fashioned attacks tightly bundled exploits and payloads together. An attack might exploit a database buffer overflow with the purpose of adding a user for the attacker to the local administrators group. But, with this tight integration, the attackers were stuck with the given payload attached to the given exploit for the given vulnerability. Taking the payload from one attack and embedding it with another exploit required some serious machine-language fine tuning, and was often impossibly difficult. To remedy the situation, today's exploit frameworks include an arsenal of different exploits and an arsenal of different payloads, each offering a different effect the attacker wants to have on the victim. So today, the attacker can use a tool like Metasploit to choose an exploit, such as a buffer overflow in lsass.exe, originally used by the Sasser worm last year. Then, the attacker can choose from more than a dozen different payloads. Metasploit packages the payload with the exploit, and then launches it at the target. The real effect of these frameworks in separating the exploits and the payloads is now reverberating through the industry. Developers who create fresh exploits for new flaws don't have to reinvent the payload wheel every time. Thus, they can focus their time on perfecting their exploits and producing them much more quickly. Moreover, those developers who don't focus on exploits can now zoom in on the production of high-quality payloads.

Defence Evolution

Computer security has been reactive for most part. That is, system administrators and security professionals are usually reacting to the latest attack. After they fix the vulnerability that allowed the attack, the attackers look for new vulnerabilities to exploit for new attacks. Trends in worm and virus delivery mechanisms and infection speed have also changed. Not long ago, a virus warning and the patch to vaccinate computers against it would appear days before the virus began spreading. Today, too often the first sign of a virus is that a part of the network goes down. Flash worms such as SQL Slammer have paved the way for future worms to carry payloads that directly target their victims and wreak havoc on government, business, and societal structures. Existing technologies such as firewalls, intrusion detection systems, intrusion protection systems, virtual private networks (VPNs), and virus scanners provide integrated security solutions.

Not surprisingly, security has become a massive industry, and it is now a focal point for virtually every organisation. Proactively eliminating just the known threats places an impractical burden on existing server and network infrastructures. Eliminating unknown threats or zero day attacks, which as the name implies reveal themselves only when they first occur, requires real-time solutions that can identify unique attacks without overburdening the network with security and management overhead. The imagination of social engineers knows no bounds. Social engineers are highly aware of Internet user psychology and are well able to exploit current anxieties. In connection with this it should be stressed that the attempts of some companies to create a browser which is capable of determining the veracity of any site visited, or a browser which protects information stored on the potential victim machine is very hard to be one hundred per cent successful.

CYBER VICTIMS

Early exploits were mass attacks which affected the whole Internet community. Between 1996 and 2000, high-profile web sites such as eBay, the U.S. Department of Commerce, UNICEF, the New York Times and Microsoft all fell victim to hackers or defacers. The Melissa virus caused company e-mail servers to shut down. A fraudulent web page that was designed to appear to be a Bloomberg financial news story resulted in the shares of a small tech company increasing 31 per cent in response to the "news." As the new millennium began, a huge, distributed DoS attack shut down major Web sites such as Yahoo! and Amazon. Apache, RSA Security, and Western Union were hacked. The Code Red worm attacked thousands of web servers, and the Sircam virus hit e-mail accounts all over the world. As of today, spam accounts for fifty per cent of all e-mail sent, a staggering 12.4 billion messages a day, worldwide. Malicious users are now changing their focus from conducting mass attacks to targeting specific business structures, and these attacks are tailored to each individual case.

Identity thefts and credit card fraud are prevalent attacks affecting the public directly. Social engineering remains a threat, and the methods used are continuing to evolve. The biggest mass mailings were comparable in size to the activity shown in December of 2004 through and January, when cyber scammers exploited the tsunami in South East Asia. Cyber criminals target people who are new to the Internet gullible. With huge numbers of people connecting to the Internet for the first time every year, cyber criminals always have a fresh crop of Net newbies on which to prey. Elderly people, youngster and kids are also among the top targets.

Current Situation

The Computer Security Institute (CSI) announced the results of its 10th annual Computer Crime and Security Survey. The survey showed that virus attacks continue as the source of the greatest financial losses, accounting for 32 per cent of the overall reported losses. Theft of proprietary information also showed a significant increase in average loss per respondent, more than double that of last year. Also unauthorised access showed a dramatic increase and replaced denial of service as the second most significant contributor to computer crime losses, accounting for 24 per cent of overall reported losses and showing a significant increase in average dollar loss. On a better note the total dollar amount of financial losses resulting from security breaches is decreasing, with an average loss of $204,000 per respondent, down 61 per cent from last year's average loss of $526,000. However the percentage of organisations reporting computer intrusions to law enforcement has continued its multiyear decline. Respondents cited the concern over negative publicity as the key reason for not reporting intrusions to law enforcement.

CATEGORIES OF CYBER CRIME

Cyber crime has manifested itself in many different forms over the years.

The following points are illustrative of some of the different categories that criminals have entered:

- Spam - Although for much of history, spam was not technically a crime, the 2003 CAN-SPAM Act changed legal definitions on what is acceptable. Spam now represents more than 50 per cent of all e-mail transmitted over the Internet. It's costs, which Internet service providers (ISPs) pass on to their customers, are enormous. With spam's ubiquity comes a whole culture and industry devoted to fighting it. Large groups of people, such as the Spamhaus Project, spend enormous effort to identify the sources of spam so as to block their activity. New technologies have been created to flag its sources, like blacklists, and spam identification through Bayesian filters, distributed checksum databases, and other advanced heuristics. Increasingly on the defensive, spammers are fighting back by becoming more sophisticated, generating unique messages, and using subverted computers to send messages.

- Extortion and Damaging Reputations - In the Internet variant of a blackmail, criminal gangs will threaten companies with disruption of their networks, through denial of service attacks, or the theft of valuable information, unless they pay ransom into offshore bank accounts. Defacement of a company's web site can cause not just embarrassment but loss of sales. In other cases, spite or a desire to inflict harm means that the attack will be executed without warning.
- Fraud and Phishing - The anonymity and opportunities for misrepresentation found on the Internet make fraud easy. Consumer Sentinel, a complaint database developed and maintained by the US Federal Trade Commission, has recorded more than 390,000 Internet-related fraud complaints regarding transactions involving over US$540 million losses in 2004 alone. Fraud schemes are usually peddled by individuals who spam potential victims, such as the Nigerian, or 419, scam. But as the number of fraud cases has increased, so has the public's awareness of them; fraudsters are increasingly forced to resort to more intricate schemes. New practices like "phishing" are gaining popularity with fraudsters. Using this scheme, criminals create e-mail messages with return addresses, links, and branding that seem to come from trusted, well-known organisations with the hope to convince victims to disclose sensitive information. This practice originates in attempts to fool America Online users into parting with their screen names and passwords in the mid-1990s. The goal these days is to extract information from a victim that crackers can use for financial gain. A commonly targeted item is victim's credit card information. Criminals also want access to Internet payment systems such as e-Bullion, egold, or

PayPal; online transaction services such as Authorise.Net, iBill, and Verotel; and Internet accessible banks which includes almost all major banks today.

- Service Disruption - A cyber criminal can use an Internet attack to disrupt a key service. Denial of service attacks are one method, worms and viruses containing malicious code are another. A major auto manufacturer was one of many companies that had to shutdown its e-mail network for a few days because of the Love Letter virus.
- Information Theft - The most damaging category of Internet crime, information theft can take several forms. Cyber criminals can extract personal identification information or credit information from a company's database and affect thousands of consumers. Cyber criminals can also extract a company's own financial information. Finally, cyber criminals can steal valuable intellectual property from a company. While the reported cost of information theft is declining, it remains one of the greatest Internet risks a company can face.
- Money Laundering - The growth of global financial services makes it easy to conduct banking operations across borders over the Internet. The Financial Action Task Force, a group of national law enforcement agencies, notes that "within the retail banking sector, services such as telephone and Internet banking allow customers to execute transactions on a non face-to-face basis from any location with telephone or Internet access." While use of the Internet provides law enforcement agencies a greater ability to trace transactions through electronic records, the volume of transactions, the anonymity, and the lack of consistent record-keeping make it attractive to criminals and terrorists.
- Child Pornography – The Internet has become an important tool for sex offenders in order to facilitate the making, collection, trading and distribution of abusive images engaging children. It constitutes a vehicle to simplify the contact between child pornographers mutually, on the one hand, and with their victims, on the other hand.

Consequently, the Internet linked with other technological advances has an enormous impact on both the volume and the nature of child pornography.

CYBER CRIME TOOLS

Cyber criminals have developed a wide array of potential tools that have had varying degrees of success over the years.

The following are a short list of some of these techniques:

- Bots – A bot (short for robot) is a computer on which a worm or virus has installed programmes that run automatically and allow cyber criminals access and control. Cyber criminals use viruses or other bots to search for vulnerable computers where they can load their own programmes or store data. A botnet is a collection of these infected machines that can be centrally controlled and used to launch simultaneous attacks. Spammers, hackers, and other cyber criminals are acquiring or renting botnets, making it harder for authorities to track down the real culprits.
- Keylogging – Keyloggers are programmes that covertly recover the keys typed by a computer user and either stores the data for later access or secretly sends the information to the author. The advantage of a keylogger programme is that the cyber criminal does not need to trick a user into supplying sensitive information.
- Bundling – Covertly attaching a virus or spyware to a benign or legitimate download, such as a screensaver or a game. When the computer user downloads and installs the legitimate file, they are unwittingly also giving permission to install the criminal programme.
- Denial of Service – An attack specifically designed to prevent the normal functioning of a computer network or system and to prevent access by authorised users. A distributed denial of service attack uses thousands of computers captured by a worm or trojan to send a landslide of data in a very short time. Attackers can cause denial of service attacks by destroying or modifying data or by

using zombie computers to bombard the system with data until its servers are overloaded and cannot serve normal requests.

- Packet Sniffers — Software programmes that monitors network traffic. Attackers use packet sniffers to capture and analyse data transmitted via a network. Specialised sniffers capture passwords as they cross a network.
- Rootkit — A set of tools used by an intruder after hacking a computer. The tools allow the cyber criminal to maintain access, prevent detection, build in hidden backdoors, and collect information from both the compromised computer.
- Spyware — Software that gathers information without the users' knowledge. Spyware is typically bundled covertly with another programme. The user does not know that installing one also installs the other. Once installed, the spyware monitors user activity on the Internet and transmits that information in the background to someone else.
- Social Engineering — Social engineering is not limited to cyber crime, but it is an important element for cyberfraud. Social engineering tricks deceives the recipient into taking an action or revealing information. The reasons given seem legitimate but the intent is criminal. Phishing is an obvious example, a certain percentage of users will respond unthinkingly to a request that appears to be from a legitimate institution.
- Worms and Trojans — A trojan is a malicious programme unwittingly downloaded and installed by computer users. Some trojans pretend to be a benign application. Many hide in a computer's memory as a file with a non-descript name. Trojans contain commands that a computer automatically executes without the user's knowledge. Sometimes it can act as a zombie and send spam or participate in a distributed denial of service attack. It may be a keylogger or other monitoring programme that collects data and sends it covertly to the attacker. Worms are wholly contained viruses that travel through networks,

automatically duplicate themselves and send themselves to other computers whose addresses are in the host computer. In the past, cyber criminals occasionally use worms and trojans to hijack a victim's Web browsers. They replace the victims' home and search pages with links to Web spam, as well as drop links to the spam in the victims' bookmarks and on their desktops. To make money, they infect computers with malicious code that generates fraudulent ad views.

- Virus—A programme or piece of code that spreads from computer to computer without the users' consent. They usually cause an unexpected and negative event when run by a computer. Viruses contaminate legitimate computer programmes and are often introduced through e-mail attachments, often with clever titles to attract the curious reader.
- Internet message boards – Internet message boards dedicated to stocks are fertile ground for impersonators. A habit of many posters to these boards is to cut-and-paste press releases and news stories from other electronic sources into their posts to alert other posters and visitors to that information. Frequently, posters will paste in a hyperlink to direct a reader to a source directly, as Hoke did in the PairGain hoax. In addition to the rising threat, as national level attacks become more plausible, the vulnerabilities have also increased.

CYBER LAUNDERING

Money laundering is said to be the "process by which one conceals the existence, illegal source, or illegal application of income, and then disguises that income to make it appear legitimate" As money technology has evolved, methods of payment have also changed, but cash still often remains a preferred method of payment by many people. Over the past few decades various media and industry experts have predicted the demise of cash and the advent of the "cashless" society. Since, money in a modern economy exists chiefly in the form of electronic entries in computerized recordkeeping systems or data bases so conventional laundering has paved way for cyber laundering comprising the use of internet. One of its potential key features is anonymity. The proceeds of crime that are in the form of e-money could therefore be used, for example, to buy foreign currency and high value goods to be resold.

E-money may therefore be used to place dirty money without having to smuggle cash or conduct face to face transactions. The money launderer can control transactions from his PC. He can transfer money virtually instantaneously and thereby build up an extensive audit trail in a short space of time. The transfers can be made through many jurisdictions making it harder for prosecutors from one jurisdiction to follow the audit trail.

Therefore the features of the Internet that makes it ideal for commerce also make it ideal for money laundering:

- Speed
- Access
- Anonymity
- Capacity to extend beyond national border.

As a result cyber-launderers benefit for the following reasons:

- Inability to identify and authenticate parties.
- Lack or inadequacy of audit trails, record keeping or suspicious transaction reporting by the technology provider.
- Use of higher level encryption to block out law enforcement.
- Transactions that fall outside the existing regulatory definitions.

Intellectual Property crimes/Distribution of pirated software

Intellectual property consists of a bundle of rights. Any unlawful act by which the owner is deprived completely or partially of his rights is an offence. This is the traditional type of intellectual property theft where one producer copies material or process from another for profit.

The common form of IPR violation may be said to be software piracy, copyright infringement, trademark and service mark violation, theft of computer source code, etc. The Hyderabad Court has in a land mark judgement has convicted three people and sentenced them to six months imprisonment and fine of 50,000 each for unauthorized copying and sell of pirated software.

Defamation

It is an act of imputing any person with intent to lower the person in the estimation of the right-thinking members of society generally or to cause him to be shunned or avoided or to expose him to hatred, contempt or ridicule. Cyber defamation is not different from conventional defamation except the involvement of a virtual medium.

NETSPIONAGE

Unscrupulous companies have always been delighted to take advantage of new opportunities to sabotage or steal from a dangerous competitor.

The development of information networks and vulnerable points of attack merely emphasizes this and increases the opportunities. Netspionage is where confidential information is stolen by hackers, to sell to a competitor or for the use of individuals business exploits.

Espionage was originally limited to governments, but with the information age, the rise of corporate espionage has been rapid. One tool used to steal secrets is TEMPEST (Transient Electromagnetic Pulse Emanation Surveillance Technology) that allows a scanner to read the output from a computer up to a kilometer away. It is non-invasive and virtually undetectable.

According to recent surveys, worldwide losses suffered through misappropriation of computerized intellectual property cost copyright owners close to $20 billion last year.

One of the most recent and publicized cases is where hackers broke into Microsoft's computer system and allegedly had access to source codes behind Microsoft's software for some considerable time and could have stolen blue prints of the firm's window and office products. Microsoft commented that "this is a deplorable act of industrial espionage".

In a recent case involving two major stockbrokers and a large European Bank, one of the brokers decided to set up a system dealing in government bonds and began building a network across Europe, which meant placing servers in all of the major banks to transfer information to the dealing rooms. The network manager was known to many of the banks because he had once worked for a rival, and he was given access to top-security computer rooms. In one of the banks, the space allocated for the server was next to one of its rivals, which already had a government bond operation. After a quiet chat with his boss, the network manager was given a discreet nod and told to lose? 10,000 on expenses to place a connection from the rival's server to his company's server. Because of his time at the rival he was able to decipher the code, and thus gave his company real time access to its rival's buy and sell prices, allowing it to undercut and make a killing. In China, the government is so concerned with the threat of the Internet as a vehicle for Netspionage that it shut down 127 net cafes, to curb the spread of online information, and to halt the spread of state secrets.

Social Networking Sites and Cyber Crime

The majority of adults who use of social networking sites like MySpace and Face Book engage in dangerous behavior that exposes them to cyber crime. It is not just the average net user who is a fan of social network sites, so are hi-tech criminals.

The quasi-intimate nature of the sites makes people share information readily leaving them open to all kinds of other attacks, warn security firms. Detailed information gathered via the sites will also help tune spam runs or make phishing e-mail more convincing. Cyber criminals are getting personal, aiming malicious attacks at social networking sites - targeting them as honey pots of confidential personal data, instead of targeting more traditional financial-based websites with phishing scams, e-criminals are now more frequently looking to source a wide range of consumer data by compromising social networking accounts. In addition, by targeting sites that consumers trust, these criminals are cleverly increasing the chances that their schemes will be successful and consumers will accidentally hand over personal information.

Social Networking Sites top Targets for Identity Theft

About 74 percent of adults who use social networking sites have given out personal information like an e-mail address, birthday or social security number. Giving out a social security number, paired with a birthday and name could provide enough ammunition for criminals to hack into financial records and compromise users' personal information, besides compromising their personal information adults are also leaving their computers vulnerable to attacks by downloading files from other profiles. And it isn't only personal computer networks at risk, as many of the people visit social networking sites when they're at work - jeopardizing business networks. This data can give criminals knowledge about the names of employees at a company, insight in its managerial make-up or information about its processes to lend credibility to other attacks.

This information could help attackers embarking on social engineering attacks which attempt to con employees by posing as another worker or a business partner.

Already at the end of 2007 Brazilian users of Google's Orkut were subject to an attack by a worm that tried to steal bank account details. The malicious program, which also tried to hijack compromised computers, propagated via booby-trapped links placed on the personal page of Orkut users.

With the growth of social networking sites, blogging, chat rooms, or instant messaging, children today are more in danger. Over 50 percent of teenagers in USA visit social networking sites and most of them do so on a daily basis! Indian children are catching the social networking bug too. Some children visit these sites to increase their friend's circle, some to keep in touch with friends they cannot meet, and to make plans, socialize, or share information. Unfortunately, most children reveal a lot of personal details on their profiles which can easily be misused and their personal details can harm them even. On the one hand where they increase a person's friend circle, they can also increase exposure to people who could be dangerous and many a times this type of information has lead to dire consequences when people have been stalked and in extreme cases murders have also been committed.

The orkut angle in the kidnapping and murder of Adnan Patrawla, is an example of how dangerous it can become to befriend a stanger and then going out to meet them even more dangerous.

We need to understand that coming across even one wrong person in our entire life can have serious implications. There are certain norms that we need to adhere to both in our personal as well as social lives and if we breach them by ourselves, the consequences can affect all those around us. Social networking sites are all over the internet and a number of youngsters tend to be misled. But one cannot blame the internet or these sites for individual actions. It is important for us to be alert and take care about the information we are passing on to others. As a ground rule one must never pass on information without knowing anything about the other person. One can ask for the other person's phone number or address in order to get to know them better. It is better to build upon healthy contacts rather than falling in wrong hands. One needs to take several things in account while interacting with people on social networking sites:

- Do not reveal confidential information on the site.
- Never agree to meet a stranger all by yourself.
- If at all, you have to go, then, do take someone along.
- Trust your instincts. If you get the slightest hint of getting threatened or feel uncomfortable, confide in an adult, report to the police and to the social networking site.
- Do not flirt on the site as people have fake identities.
- Remember that once you post information, you cannot delete it as older versions exist on other people's computers.
- Try not to post your photo as it can be altered and transmitted in various unethical ways
- Before you try to meet someone, try to gather as much information about him/her as possible. Meet the stranger only when you are satisfied that you know enough about him/her.

THE CYBER CRIME LAWS OF NATIONS

Based on its findings in the E-Readiness study, and in the wake of the Philippines inability to prosecute the student responsible for the "I Love You" virus, McConnell International surveyed its global network of information technology policy officials to determine the state of cyber security laws around the world. Countries were asked to provide laws that would be used to prosecute criminal acts involving both private and public sector computers. Over fifty national governments4 responded with recent pieces of legislation, copies of updated statutes, draft legislation, or statements that no concrete course of action has been planned to respond to a cyber attack on the public or private sector. Countries were provided the opportunity to review the presentation of the results in draft, and this report reflects their comments.

Countries that provided legislation were evaluated to determine whether their criminal statutes had been extended into cyberspace to cover ten different types of cyber crime in four categories: data-related crimes, including interception, modification, and theft; network-related crimes, including interference and sabotage; crimes of access, including hacking and virus distribution; and associated computer-related crimes, including aiding and abetting cyber criminals, computer fraud, and computer forgery.

Thirty-three of the countries surveyed have not yet updated their laws to address any type of cyber crime. Of the remaining countries, nine have enacted legislation to address five or fewer types of cyber crime, and ten have updated their laws to prosecute against six or more of the ten types of cyber crime.

Law is Only Part of the Answer

Extending the rule of law into cyberspace is a critical step to create a trustworthy environment for people and businesses. Because that extension remains a work in progress, organizations today must first and foremost defend their own systems and information from attack, be it from outsiders or from within. They may rely only secondarily on the deterrence that effective law enforcement can provide.

To provide this self-protection, organizations should focus on implementing cyber security plans addressing people, process, and technology issues. Organizations need to commit the resources to educate employees on security practices, develop thorough plans for the handling of sensitive data, records and transactions, and incorporate robust security technology--such as firewalls, anti-virus software, intrusion detection tools, and authentication services-- throughout the organizations' computer systems.

These system protection tools--the software and hardware for defending information systems--are complex and expensive to operate. To avoid hassles and expense, system manufacturers and system operators routinely leave security features "turned off," needlessly increasing the vulnerability of the information on the systems. Bugs and security holes with known fixes are routinely left uncorrected. Further, no agreed-upon standards exist to benchmark the quality of the tools, and no accepted methodology exists for organizations to determine how much investment in security is enough. The inability to quantify the costs and benefits of information security investments leave security managers at a disadvantage when competing for organizational resources. Much work remains to improve management and technical solutions for information protection. Industry-wide efforts are underway to address prevention, response, and cooperation.

Around the world, various industries have been establishing information sharing and analysis centers (ISACs) to share real-time information related to threats, vulnerabilities, attacks, and countermeasures. A recent Global Information Security Summit sponsored by the World Information Technology and Services Alliance (www.witsa.org) brought together industry, governments, and multilateral organizations across economic sectors to share information and build partnerships.

Post-summit working groups are now developing cooperative approaches to addressing the most critical information security problems. The results of that work will be taken up at a second summit in Belfast in May 2001. That summit will also provide an opportunity to revisit the progress of nations in updating their laws to cover cyber crimes.

1. Reliance on terrestrial laws is an untested approach. Despite the progress being made in many countries, most countries still rely on standard terrestrial law to prosecute cyber crimes. The majority of countries are relying on archaic

statutes that predate the birth of cyberspace and have not yet been tested in court.

2. Weak penalties limit deterrence. The weak penalties in most updated criminal statutes provide limited deterrence for crimes that can have large-scale economic and social effects.
3. Self-protection remains the first line of defence. The general weakness of statutes increases the importance of private sector efforts to develop and adopt strong and efficient technical solutions and management practices for information security.
4. A global patchwork of laws creates little certainty. Little consensus exists among countries regarding exactly which crimes need to be legislated against. Unless crimes are defined in a similar manner across jurisdictions, coordinated efforts by law enforcement officials to combat cyber crime will be complicated.
5. A model approach is needed. Most countries, particularly those in the developing world, are seeking a model to follow. These countries recognize the importance of outlawing malicious computer-related acts in a timely manner in order to promote a secure environment for ecommerce. But few have the legal and technical resources necessary to address the complexities of adapting terrestrial criminal statutes to cyberspace. A coordinated, public-private partnership to produce a model approach can help eliminate the potential danger from the inadvertent creation of cyber crime havens.

Recommendations

The weak state of global legal protections against cyber crime suggests three kinds of action.

Firms should secure their networked information.

Laws to enforce property rights work only when property owners take reasonable steps to protect their property in the first place. As one observer has noted, if homeowners failed to buy locks for their front doors, should towns solve the problem by passing more laws or hiring more police? Even where laws are adequate, firms dependent on the network must make their own information and systems secure. And where enforceable laws are months or years away, as in most countries, this responsibility is even more significant.

Governments should assure that their laws apply to cyber crimes.

National governments remain the dominant authority for regulating criminal behaviour in most places in the world. One nation already has struggled from, and ultimately improved, its legal authority after a confrontation with the unique challenges presented by cyber crime. It is crucial that other nations profit from this lesson, and examine their current laws to discern whether they are composed in a technologically neutral manner that would not exclude the prosecution of cyber criminals. In many cases, nations will find that current laws ought to be updated. Enactment of enforceable computer crime laws that also respect the rights of individuals are an essential next step in the battle against this emerging threat.

Firms, governments, and civil society should work cooperatively

To be prosecuted across a border, an act must be a crime in each jurisdiction. Thus, while local legal traditions must be respected, nations must define cyber crimes in a similar manner. An important effort to craft a model approach is underway in the Council of Europe, comprising 41 countries.

The Council is crafting an international Convention on Cyber Crime. The Convention addresses illegal access, illegal interception, data interference, system interference, computer-related forgery, computer-related fraud, and the aiding and abetting of these crimes. It also addresses investigational matters related to jurisdiction, extradition, the interception of communications, and the production and preservation of data. Finally, it promotes cooperation among law enforcement officials across national borders.

Late in its process, the Council began to consider the views of affected industry and civil society. This process is making the Council's product more realistic, practical, efficient, balanced, and respectful of due process that protects individual rights.

At this point, most observers support provisions to improve law enforcement cooperation across borders. However, industry, through the World Information Technology and Services Alliance, argues that the requirements on service providers to monitor communications and to provide assistance to investigators, as outlined in the Draft Convention, would be unduly burdensome and expensive. Another provision considered objectionable could criminalize the creation and use of intrusive software, or hacking programs, which are designed for legitimate security testing purposes.

This action could stifle the advances in technology vital to keep up with evolving cyber threats. Privacy and human rights advocates object to the Draft Convention's lack of procedural safeguards and due process to protect the rights of individuals, and to the possibility that the ensuing national laws would effectively place restrictions on privacy, anonymity, and encryption.

The Council plans to release a final draft of the Convention in December 2000. In 2001, a political process involving national governments will determine the scope and coverage of the final Convention.

Because of cyber crime's international potential, all countries, and all companies, are affected. Interested parties, including national governments from outside Europe, and businesses and non-governmental organizations from around the world, should participate vigorously in a consensus process to develop measures that support effective international law enforcement and foster continued growth and innovation.

3

Computer Crime Legislation

Because of the versatility of the computer, drawing lines between criminal and noncriminal behaviour regarding its use can be difficult. Behaviour that companies and governments regard as unwanted can range from simple pranks, such as making funny messages appear on a computer's screen, to financial or data manipulation producing millions of dollars in losses. Early prosecution of computer crime was infrequent and usually concerned Embezzlement, a crime punishable under existing laws. The advent of more unique forms of abuse, such as computer worms and viruses and widespread computer hacking, has posed new challenges for government and the courts.

The first federal computer crime legislation was the Counterfeit Access Device and Computer Fraud and Abuse Act (18 U.S.C.A. § 1030), passed by Congress in 1984. The act safeguards certain classified government information and makes it a misdemeanor to obtain through a computer financial or credit information that federal laws protect. The act also criminalizes the use of computers to inflict damage to computer systems, including their hardware and software.

In the late 1980s, many states followed the federal government's lead in an effort to define and combat criminal computer activities. At least 20 states passed statutes with similar definitions of computer crimes. Some of those states might have been influenced by studies released in the late 1980s. One report, made available in 1987 by the accounting firm of Ernst and Whinney, estimated that computer abuse caused between $3 billion and $5 billion in losses in the United States annually. Moreover, some of those losses were attributable to newer, more complicated crimes that usually went unprosecuted.

The number of computer crimes continued to increase dramatically in the early 1990s. According to the Computer Emergency and Response Team at Carnegie-Mellon University, the number of computer intrusions in the United States increased 498 percent between 1991 and 1994. During the same time period, the number of network sites affected by computer crimes increased by 702 percent. In 1991, Congress created the National Computer Crime Squad within the Federal Bureau of Investigation (FBI). Between 1991 and 1997, the Squad reportedly investigated more than 200 individual cases involving computer hackers.

Congress addressed the dramatic rise in computer crimes with the enactment of the National Information Infrastructure Act of 1996 as title II of the Economic Espionage Act of 1996, Pub. L. No. 104-294, 110 Stat. 3488. That Act strengthened and clarified provisions of the original Computer Fraud and Abuse Act, although lawmakers and commentators have suggested that as technology develops, new legislation might be necessary to address new methods for committing computer crimes. The new statute also expanded the application of the original statute, making it a crime to obtain unauthorized information from networks of government agencies and departments, as well as data relating to national defense or foreign relations.

Notwithstanding the new legislation and law enforcement's efforts to curb computer crime, statistics regarding these offenses remain stag-gering. According to a survey in 2002 conducted by the Computer Security Institute, in conjunction with the San Francisco office of the FBI, 90 percent of those surveyed (which included mostly large corporations and government agencies) reported that they had detected computer-security breaches. Eighty percent of those surveyed acknowledged that they had suffered financial loss due to computer crime. Moreover, the 223 companies and agencies in the survey that were willing to divulge information about financial losses reported total losses of $455 million in 2002 alone.

Concerns about Terrorism have also included the possibility that terrorist organizations could perform hostile acts in the form of computer crimes. In 2001, Congress enacted the Uniting and Strengthening America by Providing Appropriate Tools Required to Intercept and Obstruct Terrorism Act (USA PATRIOT ACT), Pub. L. No. 107-56, 115 Stat. 277, to provide law enforcement with the necessary tools to combat terrorism. The Act includes provisions that allow law enforcement greater latitude in hunting down criminals who use computers and other communication networks. The Homeland Security Act of 2002, Pub. L. No. 107-296, 116 Stat. 2135 also directed the UNITED STATES SENTENCING COMMISSION to review, and possibly to amend, the sentencing provisions that relate to computer crimes under 18 U.S.C.A. § 1030.

The Department of Justice's Computer Crime and Intellectual Property Section prosecutes dozens of computer-crime cases each year. Many of those cases involve instances of computer hacking and other unauthorized intrusions, as well as software Piracy and computer fraud.

One set of especially destructive crimes—internal computer crimes—includes acts in which one computer's program interferes with another computer, thus hindering its use, damaging data or programs, or causing the other computer to crash (i.e., to become temporarily inoperable). Two common types of such programs are known in programming circles as "worms" and "viruses." Both cause damage to computer systems through the commands written by their authors. Worms are independent programs that create temporary files and replicate themselves to the point where computers grow heavy with data, become sluggish, and then crash. Viruses are dependent programs that reproduce themselves through a computer code attached to another program, attaching additional copies of their program to legitimate files each time the computer system is started or when some other triggering event occurs.

The dangers of computer worms and viruses gained popular recognition with one of the first cases prosecuted under the Computer Fraud and Abuse Act. In *United States v. Morris*, 928 F.2d 504 (2d Cir. 1991), Cornell University student Robert T. Morris was convicted of violating a provision of the act that punishes anyone who, without authorization, intentionally accesses a "federal interest computer" and damages or prevents authorized use of information in such a computer, causing losses of $1,000 or more. Morris, a doctoral candidate in computer science, had decided to demonstrate the weakness of security measures of computers on the Internet, a network linking university, government, and military computers around the United States. His plan was to insert a worm into as many computers as he could gain access to, but to ensure that the worm replicated itself slowly enough that it would not cause the computers to slow down or crash. However, Morris miscalculated how quickly the worm would replicate. By the time he released a message on how to kill the worm, it was too late: Some 6,000 computers had crashed or become "catatonic" at numerous institutions, with estimated damages of $200 to $53,000 for each institution. Morris was sentenced to three years' Probation and 400 hours of community service, and was fined $10,500.

Computer hackers often share Morris's goal of attempting to prove a point through the clever manipulation of other computers. Hackers, who, typically, are young, talented, amateur computer programmers, earn respect among their peers by gaining access to information through Telecommunications systems. The information obtained ranges from other individuals' E-Mail or credit histories to the Department of Defense's secrets.

A high-profile case in 1992 captured national headlines. In what federal investigators called a conspiracy, five young members of an underground New York City gang of hackers, the Masters of Deception (MOD), faced charges that they had illegally obtained computer passwords, possessed unauthorized access devices (long-distance calling-card numbers), and committed wire fraud in violation of the Computer Fraud and Abuse Act. Otto Obermaier, the U.S. attorney who prosecuted the youths, described their activities as "the crime of the future," and said that he intended to use the case to make a critical statement about computer crime. The indictment contained 11 counts, each punishable by at least five years in prison and individual fines of $250,000. Supporters of MOD's civil liberties questioned whether the gang members had done anything truly illegal.

MOD members Paul Stira and Eli Ladopoulos pleaded guilty to the charges against them. They confessed that they had broken the law but insisted that they had not done anything for personal profit. They were sentenced to six months in a federal penitentiary, followed by six months' home detention. John Lee and Julio Fernandez faced specific charges of illegally selling passwords for personal profit. Lee pleaded guilty and received a year behind bars, followed by 300 hours of community service. Fernandez bargained with prosecutors, offering them information on MOD activities, and thus received no jail time. Gang leader Mark Abene, who was notorious in computer circles by his handle Phiber Optik, pleaded guilty to charges of fraud. A U.S. District Court judge sentenced Abene to a year in federal prison, hoping to send a message to other hackers. However, by the time Abene was released from prison in 1995, his notoriety had grown beyond the hacker underground. Many in the computer world hailed him as a martyr in the modern web of computer technology and criminal prosecution. Abene subsequently found employment as a computer technician at a New York-based on-line service.

Computer crime can become an obsession. Such was the case for Kevin Mitnick, a man federal prosecutors described prior to his arrest as the most wanted computer hacker in the world. In the early 1980s, as a teenager, Mitnick proved his mettle as a hacker by gaining access to a North American Air Defense terminal, an event that inspired the 1983 movie *War Games*. Like the MOD gang, Mitnick gained access to computer networks through telecommunications systems. In violation of federal law, he accessed private credit information, obtaining some 20,000 credit numbers and histories. Other break-ins by Mitnick caused an estimated $4 million in damage to the computer operations of the Digital Equipment Corporation. The company also claimed that Mitnick had stolen more than one million dollars in software.

Mitnick was convicted, sentenced to one year in a minimum-security prison, and then released into a treatment program for compulsive-behaviour disorders. Federal investigators tried to keep close track of him during his probation, but in November 1992, he disappeared. Authorities caught up with his trail when

Mitnick broke into the system of computer-security expert Tsutomu Shimomura at the San Diego Supercomputer Centre—a move that was clearly intended as a challenge to another programming wizard. Shimomura joined forces with the Federal Bureau of Investigation to pursue their elusive quarry in cyberspace. Using a program designed to record activity in a particular database that they were sure that Mitnick was accessing, while monitoring phone activity, Shimomura and authorities narrowed their search to Raleigh, North Carolina. A special device detecting cellular-phone use ultimately led them to Mitnick's apartment. Mitnick was arrested and was charged on 23 federal counts. He pleabargained with prosecutors, who agreed to drop 22 of the counts in exchange for Mitnick's guilty plea for illegally possessing phone numbers to gain access to a computer system. Mitnick was sentenced to eight months in jail.

Mitnick's case illustrates the difficulties that legislatures and courts face when defining and assigning penalties for computer crime. Using a computer to transfer funds illegally or to embezzle money is clearly a serious crime that merits serious punishment. Mitnick broke into numerous services and databases without permission and took sensitive information, in violation of federal laws; however, he never used that information for financial gain. This type of behaviour typically has no counterpart outside of cyberspace—for example, people do not break into jewelry stores only to leave a note about weak security.

Some instances of computer crimes demonstrate the way in which small computer files that require relatively little effort on the part of the perpetrator can cause millions of dollars' worth of damage to computer networks. In March 1999, David L. Smith of New Jersey created a virus that lowered the security levels of certain word-processing programs and caused infected computers to send e-mail messages containing attachments with the virus to e-mail addresses contained in the infected computer's e-mail address book. The virus was activated on an infected computer when the user opened the word-processing program.

Smith posted a message on March 26, 1999, to an Internet newsgroup called "Alt.Sex." The message claimed that if a user opened an attachment, it would provide a list of passcodes to pornographic websites. The attachment contained the virus, which became known as the "Melissa" virus. Smith was arrested by New Jersey authorities on April 1, 1999, but not before the virus had infected an estimated 1.2 million computers and affected one-fifth of the country's largest businesses.

The total amount of damages was $80 million. Smith pleaded guilty in December 1999 to state and federal charges. He faced 20 months in a federal prison and a fine of approximately $5,000 for his crime. He faced additional time in state prison. According to U.S. Attorney Robert J. Cleary, "There is a segment in society that views the unleashing of computer viruses as a challenge, a game. Far from it; it is a serious crime. The penalties Mr. Smith faces—including potentially five years in a federal prison—are no game, and others should heed his example." Others have continued to commit such crimes. In February 2000, a computer hacker stunned the world by paralyzing the Internet's leading U.S. web sites. Three days of concentrated assaults upon major sites crippled businesses like Yahoo, eBay, and CNN for hours, leaving engineers virtually helpless to respond. When the dust had settled, serious doubts were raised about the safety of Internet commerce. An international hunt ensued, and web sites claimed losses in the hundreds of millions of dollars. After pursuing several false leads, investigators ultimately charged a Canadian teenager in March 2000 in one of the attacks.

On February 7, engineers at Yahoo, the popular portal web site, noticed traffic slowing to a crawl. Initially, suspecting faulty equipment that facilitates the thousands of connections to the site daily, they were surprised to discover that it was receiving many times the normal number of hits. Buckling under exorbitant demand, the servers—the computers that receive and transmit its Internet traffic—had to be shut down for several hours. Engineers then isolated the problem: Remote computers had been instructed to bombard Yahoo's servers with automated requests for service. Over the next two days, several other major web sites suffered the same fate. Hackers hit the auction site eBay, the bookseller Amazon.com, the computer journalism site ZDnet, stock brokerages

E*Trade and Datek, the computer store Buy.com, the web portal Excite at Home, and the flagship site for news giant CNN. As each site ground to a halt or went offline, engineers tried in vain to determine where the digital bombardment had originated.

Experts expressed amazement at the attacks' simplicity as well as at the inherent vulnerabilities that they exposed in the Internet's architecture. Hackers had launched what quickly came to be known as a distributed Denial-of-Service (DOS) attack—essentially a remote-controlled strike using multiple computers. First, weeks or months in advance, they had surreptitiously installed commonly available hacking programs called "scripts" on 50 or more remote computers, including university systems chosen for their high-speed connections to the Internet. Later, they activated these scripts, turning the remote computers into virtual zombies that were ordered to send unfathomably large amounts of data—up to one gigabyte per second—continuously to their victims. These data asked the target web sites to respond, just as every legitimate connection to a web site does. The sheer multitudes of requests and responses overwhelmed the victim sites. To escape detection, the "zombies" forged their digital addresses.

Federal investigators were initially stymied. They had legal authority to act under 18 U.S.C.A. § 1030, which criminalizes "knowingly transmit(ting) a program information code or command" that "intentionally causes damage." Sleuthing was difficult, however. Not only had the hackers covered the trail well, but also the FBI had suffered numerous personnel losses to private industry. The bureau had to hire consultants and had to develop special software to assist in its manhunt. Moreover, as FBI official Ron Dick told reporters, the proliferation of common hacking tools meant that even a teenager could have orchestrated the crime. In early March 2000, authorities arrested 17-year-old New Hampshire resident Dennis Moran, allegedly known online as "Coolio." The lead proved false. In mid-April, claiming to have found "Mafia boy," Royal Canadian Mounted Police arrested a 15-year-old Montreal hacker. The youth, whose real name was not divulged, allegedly had boasted of his exploits online while trying to recruit helpers. Officials charged him with a misdemeanor for launching the attack upon CNN's website.

Although the department of justice continued its hunt, this denial-of-service attack was never completely resolved. Analysts have noted that DOS attacks have occurred for several years, although not to the extent as that of February 2000. In May 2001, for instance, the White House's web page was hit with a DOS attack that blocked access to the site for about two hours.

Based upon the sheer number of cases involving computer crime, commentators remain puzzled as to what is necessary to curb this type of activity. Clearly, technology for law enforcement needs to stay ahead of the technology used by the hackers, but this is not an easy task. A number of conferences have been held to address these issues, often attracting large corporations such as Microsoft and Visa International, but the general consensus is that the hackers still hold the upper hand, with solutions still elusive.

SPECIAL PROBLEMS WITH COMPUTER-RELATED CRIME

Discussions of computer-related crime refer with increasing frequency to intellectual property. While the term is familiar to many, its actual meaning may be somewhat elusive. Intellectual property consists of concepts, ideas, planning documents, designs, formulas, and other information-based materials intended for products or services that have some commercial value or represent original thoughts or theses.

Crimes associated with intellectual property focus primarily on theft when the product has commercial value, as opposed to basic research or research for private use.

In some instances, the theft takes place when a competitor manufactures a similar product developed from stolen intellectual property. In other cases, the crime occurs when the offender mounts countermarketing strategies after learning of a competitor's product through illegal, electronic means, oftentimes referred to as competitive intelligence. Frequently, these crimes are difficult to discover and even more difficult to prove. The problem becomes further complicated when the property is still in the developmental stages with its final design or application still incomplete. The investigation and prosecution of thefts of intellectual property with clear protection_such as intellectual property that is copyrighted or has a trademark, patent, or registered trade secret_have more of an advantage than when the protection of such property can be debated. This latter category includes unprotected research and development, original concepts and ideas yet to be realized, and public domain information modified with individual refinements. These areas provide particular challenges for investigating and proving a wrongdoing.

Intellectual property can be divided into two broad categories. The first involves formulas, processes, components, structure, characteristics, and applications of new technologies and covers such areas as fiber optics, computer chip designs and conductivity, and telecommunications equipment, protocols, and technologies, to name a few. The second category of intellectual property takes in factors associated with the marketing and pro-duction of new technologies. Pricing information, marketing targets, product release dates, and production timetables would be included in this category.

Malfeasance by Computer

The concept of malfeasance by computer means that computer-related behaviour stretches the bounds of legality and may be viewed as only technically wrong, despite its widespread, potentially negative impact. Without question, a variety of computer-related behaviours border on illegality but are not clearly defined as such. Although sometimes done with the best intent, the behaviour poses ethical problems, at the very least. The following scenarios illustrate the problem:

- A parent offers to copy a computer program for a school that cannot afford to buy the software
- An employee secretly maintains a small database in an office computer as part of a sideline business
- An individual uses someone else's computer account number and password to view the contents of a database
- A customer gives her unlisted telephone number as part of a sales transaction at a store. The store enters the number

into a computerized database and later sells the data to a telemarketing firm without the customer's permission

- A university computer programmer develops a program to schedule classes as part of a job assignment. The programmer then accepts a job with another university and leaves with a copy of the program for use at the new place of employment.

These illustrations point to the "gray" areas of computer abuse—areas that fall increasingly on the shoulders of law enforcement to address and resolve.

International Issues

Americans tend to have a provincial view that the United States is ahead of the rest of the world in many areas, especially technological development. While this is true to some extent, the lead is not as great as many would believe. Japan and Germany, in particular, have shown themselves to be strong technological innovators and consumers. In general, technological knowledge and expertise contribute to the growth of computer-related crime on an international level.

Americans must be concerned about the growth of computer-related crime capabilities emerging outside U.S. borders because of the ease of information exchange and the high concentration of computer-driven businesses and research projects in the United States. However, it appears that the area of most rapid growth will be in Europe as a result of the treaties signed to create the European Community. Among the important elements of the act that established the basis for unification are open communications, a single, European-wide communication protocol, a strong profit-oriented market spanning 12 countries, open borders, unification of technology standards, and easier banking, including monetary transfers between countries. While businesses can make great use of these unifying measures, so can criminals. Emerging international crime-related issues most probably will accompany the unification of Europe. These issues include industrial espionage (competitive intelligence), economic/political espionage, expansion of international organized crime beyond traditional areas, and theft of technological hardware.

COMPUTER FRAUD VS. COMPUTER CRIME

There is a difference between computer fraud and computer crime. These terms are often used interchangeably with little distinction made between them although substantial differences between them exist.

A general definition of *computer fraud* is: Any defalcation or embezzlement accomplished by tampering with computer programs, data files, operations, equipment, or media, and resulting in losses sustained by the organisation whose computer system was manipulated.

The distinguishing characteristic of computer fraud is that access occurs with the intent to defraud. About half of reported frauds are committed by insiders who have authorised access to the computer system. When investigating cases of potential computer fraud, it is vital to establish the system of the organisation's authorisation procedures.

Computer Fraud

At a basic level, computer fraud is the use of computer systems to perpetrate a fraud. In many cases, the computer has replaced manual records, and the fraudulent input document has been substituted by manipulating data held in a computer system. This manipulation does not need to be sophisticated. The dramatic erosion of clearly segregated duties in different locations to people in the same office with different user ID and passwords on the same PC means that a forged payment instruction may be approved simply by logging on to a computer with a stolen supervisor's logon.

At the other extreme, the use of the Internet and e-mail with "sniffer" programs to capture user's passwords and credit card details can only exist because of the global explosion in the use of networked computers. Many industries will be at risk from a specific type of computer fraud, but by reducing the crime to its basic elements–input, manipulation, and output–the investigator should be able to identify the likely culprits, the methods of manipulation, and the means of conversion or diversion of funds.

Computer Crime

Computer crime differs from computer fraud in two major ways. Employees who as a part of their normal duties have access to the computers are deemed to have authorised access and thus do not come under the law against access. Manipulation (alteration) or destruction of data (including computer software) is independent of fraudulent or other schemes. Such action does not fit into the normal vandalism crimes because the data is intangible.

COMPUTER-ASSISTED CRIME

It is sometimes said that most computer fraud is not "computer crime" but involves the use of computers instead of other means to break the law. In some cases these traditionally illegal acts can yield more because of the high speed of the computer. These are in reality computer-assisted crimes, and the existing criminal statutes can be appropriately applied to them. However, where detection and proof problems are complicated by the involvement of electronic media, computer fraud laws are useful for effective prosecution.

Information Crime

In some cases, the computer is an active weapon. Here, the crime would not be possible without computer technology. Examples of information crimes include the theft of computer time, software, and data.

Misuse of Computer Assets

This is another form of computer crime, although it may be more correctly described as computer abuse. It involves the use of company assets, in this case computers, by employees for non-authorised activities. Again, this is very much dependent on the policies and procedures within a company. At the trivial end of the spectrum is the use of computers to generate personal correspondence. However, e-mail is now widely regarded as a corporate asset, provided by the employers to enable employees to be more productive. Many employers do not regard the abuse of e-mail privileges as a trivial matter since the cost to the company in lost productivity by employees can be considerable. At the other extreme is the use of computer facilities to run an unofficial business venture.

Theft of Computer Hardware

There have been occasions where the theft of computer hardware, specifically computer memory chips, made them more valuable than cocaine on a pound for pound weight basis. This occurred after the fire and earthquake in Kobe where one of the major memory production plants was destroyed and this disrupted some 25% of the world memory supply. Ram raiding of premises with computers became common and either the computers were stolen completely or shipments of memory were hijacked from container lorries. Some specialised hardware is often stolen 'to order', typically this has been Sun and Apple equipment. Often the premises are burgled again just days after the new equipment is installed.

Information Theft

This type of computer crime covers the activities of the following:

- Disgruntled employees: Planning their next move to a competitor and copying (either as a paper document or electronically) commercially sensitive material;
- Political activists, journalists, and minority action groups: Who wish to discredit the activities of an organisation by releasing potentially damaging information into the public domain;
- Hackers and Phishers: Obtaining and trading or publishing passwords, credit card details or other valuable information for sale or trade (or even for free) on web sites or similar. This also applies to the publishing of 'exploits' on the internet so that others can use hacking methods developed by more knowledgeable hackers–these are called 'script kiddies' as all they do is find the script and run it as any kid could do;
- Information brokers: A term which originated in the petrochemical industry where the contracts to build oil

platforms and geological exploration information was worth millions of pounds. The information brokers would buy and gather information using a variety of techniques to sell to the highest bidder.

While information theft has been referred to above as a computer crime, the investigator should be aware that when a company's information has "leaked" to a competitor, there might have been no criminal act committed. A company may find it very difficult to bring a case for information theft if:

- The employee had access to such data in the course of a normal working day;
- The company had no information classification policy to define what company sensitive material was;
- The company does not have clear policies for the storage and management of sensitive materials, for example a clean desk policy, and an information security policy;
- There are no secure document disposal mechanisms (i.e. cross cut shredders);
- The terms and conditions of employment did not include clauses on confidentiality and proprietary information and make reference to the Data Protection Act 1998 or the Computer Misuse Act 1990;
- There was no proper exit interview when such information and media containing it could be recovered.

COMPUTER CRIME BACKDOORS

When attackers obtain root-level access to a server, by whatever means, they will want to do two things:

- Install a backdoor;
- Cover their tracks.

Backdoors allow attackers to remotely access a system again in the future. For example, the attacker may have used a particular security hole to get root-level or Administrator-level access to a computer. However, over time, that particular security hole may be closed, preventing the attacker from accessing the system again using that specific method. To overcome this, attackers install 'backdoors'. These backdoors take different forms, but all allow an attacker to access the server again without going through the standard login procedures and without having to repeat the attack that gave them access in the first place. Many worms install backdoors as a part of their malicious payload. Common backdoor programs are 'Netbus' and 'BackOrifice', which allow attackers to remotely control a compromised server.

HTTP Exploits

HTTP exploits involve using the Web server application to perform malicious activities. These attacks are very common and are growing in popularity because firewalls typically block most traffic from the Internet to keep it away from corporate servers. However, HTTP traffic, used for Web browsing, is almost always allowed to pass through firewalls, on Port 80, unhindered. Thus, attackers have a direct line to the Web server. If they can coerce the Web server into performing malicious activities, they can access resources that would otherwise be unavailable.

Insider Threats

By far the greatest threat to information systems in terms of computer crime comes from employees inside an organisation. It is not uncommon for operators, media librarians, hardware technicians and other staff members to find themselves in positions of extraordinary privilege in relation to the key functions and assets of their organisations. A consequence of this situation is the probability that such individuals are frequently exposed to temptation.

A further complication is the tendency on the part of management to tolerate less stringent supervisory controls over information system personnel, often allocating them to contractors or other third parties.

The premise is that the work is not only highly technical and specialized but difficult to understand and control. As an example, systems or applications software support is often entrusted to a single programmer who generates the version of the operating system or application in use, establishes password or other control lists, and determines the logging and accounting features to be used. In addition, such personnel are often permitted, and sometimes encouraged, to perform these duties during non-prime shift periods or other times when demands on computer time are light.

As a result, many of the most critical software development and maintenance functions are performed in an unsupervised environment. It is also clear that operators, librarians, and technicians often enjoy a degree of freedom quite different from that which would be considered normal in a more traditional employment area.

Insiders typically are aware of the "holes" in the system of internal controls and often exploit weaknesses "just to see if they can get away with it."

The most prevalent method of committing computer fraud probably is alteration or falsification of input transactions (and/ or documents), including:

- Alteration of input;
- Alteration of output;
- Communications systems;
- Computer operations;
- Data file manipulation;
- Operating systems.

Characteristics

The characteristics of the traditional inside computer fraudster are very similar to those of the hacker or other computer criminal, they are usually:

- Bored with the routine of the job;
- Hard workers;
- Have large ego;
- Intelligent;
- Seldom take time off.

Many computer technicians have demonstrated a greater loyalty to the technology than to the organisation for which they work. This technology loyalty can create an attitude that any behaviour is acceptable if it is in the name of technology.

The following are possible indicators of insider computer fraud:

- Access logs not reviewed;
- Access privileges beyond those required to perform assigned job functions;
- Exception reports not reviewed and resolved;
- Lack of separation of duties in the data centre;
- Production programs run at unusual hours.

COMPUTER CRIME CATEGORIES

"The world isn't run by weapons anymore, or energy, or money. It's run by ones and zeros—little bits of data—it's all electrons....There's a war out there, a world war. It's not about who has the most bullets. It's about who controls the information—what we see and hear, how we work, what we think. It's all about information." Lines from the character "Cosmos," in the movie Sneakers, MCA/Universal Pictures, 1992. The motion picture Sneakers focused on computerized information as a valuable commodity and on the technological means to invade and steal that commodity. To many, the high-tech wizardry of the movie probably appears exotic; however, it is much more realistic than some assume. If there is a lesson to be learned from the movie, it is that the potential criminality associated with computers can be eclipsed only by the difficulty in identifying and investigating these crimes. Discussions of emerging technological crimes centre mostly on computer crime, with the inference that there is only one type of offense. This is not, however, the case, because specific categories of computer crime exist. As computer-related crimes become more prevalent, an increasing need emerges for police personnel—particularly those who do not have expertise in computer technology—to understand how these crimes vary. An understanding of the types of computer-related crimes will assist law enforcement by providing insight for investigative strategies.

TYPES OF COMPUTER CRIMES

There are primarily four general types of computer crimes. However, in practice, multiple crimes, that is, concurrent criminality or lesser offenses, can occur during any given criminal transaction, resulting in an overlap between the classifications.

Computer as the Target

Crimes in which the computer is the target include such offenses as theft of intellectual property, theft of marketing information (e.g., customer lists, pricing data, or marketing plans), or blackmail based on information gained from computerized files (e.g., medical information, personal history, or sexual preference). These crimes also could entail sabotage of intellectual property, marketing, pricing, or personnel data or sabotage of operating systems and programs with the intent to impede a business or create chaos in a business' operations. Unlawful access to criminal justice and other government records is another crime that targets the computer directly. This crime covers changing a criminal history; modifying want and warrant information; creating a driver's license, passport, or another document for identification purposes; changing tax records; or gaining access to intelligence files.

Techno-vandalism occurs when unauthorized access to a computer results in damage to files or programs, not so much for profit but for the challenge. In such cases, the damage or loss may be intentional or accidental. Another crime in this category is techno-trespass, that is, "walking" through a computer just to explore. In such cases, the intruder only looks at a file, but even this violates the owner's privacy. This would be the technological equivalent of a criminal trespass.

In all of these crimes, the offender uses the computer to obtain information or to damage operating programs. The offender commits the crime either by "superzapping" or by becoming a "super user." These labels mean that the offender accesses the operating program by masquerading as the system's manager, thus giving the intruder access to virtually every file in the system. Not surprisingly, becoming a super user is relatively easy for individuals experienced in computer operations, because virtually every operating system has a trap door that allows individuals to enter a system and declare themselves the system's manager. Trap doors permit access to systems should a problem, either a human or technological one, arise. Unfortunately, this device also poses a threat to the system's integrity.

One of the best examples of a crime in which the computer is the target can be found in the book The Cuckoo's Egg by Cliff Stoll. The book recounts the true story of a hacker from Hanover, Germany, who infiltrated a number of computers in the United States, including those of universities, the military, and government contractors. The hacker attempted to locate and steal national security information in order to sell it to foreign governments, a clear illustration of making computers the targets of crime.

Computer as the Instrumentality of the Crime

In common law, instrumentality refers to the diversion of a lawfully possessed item, that is, an instrument, to facilitate committing a crime. In this category, the processes of the computer, not the contents of computer files, facilitate the crime. Essentially, the criminal introduces a new code (programming instructions) to manipulate the computer's analytical processes, thereby facilitating the crime. Another method involves converting legitimate computer processes for illegitimate purposes. Crimes in this category include fraudulent use of automated teller machine (ATM) cards and accounts; theft of money from accrual, conversion, or transfer accounts; credit card fraud; fraud from computer transactions (stock transfers, sales, or billings); and telecommunications fraud.

One example of using a computer as the instrument to commit a crime is the growing problem of individuals' using cellular phones and electronically billing charges to other customers. In these cases, offenders obtain cellular billing identification codes by using scanning devices, which are small parabolic (curve-shaped) antennae connected to portable computers. When activated, these scanners capture and store account numbers transmitted by cellular phones. The offenders operate near highways, because motorists frequently make calls from their cars. Once they capture the computerized billing codes, they program these codes into other cellular phones simply by hooking up the phone to a personal computer. Then, using software originally developed by programmers in London, they reprogram the signal chip in the cellular phone. The use of this software, which is easy to copy and to use, is spreading across the United States and Canada, sometimes being shared through underground computer bulletin board services (BBS).

Computer is Incidental to Other Crimes

In this category of computer crime, the computer is not essential for the crime to occur, but it is related to the criminal act. This means that the crime could occur without the technology; however, computerization helps the crime to occur faster, permits processing of greater amounts of information, and makes the crime more difficult to identify and trace. Such crimes include money laundering and unlawful banking transactions, BBSs supporting unlawful activity, organized crime records or books, and bookmaking. In one case, a suspect committed murder by changing a patient's medication information and dosage in a hospital computer. Cases involving drug raids, money laundering seizures, and other arrests also have produced computers and electronic storage media containing incriminating information. Many times, the criminals encrypt the data or design the files to erase themselves if not properly accessed. In some instances, criminals even destroy the storage media, such as disks, to eliminate evidence of their illegal activities.

All of these situations require unique data recovery techniques in order to gain access to the evidence. And, in every case, the crimes could occur without the computers; the systems merely facilitate the offenses. Another illustration of how criminals use technology to further their illegal activities involves child pornography. Historically, consumers of child pornography have trafficked photographs and related information through newsletters and tightly controlled exchange networks. Now, with the advancement of computer technology, child pornographers exchange this information through BBSs.

Recently, U.S. Customs agents raided 40 locations in 15 States serviced by a Denmark-based, child pornography BBS. These criminals used the computer to facilitate the distribution of pornographic material and to increase the efficiency of criminal activity already occurring via other methods.

Crimes Associated with the Prevalence of Computers

The simple presence of computers, and notably the widespread growth of microcomputers, generates new versions of fairly traditional crimes. In these cases, technological growth essentially creates new crime targets. Software piracy/counterfeiting, copyright violation of computer programs, counterfeit equipment, black market computer equipment and programs, and theft of technological equipment fall into this category of computer crime. One offense in this category occurs with relative frequency—the violation of copyright restrictions of commercial software. Initially, this offense may not seem like a serious crime; yet, the potential loss to businesses can be quite staggering.

A software package usually costs about $400; a strong-arm robbery usually yields about $50 or less for the thief. Thus, one copyright violation is the economic equivalent of eight strong-arm robberies. However, because the emotional trauma experienced in a piracy is almost nonexistent, many people do not view this as a serious crime. Evidence exists that software also is being written and sold explicitly to help hackers break into computers. In another area, successful computer programs—notably word processing, spreadsheets, and databases—are being duplicated, packaged, and sold illegally on a large scale, just as audio and video tapes are pirated. Similarly, counterfeit computers and peripherals (items such as modems and hard disks) are being manufactured and sold as originals in much the same manner as imitation Rolex watches and Gucci shoes.

COMPUTER FRAUD

Computer fraud is any dishonest misrepresentation of fact intended to induce another to do or refrain from doing something which causes loss. In this context, the fraud will result in obtaining a benefit by:

* altering computer input in an unauthorized way. This requires little technical expertise and is not an uncommon form of theft by employees altering the data before entry or entering false data, or by entering unauthorized instructions or using unauthorized processes;

* altering, destroying, suppressing, or stealing output, usually to conceal unauthorized transactions: this is difficult to detect;
* altering or deleting stored data; or
* altering or misusing existing system tools or software packages, or altering or writing code for fraudulent purposes. This requires real programming skills and is not common.

Manipulating banking systems to make unauthorized identity theft with reference to ATM fraud.

Offensive Content

The content of websites and other electronic communications may be harmful, distasteful or offensive for a variety of reasons. Most countries have enacted law that place some limits on the freedom of speech and ban racist, blasphemous, politically subversive, seditious or inflammatory material that tends to incite hate crimes. This is a sensitive area in which the courts can become involved in arbitrating between groups with entrenched beliefs, each convinced that their point of view has been unreasonably attacked.

In England, s28 Crime and Disorder Act 1998 defines a racial group, following Mandla v Dowell-Lee (1983) 2 AC 548 (in which a requirement to wear a cap as part of a school uniform had the effect of excluding Sikh boys whose religion required them to wear a turban), as a group of persons defined by reference to race, color, nationality (including citizenship) or ethnic or national origin; and a religious group as a group of persons defined by reference to religious belief or lack of religious belief. Therefore, it is equally an offense to show hostility to a person who practices a particular faith as to a person who has no religious belief or faith.

Harassment

Whereas content may be offensive in a non-specific way, harassment directs obscenities and derogatory comments at specific individuals focusing for example on gender, race, religion, nationality, sexual orientation. This often occurs in chat rooms, through newsgroups, and by sending hate e-mail to interested parties (see cyber bullying, harassment by computer, stalking, and cyberstalking). In England, in a broader form than s43 Telecommunications Act 1984, s1 Malicious Communications Act 1988 makes it an offense to send an indecent, offensive or threatening letter, electronic communication or other article to another person. Now, s2 Protection from Harassment Act 1997 criminalizes a course of conduct amounting to harassment which the defendant knows, or ought to know, amounts to harassment of another. If a reasonable person in possession of the same information would think the course of conduct amounted to harassment of the other, the knowledge will be imputed to the defendant. Although harassment is not defined, s7 states that it includes causing alarm or distress, and conduct is defined as including speech in all its forms.

In DPP v Collins (2006) 1 WLR 308 the defendant repeatedly telephoned the offices of his MP on a wide range of political matters. In conversations with employees at the office and on messages left on the telephone answering machine, he used racist terms to show the frustration he felt at the way in which his affairs were being handled. No-one was personally offended, but the staff became depressed. Charged under s127(1) Communications Act 2003, the magistrates found that the terms were offensive but that a reasonable person would not find them grossly offensive. To determine whether any message content is merely offensive or grossly offensive depended on their particular circumstances and context, i.e. in the wider society which is an open and just multi-racial society, the test of offensiveness was objective.

More problematic are deliberate attacks which amount to defamation although, in March 2006, Michael Keith-Smith became the first person to win damages from an individual internet user after she accused him of being a 'sex offender' and 'racist blogger' on a Yahoo! discussion site. She also claimed that his wife was a prostitute. The High Court judge decided that Tracy Williams, of Oldham, was "particularly abusive" and "her statements demonstrated that ... she had no intention of stopping her libellous and defamatory behavior". She was ordered to pay £10,000 in damages, plus £7,200 costs. In general, libel is not treated as a criminal matter except when it may provoke the person defamed into retaliatory violence (see cybersmearing as it affects business. All forms of unsolicited e-mail and advertisements can also be considered to be forms of Internet harassment where the content is offensive or of an explicit sexual nature. Now termed spam, it has been criminalized in various countries.

Drug Trafficking

Drug traffickers are increasingly taking advantage of the Internet to sell their illegal substances through encrypted e-mail and other Internet Technology. Some drug traffickers arrange deals at internet cafes, use courier Web sites to track illegal packages of pills, and swap recipes for amphetamines in restricted-access chat rooms.

The Internet's easy-to-learn, fast-paced character, global impact, and fairly reliable privacy features facilitate the marketing of illicit drugs. Detecting money laundering of cash earned by drug traffickers is very difficult, because dealers are now able to use electronic commerce and Internet banking facilities.

Also, traffickers have been using online package tracking services offered by courier companies to keep tabs on the progress of their shipments.

If there happened to be some sort of undue delay, this could signal authority interception of the drugs, which would still allow the dealers time to cover their tracks. Law enforcement is also more deficient because illicit drug deals are arranged instantaneously, over short distances, making interception by authorities much more difficult.

The rise in Internet drug trades could also be attributed to the lack of face-to-face communication. These virtual exchanges allow more intimidated individuals to more comfortably purchase illegal drugs. The sketchy effects that are often associated with drug trades are severely minimized and the filtering process that comes with physical interaction fades away. Furthermore, traditional drug recipes were carefully kept secrets. But with modern computer technology, this information is now being made available to anyone with computer access.

COMPUTER INSECURITY

Security and Systems Design

Most current real-world computer security efforts focus on external threats, and generally treat the computer system itself as a trusted system. Some knowledgeable observers consider this to be a disastrous mistake, and point out that this distinction is the cause of much of the insecurity of current computer systems - once an attacker has subverted one part of a system without fine-grained security, he or she usually has access to most or all of the features of that system.

Because computer systems can be very complex, and cannot be guaranteed to be free of defects, this security stance tends to produce insecure systems.

The 'trusted systems' approach has been predominant in the design of many Microsoft software products, due to the long-standing Microsoft policy of emphasizing functionality and 'ease of use' over security. Since Microsoft products currently dominate the desktop and home computing markets, this has led to unfortunate effects. However, the problems described here derive from the security stance taken by software and hardware vendors generally, rather than the failing of a single vendor. Microsoft is not out of line in this respect, just far more prominent with respect to its consumer marketshare.

It should be noted that the Windows NT line of operating systems from Microsoft contained mechanisms to limit this, such as services that ran under dedicated user accounts, and Role-Based Access Control (RBAC) with user/group rights, but the Windows 95 line of products lacked most of these functions. Before the release of Windows 2003 Microsoft has changed their official stance, taking a more locked down approach.

On 15 January 2002, Bill Gates sent out a memo on Trustworthy Computing, marking the official change in company stance. Regardless, Microsoft's operating system Windows XP is still plagued by complaints about lack of local security and inability to use the fine-grained user access controls together with certain software (esp. certain popular computer games).

Financial Cost

Serious financial damage has been caused by computer security breaches, but reliably estimating costs is quite difficult. Figures in the billions of dollars have been quoted in relation to the damage caused by malware such as computer worms like the Code Red worm, but such estimates may be exaggerated. However, other losses, such as those caused by the compromise of credit card information, can be more easily determined, and they have been substantial, as measured by millions of individual victims of identity theft each year in each of several nations, and the severe hardship imposed on each victim, that can wipe out all of their finances, prevent them from getting a job, plus be treated as if they were the criminal. Volumes of victims of phishing and other scams may not be known.

Individuals who have been infected with spyware or malware likely go through a costly and time-consuming process of having their computer cleaned. Spyware and malware is considered to be a problem specific to the various Microsoft Windows operating systems, however this can be explained somewhat by the fact that Microsoft controls a major share of the PC market and thus represent the most prominent target.

Reasons

There are many similarities (yet many fundamental differences) between computer and physical security. Just like real-world security, the motivations for breaches of computer security vary between attackers, sometimes called hackers or crackers. Some are teenage thrill-seekers or vandals (the kind often responsible for defacing web sites); similarly, some web site defacements are done to make political statements. However, some attackers are highly skilled and motivated with the goal of compromising computers for financial gain or espionage. An example of the latter is Markus Hess who spied for the KGB and was ultimately caught because of the efforts of Clifford Stoll, who wrote an amusing and accurate book, The Cuckoo's Egg, about his experiences. For those seeking to prevent security breaches, the first step is usually to attempt to identify what might motivate an attack on the system, how much the continued operation and information security of the system are worth, and who might be motivated to breach it. The precautions required for a home PC are very different for those of banks' Internet banking system, and different again for a classified military network. Other computer security writers suggest that, since an attacker using a network need know nothing about you or what you have on your computer, attacker motivation is inherently impossible to determine beyond guessing. If true, blocking all possible attacks is the only plausible action to take.

Vulnerabilities

To understand the techniques for securing a computer system, it is important to first understand the various types of "attacks" that can be made against it. These threats can typically be classified into one of these seven categories:

Exploits

Software flaws, especially buffer overflows, are often exploited to gain control of a computer, or to cause it to operate in an unexpected manner. Many development methodologies rely on testing to ensure the quality of any code released; this process often fails to discover extremely unusual potential exploits. The term "exploit" generally refers to small programs designed to take advantage of a software flaw that has been discovered, either remote or local. The code from the exploit program is frequently reused in trojan horses and computer viruses. In some cases, a vulnerability can lie in certain programs' processing of a specific file type, such as a non-executable media file.

Eavesdropping

Any data that is transmitted over a network is at some risk of being eavesdropped, or even modified by a malicious person. Even machines that operate as a closed system (ie, with no contact to the outside world) can be eavesdropped upon via monitoring the faint electro-magnetic transmissions generated by the hardware such as TEMPEST. The FBI's proposed Carnivore program was intended to act as a system of eavesdropping protocols built into the systems of internet service providers.

4

Critical Infrastructure Protection and Cyber Security

The Internet infrastructure relies on primarily on the Border Gateway Protocol (BGP) and the Domain Name System (DNS). The secure remote administration of routers relies mostly on the Secure Shell (SSH) protocol. Attacks against any of these technologies may impact on the availability of Internet-based services. As we do not know how to guarantee software correctness, it is a reasonable to assume that exploitable programming errors exist in applications.

To reduce the ability of an adversary to cause damage, we need to limit the impact of such programming errors. We offer *Privilege Separation* as one solution. Services that authenticate remote users to system resources are difficult to contain via external application confinement mechanisms. Privilege Separation is a protection mechanism at the application level that separates the privileged code path from the unprivileged code path. An adversary interacts with the unprivileged part only; an exploitable programming error in the unprivileged code path does not lead to immediate privilege escalation.

Privilege separation may also be employed to increase the resilience of domain name service implementations like bind. Privilege Separation is very portable as most modern Unix operating system provide address space protection between processes and inter-process communication, privilege separation.

Intrusion Prevention

While Privilege Separation increases an application's resilience against programming errors, it does not prevent all possible intrusions. Many system services and applications perform specific tasks. By confining applications to only those operations that required for its correct execution, we prevent adversaries who gain control over these system services from causing damage to the system. In Unix operating systems, persistent changes are possibly only via *System Calls*. By carefully monitoring and restricting an application's system calls, we can limit or even prevent an adversary from causing damage. We offer *Systrace* as solution. Systrace provides fine-grained application confinement based on configurable security policies. Additionally, it can detect and prevent intrusions. It also records audit trails that can used in forensic analysis.

Threat Assessment

The impact of new security problems can be reduced by early threat detection. Threat detection and assessment allows us to quickly identify so far unknown attacks, prioritize their threat and protect vulnerable systems. Honeypot technology serves this purpose by providing computer systems that we expect to be compromised. The honeypot systems are network sensors that allows us to detect new attacks. As computer security problems are inherently repeatable, we obtain threat detection by populating our network with honeypots. New attacks can easily be identified by monitoring the state of deployed honeypots including new worms or widespread scans for vulnerabilities.

MODEL OF CYBER-PROTECTION

The cyber-threat to British business and government is growing. Statistics from Symantec, the internet protection software company, show that during 2010 over 286 million unique malicious internet threats were observed globally, with a 93 per cent increase in the volume of web-based attacks from the previous year. This translates to a growing economic threat, with the UK's Office of Cyber Security and Information Assurance estimating the cost of cybercrime to British business at over £20 billion a year. This rising burden on the British economy cannot be ignored or dismissed as an acceptable cost of conducting business online.

There is also widespread acknowledgement that better public-private cooperation is an important element in improving security in cyberspace. At a meeting in February hosted by the Prime Minister, representatives from a cross section of British industry and government ministers agreed on the need for increased information sharing as part of a new approach to protecting the UK's economic and national security interests against cyber threats.

Research conducted by RUSI's Cyber-Security Programme has confirmed the need for sharing information on threats and responses, not just between government and industry, but between companies and other organisations, especially across sector boundaries. This research has also shown that it is vital to extend protection beyond what is traditionally perceived to be national infrastructure (*e.g.*, defence, telecommunications, food and water supply) to include often neglected sectors. These overlooked areas of vulnerability encompass those sectors which act as service providers (*e.g.*, lawyers and accountants) and collaborators (in particular academia), and potentially represent weak links in the cyber-security chain. Moreover, these sectors also represent vital components of the economy, and should be protected accordingly. Any critical breach of security from these companies, such as the theft of sensitive client data from a law firm or a doctor's practice, could have a damaging impact upon public confidence in the industry as a whole. Furthermore, sectors such as academia are entirely based upon the knowledge they generate through research, and hence it is vital to safeguard this from theft. There is therefore a clear need to extend protection across and within sectors to provide collective security.

RUSI's research has, however, also revealed equally widespread agreement among stakeholders and others that effective information sharing is hard to achieve, and that the costs often outweigh the benefits, as highlighted in Thomas and Walport's Data Sharing Review for the Ministry of Justice. This problem afflicts many areas where collective action is crucial for security (not just cyberspace), but is rarely acknowledged publicly. The idea is attractive, but there are many examples in various fields of systems that fail to deliver. However, RUSI's research into models for information sharing shows that, whilst it is undoubtedly challenging to do it well, outstandingly effective and efficient systems do exist, and a study of these can help identify the criteria that are key to success.

Understanding the Requirement

The overarching problem for security in cyberspace is that whilst a networked world brings many benefits, those benefits are accompanied by risks. How do we manage those risks intelligently and efficiently? The immediate problem is that our knowledge of those risks is dispersed, and our understanding fragmentary.

Without adequate knowledge, countermeasures will be ineffectual, if not counter-productive, and policy will be based merely on plausible ideas and guesswork. Success will be the result of luck, not judgement. But from greater shared knowledge will follow better countermeasures (both in their design and implementation) and better policy. Thus the absolutely necessary precursor to any sensible intervention in cyber-security is: Get knowledge.

Genuine knowledge is rooted in accurate, timely information, but how are we to understand 'information sharing'? It covers a wide range of actions, from the exchange of high-level generalised conclusions (*e.g.* at conferences or liaison meetings) to the automated transfer of large volumes of data. We would suggest that the latter is not appropriate in this instance, two major objections being the horrendous privacy implications and the technical infrastructure needed. High-level exchanges have their place but experience (*e.g.* from financial crime) suggests that by themselves they are inadequate. The answer lies somewhere between these two extremes: in essence, the reporting of incidents by individuals at the operational level. This does not rule out deeper analysis and higher level exchanges, but is a necessary precursor: a firm foundation of hard information on which they can be based.There is, indeed, much good co-operation and information sharing already in the field of cyber-security, often of an informal sort. But this activity tends to be confined to a particular sector (*e.g.*, banking or academia) and even then it is rarely comprehensive. The sharing of knowledge is fairly high level or anecdotal: what is lacking is a foundation of hard information upon which a solid body of knowledge can be built. It will be important, however, to ensure that any new initiative(s) do not harm or disrupt the good work that is already being done: they should enhance and improve, not replace. Especially important will be avoiding a form of moral hazard where reporting, analysing and solving problems become 'someone else's business'. This will easily happen if the wrong model is adopted. Systemic flaws produce perverse outcomes, no matter how commendable the aims or how strong the commitment to them.

Principles

There are several guiding principles upon which we believe any solution to the problem of wider cyber-security should be based. The first is that the process should be fundamentally based upon active collaboration between the public and private sectors, whereby the government and its relevant agencies are equal stakeholders rather than controlling entities. This is designed to ensure a more level playing field to engender trust between public and private agencies, and to help facilitate greater information sharing, to the mutual benefit of all.

The second principle concerns the shifting of responsibility for cyber-security from central government agencies to companies themselves. This is designed to empower companies so that they may look after their own interests and not have to rely on the resources and direction of some central entity. This will help overcome the crucial time delay which occurs whenever companies at the periphery have to defer to the centre, thus reducing the vital time between detection and response to cyber incidents, where action will need to be taken within minutes rather than hours. Therefore companies should be provided with the tools and education to protect themselves from the most prevalent threats, and also trained to recognise serious incursions so that the rest of the community can be alerted and the relevant government agencies quickly involved.

In relation to this, the third principle argues for the creation of an environment which encourages collective security that can be collectively enforced, rather than security controlled and enforced from a central entity. An ideal model of cyber-security would facilitate, rather than direct, information-sharing between companies across non-traditional sector boundaries, and would encourage a culture of 'cyber-hygiene' amongst its members. Member organisations would thus be nudged into practicing better cyber-security as part of a collective community of security, with any central agency only intervening when necessary.

The fourth and perhaps the most important principle concerns the operator 'at the coalface'. This is the person who will spot and report incidents. If the system is designed so that their interest and intelligence is engaged, it will succeed. If not, a 'box-ticking' mentality will prevail and the information entering the system will be of poor quality, which will be devastating. Positive and negative factors come into play. The most important positive factor is that the system helps the operator to do their job better: they have access to the reports it contains and can use them to locally implement better countermeasures. This is a powerful incentive to contribute to the body of information themselves. On the negative side there must be no undue obstacles or disincentives to report. Reporting must be easy, quick, not (primarily) a compliance issue, and not governed by arbitrary targets.

Comparable Models

When considering the feasibility of putting these principles into practice, it is instructive to look towards existing collective security and information sharing arrangements. Public sector models such as the Serious Organised Crime Agency's Suspicious Activities Reports (SAR) system whilst playing a vital role in combating financial crime in the UK, are incompatible with our stated principles because they employ a top-down centralised approach, with private companies relegated to merely passing on information to assist law enforcement. Furthermore the SARs regime is part of a large and costly public-sector body, which is at odds with our vision of a small and nimble public-private sector collaborative entity.

A workable model can be found in Information Sharing and Analysis Centres (ISACs), which are organisations usually set up by the owners and operators of an infrastructure within a sector to provide information analysis and data dissemination. An example of this model that can be seen in practice in the UK is CIFAS-the UK's Credit Industry Fraud Advisory Service, which is a privately run organisation consisting of over 260 UK organisations, predominantly drawn from the private sector, and is the world's first non-profit fraud prevention data-sharing scheme. This model closely adheres to our stated principles as a relatively small organisation, entirely funded through membership fees, which facilitates information sharing between public and private agencies and across different sectors such a retail and finance. It also helps to empower and educate its members about fraud prevention by providing them with reports concerning the latest fraud trends and threats, and offers a multitude of staff training and even (jointly with a university) a foundation degree in Fraud Management. CIFAS provides an attractive model of collective security whereby the system empowers and educates its members whilst also facilitating information sharing, with the centre intervening and disciplining members only in cases of serious misconduct.

PROTECTION OF CRITICAL INFORMATION INFRASTRUCTURES

The protection of critical information infrastructures is the main priority of cyber security. They are a central component of nearly all critical infrastructures and become increasingly important. The public and the private sector must create an enhanced strategic and organizational basis for closer coordination based on intensified information sharing. To this end, cooperation established by the CIP implementation plan is systematically extended, and legal commitments to enhance the binding nature of the CIP implementation plan are examined. With the participation of the National Cyber Security Council (cf. objective 5), the integration of additional sectors is examined and the introduction of new relevant technologies is considered to a greater extent. Whether and where protective measures have to be made mandatory and whether and where additional powers are required in case of specific threats have to be clarified, too. Furthermore we will examine the necessity of harmonizing rules to maintain critical infrastructures during IT crises.

Strengthening IT Security in the Public Administration

The public administration will further enhance the protection of its IT systems. State authorities have to serve as role models for data security. We will create a common, uniform and secure network infrastructure in the federal administration ("federal networks") as a basis for electronic audio and data communication. We will continue to press ahead with the implementation plan for the federal administration. Should the IT security situation get worse, this plan may be aligned accordingly. Effective IT security requires powerful structures in all federal authorities. For this reason resources must be deployed appropriately at central and local level. To facilitate implementation through uniform action by authorities, joint investments into the Federal Government's IT security will be made regularly in line with budgetary possibilities. Operational cooperation with the federal Länder, particularly with regard to CERTs (computer emergency response teams), will be further intensified by the IT planning council.

National Cyber Response Centre

To optimize operational cooperation between all state authorities and improve the coordination of protection and response measures for IT incidents we will set up a National Cyber Response Centre. It will report to the Federal Office for Information Security (BSI) and cooperate directly with the Federal Office for the Protection of the Constitution (BfV) and the Federal Office of Civil Protection and Disaster Assistance (BBK). Cooperation in the National Cyber Response Centre will strictly observe the statutory tasks and powers of all authorities involved on the basis of cooperation agreements. The Federal Criminal Police Office (BKA), the Federal Police (BPOL), the Customs Criminological Office (ZKA), the Federal Intelligence Service (BND), the Bundeswehr and authorities supervising critical infrastructure operators all participate in this centre within the framework of their statutory tasks and powers. Quick and close information sharing on weaknesses of IT products, vulnerabilities, forms of attacks and profiles of perpetrators enables the National Cyber Response Centre to analyse IT incidents and give consolidated recommendations for action. The interests of the private sector to protect itself against crime and espionage in cyberspace should also be adequately taken into account. At the same time respective responsibilities must be observed. Every stakeholder takes the necessary measures in its remit on the basis of the jointly developed national cyber security assessment and coordinates them with the competent authorities as well as partners from industry and academia. Since security preparedness is best achieved by early warning and prevention, the Cyber Response Centre will submit recommendations to the National Cyber Security Council both on a regular basis and for specific incidents. If the cyber security situation reaches the level of an imminent or already occurred crisis, the National Cyber Response Centre will directly inform the crisis management staff headed by the responsible State Secretary at the Federal Ministry of the Interior.

CYBER PROTECTION/CYBER SECURITY LIABILITY

The dawn of the internet provided many new avenues for doing business, and the protection of computer data has become a main concern in today's working environment. "Cyber Liability," as it is called, encompasses a gamut of new risks for businesses that not only conduct business over the internet, but that also may store private confidential information subject to several federal laws.

To provide some insurance protection for these new risks, most insurance companies have developed cyber security liability policies which cover both first party "the insured" and third party liabilities which can arise because of attacks by outside parties or because of losing of sensitive data due to mistakes on the part of the insured.

Up until a few years ago, these policies were available under most property and general liability policies. However, since 2005 the loss of intangible property has been excluded under standard property policies; likewise, bodily injury or property damage, previously covered under the general liability policy, is also excluded if it emanates from a cyber breach or error. Some examples of the claims that have occurred are as follows:

Theft of Digital Assets

A regional retailer contracted with a third party service provider. A burglar stole two laptops from the service provider containing the data of over 800,000 clients of the retailer. Under applicable notification laws, the retailer-not the service provider-was required to notify affected individuals. The total expenses incurred for crisis management notification of customers cost nearly $5 million.

In a second example a home health care organization had backup data, laptops and disks containing social security numbers, clinical and demographic information. In a small number of cases, patient financial data was stolen. In total, over 365,000 patient records were exposed. The organization settled with the State Attorney General and provided patients with free credit monitoring, credit restoration to patients that were victims of identity fraud, and reimbursement to patients for direct losses that resulted from the data breach.

Human Error

An employee of a private high school mistakenly distributed via e-mail the names, social security numbers, birth dates and medical information of students and faculty creating a privacy breach. Overall, 1,250 individuals' information was compromised.

Malicious Code

A juvenile released a computer worm that caused a launch of denial of service attack against a regional computing consulting and application outsourcing firm. The infection caused an 18 hour shut down of the entity's computer systems. The computer firm incurred extensive cost and expenses to repair and restore their systems, as well as business income expenses which totaled approximately $875,000.

The cyber liability policy is sufficiently flexible so that a business can buy either third party or first party coverages, or both. Here is an example of how the language in a carrier's insurance policy protects first party assets:

Loss of Digital Assets

"We will indemnify you for loss you incur, in excess of the deductible, as a result of damage, alteration, corruption, distortion, theft, misuse, or destruction of your digital assets directly caused by a covered cause of loss". In this case, digital assets mean electronic data and computer programmes that exist in a computer system. Please note that digital assets do not include computer hardware. In addition to this, protection can be provided for the business income loss that may result from any direct first party claims. Here is an example of the coverage grants available for third party protection under a typical insurance carrier's policy:

NETWORK SECURITY AND PRIVACY LIABILITY COVERAGE

The insurance company "will pay on your behalf those amounts, in excess of the applicable deductible, which you are legally obligated as damages on claim expenses arising from your acts, errors or omissions or from acts, errors or omissions for others for whom you are legally responsible, including outsourcers, or vendors provided such acts, errors or omissions follow a security breach or privacy breach". An example of this claim is the loss of a laptop containing sensitive information, which results in the public disclosure of a person's private information. Also, this insuring agreement would cover unauthorized access into your computer system, a denial of service attack against your computer system, or an infection of your computer system by malicious code.

There are a number of other coverage protection grants available on most policies, which The Fedeli Group, after an assessment of your risks, can review with you. Please contact The Fedeli Group team to arrange for this type of risk assessment and possible valuable insurance protection.

5

Cyber Security Threats in Counter Attacks

Many people have proposed methods of "counter-attack" or "active response" to deal with today's cyber security threats. There is a common belief that traditional approaches to the problem are inadequate. Patching software vulnerabilities is labour intensive, so many people don't do it until there's an attack. The legal system is slow to respond, courts lack the necessary technical expertise, and prosecutions do not occur often enough to deter attacks.

HISTORY OF CYBER SECURITY

The history of successful counterattacks in the world of cyber security is a short one. There are an increasing number of papers and publications which make proposals, but concerns over legal issues as well as technical challenges have kept the list of successes small. In Sept. 1998, the Pentagon is reported to have counterattacked some activists who were doing a Denial of Service attack of the Department of Defense's websites, responding to their requests with an applet which ran on the attackers' machines and forced them to reboot. In 1999, a California ISP Conxion wrote a script which caused DoS packets sent to the World Trade Organization's website to be sent back to the attackers.

Of course, such an attack would not have worked if the attackers had used what's known as "IP address spoofing", which would have made the packets appear that they came from a different computer from where they did.

In 2001, several defences were created in response to the Code Red II worm. One, called CRclean, if it received a probe from the worm, would make use of a back door which the worm placed on the infected machine to load a neutralizing agent and halt the spread of the worm. But it would also install itself on that machine. Another, called CodeGreen, would actually scan the internet for computers with the IIS vulnerability that allowed CodeRed, then download the patch and place it on the machine, and clean up the back doors.

It is clear that there are serious legal and ethical issues with both of these worms, even the former, which is still a worm even though it only reacts to attacks. In 2003, the Welchia worm was released onto the Internet. Welchia would remove the Blaster worm and patch the vulnerability that Blaster used to spread. However, Welchia also caused severe network congestion.

In late 2004, Lycos Europe got fed up with spammers and launched a popular campaign called "Make Love Not Spam" which attracted over 100,000 users.

Users could install a screen saver on their desktop which would send requests to websites which were known to advertise via spam. This effort was sucessful in causing some of the sites to change locations. (http://www.makelovenotspam.com) Lycos reportedly got around the illegality of DDoS attacks by claiming to only take 95% of the target sites' bandwidth, though, David Dittrich finds this reasoning dubious at best. Lycos ended this campaign in December 2004.

Some companies such as Symbiot Security are currently developing counter attack tools and devices, but there is a lot of skepticism about deployment of devices because of liability concerns.

Cyber security Incident Response

Counter-attacks are part of the overall process of cyber security incident response. This consists of five stages:

1. Intrusion detection.
2. Identifying the attacker.
3. Defending against the attack.

4. Designing and deploying a counter attack.
5. Post-conflict investigation and support.

Intrusion Detection: Intrusion detection first identifies if there is an intrusion or intrusion attempt in the network or machine connected to network. Monitoring can be done on the network or on end-hosts. Firewalls and virus scanners also contribute. There are various techniques, such as anomaly detection, and policy-based approaches. Identifying the Attacker: This very important step towards counter-attack, basically knowing who your enemy is and where is he located. Identifying the attacker can be difficult, since an attacker may use one compromised host to attack another. Also, with today's network architecture it can be quite difficult to locate the real attacker. Packets can be sent with spoofed source addresses, and tracing them through multiple hops and different autonomous systems can be a complicated process. Finding out the specific server and location can be critical in determining what the counter attack would be.

Defending against the Attack: Before an attack, software patches are used to fix vulnerabillities. More interesting are defences once an attack against a real vulnerability has happened. Diversions can be set forth to surprise an attacker. Or once the attack has been detected, countermeasures can be put in place to stop further damage. Also, diversion tactics like Honey Pots can be used to keep the rest of the network safe. The information from these diversions (or information gained during the delays caused by these tactics) can be harnessed to engineer a specific counter attack. Designing and deploying a counter attack: Counterattacks take a surprising variety of forms. Designing a counter attack should take into account the following factors: the method of attack; the support of the network infrastructure (*i.e.* are ISPs performing egress filtering); collateral damage; and costs. Post Counter attack investigation and support: In order to aid the post counter attack investigation a counter attack should have inbuilt mechanism to log its trail and its operation history. Ideally, it will also provide a means of discovering the hacker's techniques and identity. The more risk hackers have of being discovered, the less likely they are to go hacking.

Anti-worms

A worm spreads itself by sending out packets which look for certain responses from computers. It will analyse those responses to deduce if it thinks the replying machine has the vulnerability that it exploits. These packets represent a worm's 'signature.' The machine the worm is targeting can detect the signature of the worm and thus know its mode of propagation. An anti-worm is generated, which exploits the same vulnerabilities as the original worm or uses the back doors opened by the original worm. The antiworm would either fix the attacking host, neutralize the worm, or bring it down gracefully, potentially informing the owner. It may also install itself for further propagation.

In addition to the stated goal, an antiworm adheres to following guidelines to minimize collateral damage:

- It is bug-free and does leave other vulnerabilities that could be exploited further.
- It can be uninstalled gracefully when owner asks for it.
- It makes minimal changes to host that it operates on.
- It should not be able to be used for propagating malicious content.

The countermeasure, or 'Neutralizing Agent' used, can take several forms. For example, it could patch the vulnerability and remove the botnet or worm. Less invasive changes include blocking the port over which the worm sends messages, or using a mutex and rebooting the machine to lock the botnet from being able to execute.

Also, one would have to remove any backdoors left by the worm.

In addition, deployment strategy of the antiworm will determine its effectiveness and collateral damage it may cause.

- *Active Deployment*: The antiworm is itself a worm; it propagates across the network by scanning and seeking exploited vulnerabilities. This is the fastest way to remove the original worm from the network, but this also causes the most collateral damage by affecting the network traffic a lot.

- *Passive Deployment*: The anti-worm waits on a host till another host attacks it, and then the antiworm cures only the attacking host. Collateral damage is bare minimum, but the anti-worm is left behind on the new host.
- *Controlled Deployment*: The anti-worm propagation is control via some statistic of number of infected/vulnerable host to number host it cured. This can be very effective and efficient.
- *IDS base Deployment*: The anti-worm uses the intrusion detection sensors which monitor traffic and may deploy an anti-worm against an attacker. As with passive deployment, collateral damage is limited to computers actively launching attacks, but this is less invasive because it does not leave a worm, it just neutralizes the machine.

Spam

Spam is unsolicited e-mail. A virus is a programme which, when executed, installs malware such as root-kits, key-stroke loggers, etc.

These programmes are then used to send sensitive information to the attacker without the user's consent. Both spam and viruses spread through e-mail and require human interaction to activate them. Email servers as well as the hosts can detect spam with the help of spam detectors like Symantec's TurnTide. Once the spam is identified one counter attack is achieved by automatic flooding of the Sender Server with bounced e-mails and mail notification to server's administrator. (Even if sender addresses are spoofed, one may be able to identify the last mail server that forwarded a message.)

Botnet

An attacker establishes a botnet by first spreading a virus or worm that takes over the vulnerable hosts. Each worm or virus then calls Home to tell that it has successfully captured the Host. It also establishes a command channel such that the Attacker through the home can control the host. Botnets can be used for DDOS attacks, phishing etc.

Counter Attack

- Counter attack involves identifying the attacker by monitoring the compromised Host and intercepting its communication to the Home machine. The Home machine is probably the attacker's base or intermediate node for communication between the host and the attacker base machines. Once that machine is identified, you hack back into that machine bring it down. For hacking back, you can use same techniques as used by the hackers to take control of the attacking machine.
- Taking down the Home machine only removes the attacker for a short duration, the network of compromised hosts still exists. A more effective counter attack would be to takeover or monitor the command channel for communication between the Home and other compromised hosts. If possible, identify other compromised hosts and fix them or take them down as preventive measure.

TYPES OF CYBER SECURITY THREATS

Nation-sponsored Hacking

Nation-sponsored hacking specifically-targeted cyber attacks will incorporate concepts and techniques from the commercial hacker industry. These campaigns will contain a different malware payload than the traditional attacks conducted for monetary gain. However, these attacks will use similar techniques. These Advanced Persistent Threat (APT) attacks will borrow techniques, such as automation and viral distribution, making them all the more powerful and potentially more successful. An example of such an attack is Stuxnet, which was not searching for data to monetize, rather it was focused on gaining control of crucial infrastructure.

Both classes of attack (hacker industry and APT) are going to use some of the same techniques so some security controls are applicable to both. On the positive side, given you're covered against the cyber mafia you should have some of the controls to be protected from certain APT attacks. As APT is persistent, if a certain attack does not succeed, another one will come into play.

The traditional security controls do not deter these relentless, state-sponsored hacker organizations. For the enterprise as well as government, this means increasing monitoring of traffic and setting security controls across all organization layers.

The insider Threat

In this upcoming year, we expect to see a growing awareness to security incidents of an "insider job" nature. Attention will grow as a consequence of an increased flow of incident reports where data theft and security breaches are tied to employees and other insiders. The cause of this trend will be the emphasis put on new regulations covering the act of notification and disclosure (rather on the actual protection of data).

To deter insider threats, organizations should therefore:

- Enforce access controls such that access is based only a business need-to-know level. This includes eliminating excessive privileges.
- Provide the proper access auditing tools to data centres. These auditing tools should monitor who accesses what data.

Man in the Browser Attacks will man Up

Man in the Browser (MitB) attack sophistication is going to increase, as well as moving forward to more types of online applications. As a consequence, more online service providers are going to include this in their list of priorities for 2011, shifting the responsibility for mitigating the risk from the consumers to the service providers.

While avoiding infection by proxy Trojans is presumably the responsibility of consumers, MitB attacks are quickly becoming a concern of online service providers. The actual rate of infection and the proliferation of the many types of MitB malware suggest that providers must be able to serve (and protect) customers who might be infected with one type of malware or another. Just as the evolution of vehicle safety drove manufacturers to include device such as ABS, Air Bags and ESP, rather than rely on us to drive carefully, so will online service providers need to invest in mechanisms that allow them to conduct business with allegedly infected consumers. Among the technologies that we foresee as helpful are strong device identification, client profiling, fast security code evolution, session flow tracking and site-to-client authentication.

Misanthropes and Anti-socials: Privacy vs. Security in Social Networks

In 2011, we will see prominent social networks, and tools, placing more efforts into security over privacy. This is not the result of resolved privacy issues, but rather an understanding of the real threats to the existence and proliferation of social networks.

There are two key factors at stake: security and trust. While privacy concerns the ability to keep personal information hidden from other application users, security controls the way in which people use the information of others. Trust impacts our ability to make decisions based on the information we receive through social networks.

In today's social networking platform, both security and trust are in danger. Cross-site scripting (XSS) and cross-site request forgery (CSRF) vulnerabilities are quickly translating into massive worm out brakes. Next year, we expect social platforms to invest more resources in improving the security posture of the platform. These measures will provide improved protection against application layer attacks, stronger authentication and account control features, as well as better malware detection systems.

File Security takes Centre Stage

In 2011, we expect to see a growing number of data breaches where compromised data is in the form of files rather than database records. Consequently, organizations will rush to look for the proper tools to control access to repositories of unstructured data, mainly file servers. We estimate that the number of compromised files, and the number of organizations that suffer a massive file related security breach, will rise. Even PCI 2.0 has recognized the security aspect of storing data in different locations.

With today's available tools, controlling access and usage of these files can be an extremely daunting task. Since each file is an autonomous entity, with respect to content ownership and access control (contrary to a database record), maintaining control of who can access a file is almost impossible as is keeping track of access to those files that contain sensitive information. The inability to maintain control may result in excessive access privileges and an inadequate audit trail of access to sensitive information.

Data Security goes to the Cloud

We expect to see more application security offerings in the cloud throughout 2011, and predict some early data security in the cloud offerings. Offerings will need to respond to private and public clouds that are either self-serviced or managed as a service.

This trend is a late response to the move of many applications and data stores to cloud technologies, and the industrialization of hacking, which dragged many smaller online businesses into the threat zone. Taking together all the types of cloud forms (private and public, SaaS, PaaS and IaaS) we can see a set of challenges for both providers and consumers.

These can be summarized as following:

- Maintaining bulletproof partitions between datasets of different customers
- Providing different levels of data security to applications sharing the same logical or physical platforms
- Protecting customer data from the prying eyes of cloud administrators
- Providing solutions that operate over a specialized infrastructure (VM, Amazon AMI)
- Managing application and data security for a large number of applications inside the cloud.

We expect that in 2011 good technical solutions for application security in the cloud will be available and gain traction, while data security solutions (protecting data stores in the cloud) will lag behind.

Mobile Devices Compromise Data Security

The proliferation of sophisticated mobile devices is going to have a substantial effect on application and data security in the coming years. In particular, we will see organizations struggle to accommodate the increase in number and variety of these devices, while maintaining traditional data and application security practices.

The past couple of years have witnessed a dramatic surge in the number of sophisticated mobile devices being used as access points to online services and enterprise networks. Add to the mix a growing variety of applications that are a gateway to enterprise systems, including CRM, ERP, and document management. While we are used to concerning ourselves with lost or stolen laptops, it turns out that missing mobile devices may be just as big of a pain point.

As mobile devices become mainstream, online service providers will create a special version of the applications to match each device platform. We anticipate this process, will cause older vulnerabilities to surface once again. In particular, mistakes around identification and authentication. Thus, the applications will become vulnerable to mistakenly trusting attributes of the data stream that can be forged by an attacker.

Furthermore, some assumptions regarding "strong" multifactor authentication schemes are becoming obsolete. Take, for example, applications that use a one-time password (OTP) for validation of sensitive transactions being defeated by a Trojan that is able to access the OTP delivered through SMS.

Mobile malware will proliferate as malicious code becomes available for these platforms (*e.g.* Zitmo) and the complex applications (not to mention the usual human flaws) make it easy, if not easier, to infect a mobile device with malware, as with any standard desktop platform.

We expect exponential growth in the number of incidents related to mobile devices in the next few years. Organizations need to start planning to secure the devices and their interaction with the enterprise networks. Tools and procedures need to be put into place, such as anti-malware, encryption, and authentication. Special monitoring requirements should be set for access of these devices to enterprise resources (databases, files, intranets). On the other hand, application providers need to get their act together with respect to serving these devices, including vulnerability mitigation, reevaluation of trust, and incorporation of new authentication/authorization channels.

Hackers Feeling the Heat

In 2011, the cyber crime landscape will change in two ways. First, more and more smaller cyber gangs will go out of business. Why? Security researchers will continue to look into the hacker operations and will unearth the smaller or less diligent criminals. In general, the hacker industry will react by investing more resources in their attack techniques and detection evasion. The hackers that cannot make this investment will go out of business. Other cyber-criminal organizations will "buy-out" other groups or merge their operations with other groups. This will lead to the second change. The current powerful cyber crime organizations will consolidate their power and grow (after all, antitrust laws don't apply to them).

As the year 2010 draws to a close, it provides us with all the more examples of this accelerating trend:

- At the end of September, Zeus botnet ring leaders and operatives were arrested. This was the culmination of a year-long investigation that included the infiltration of the C&C servers by security researchers. Similarly, the master mind of the Bredolab botnet was arrested three weeks later.
- During mid October, the Avalanche phishing group completed their 2 year-long move from phishing techniques to distributing MitB Trojans.
- The end of October has seen the Iranian Cyber-Army (ICA), infamously known for engaging politically-motivated DDoS attacks, advertising their bots for rent.

Also, towards the end of October, the bot code developers of the ever-competing spyEye and Zeus bots were showing signs of an upcoming merger.

Cyber Security becomes a Business Process

The consolidation taking place with security vendors implies, as Intel CEO Paul Otellini put it, "We have concluded that security has become the third pillar of computing." Vendors are seeing a big shift in security, what about enterprises?

Today, cyber security can't be separated from business operations. For this reason, how security teams must view and approach their roles has changed dramatically. For example, in the past, a CIO's role was laptop distribution. Today, CIOs build supply chains. In the past, CISOs distributed anti-virus and set up firewalls. Today, they must know where data resides, where it moves and how to protect it, which requires a serious, comprehensive data security practice. This means security teams need to become business process experts to keep the bad guys disarmed while keeping the good guys productive.

Convergence of Data Security and Privacy Regulation Worldwide

As newspapers features more companies that violate data privacy on its front page and security breaches appear daily, government regulators will continue to tighten the legal screws on enterprises.

Continuing data breaches force more and more governments—and even private industries—to consider more in-depth security regulations to protect citizens. But another interesting trend seems to be flying under the radar: as enterprises contend with additional data laws, a consolidation will take place across borders. Recently, for instance, the FTC reached out to the EU to begin the process of investigating where both sides of the Atlantic can unify data security laws. Companies will comply, but will find the task of complying with multiple mandates across borders very difficult. Governments will respond—in fact already are—to define a common framework to make life easier for themselves and for enterprises housing data.

THREATS AND COUNTERMEASURES

This chapter analyses Web application security from the perspectives of threats, countermeasures, vulnerabilities, and attacks. The following set of core terms are defined to avoid confusion and to ensure they are used in the correct context.

- *Asset.* A resource of value such as the data in a database or on the file system, or a system resource
- *Threat.* A potential occurrence — malicious or otherwise — that may harm an asset
- *Vulnerability.* A weakness that makes a threat possible
- *Attack (or exploit).* An action taken to harm an asset
- *Countermeasure.* A safeguard that addresses a threat and mitigates risk

This chapter also identifies a set of common network, host, and application level threats, and the recommended countermeasures to address each one. The chapter does not contain an exhaustive list of threats, but it does highlight many top threats. With this information and knowledge of how an attacker works, you will be able to identify additional threats. You need to know the threats that are most likely to impact your system to be able to build effective threat models.

Understanding Threat Categories

While there are many variations of specific attacks and attack techniques, it is useful to think about threats in terms of what the attacker is trying to achieve. This changes your focus from the identification of every specific attack — which is really just a means to an end — to focusing on the end results of possible attacks.

STRIDE

Threats faced by the application can be categorized based on the goals and purposes of the attacks. A working knowledge of these categories of threats can help you organize a security strategy so that you have planned responses to threats. STRIDE is the acronym used at Microsoft to categorize different threat types. STRIDE stands for:

- *Spoofing. Spoofing* is attempting to gain access to a system by using a false identity. This can be accomplished using stolen user credentials or a false IP address. After the attacker successfully gains access as a legitimate user or host, elevation of privileges or abuse using authorization can begin.

- *Tampering*. *Tampering* is the unauthorized modification of data, for example as it flows over a network between two computers.
- *Repudiation*. *Repudiation* is the ability of users (legitimate or otherwise) to deny that they performed specific actions or transactions. Without adequate auditing, repudiation attacks are difficult to prove.
- *Information disclosure*. *Information disclosure* is the unwanted exposure of private data. For example, a user views the contents of a table or file he or she is not authorized to open, or monitors data passed in plaintext over a network. Some examples of information disclosure vulnerabilities include the use of hidden form fields, comments embedded in Web pages that contain database connection strings and connection details, and weak exception handling that can lead to internal system level details being revealed to the client. Any of this information can be very useful to the attacker.
- *Denial of service*. *Denial of service* is the process of making a system or application unavailable. For example, a denial of service attack might be accomplished by bombarding a server with requests to consume all available system resources or by passing it malformed input data that can crash an application process.
- *Elevation of privilege*. *Elevation of privilege* occurs when a user with limited privileges assumes the identity of a privileged user to gain privileged access to an application. For example, an attacker with limited privileges might elevate his or her privilege level to compromise and take control of a highly privileged and trusted process or account.

Network Threats and Countermeasures

The primary components that make up your network infrastructure are routers, firewalls, and switches. They act as the gatekeepers guarding your servers and applications from attacks and intrusions. An attacker may exploit poorly configured network devices. Common vulnerabilities include weak default installation settings, wide open access controls, and devices lacking the latest security patches. Top network level threats include:

Information Gathering

Network devices can be discovered and profiled in much the same way as other types of systems. Attackers usually start with port scanning. After they identify open ports, they use banner grabbing and enumeration to detect device types and to determine operating system and application versions. Armed with this information, an attacker can attack known vulnerabilities that may not be updated with security patches.

Countermeasures to prevent information gathering include:

- Configure routers to restrict their responses to footprinting requests.
- Configure operating systems that host network software (for example, software firewalls) to prevent footprinting by disabling unused protocols and unnecessary ports.

Sniffing

Sniffing or *eavesdropping* is the act of monitoring traffic on the network for data such as plaintext passwords or configuration information. With a simple packet sniffer, an attacker can easily read all plaintext traffic. Also, attackers can crack packets encrypted by lightweight hashing algorithms and can decipher the payload that you considered to be safe. The sniffing of packets requires a packet sniffer in the path of the server/client communication.

Countermeasures to help prevent sniffing include:

- Use strong physical security and proper segmenting of the network. This is the first step in preventing traffic from being collected locally.
- Encrypt communication fully, including authentication credentials. This prevents sniffed packets from being usable to an attacker. SSL and IPSec (Internet Protocol Security) are examples of encryption solutions.

Spoofing

Spoofing is a means to hide one's true identity on the network. To create a spoofed identity, an attacker uses a fake source address that does not represent the actual address of the packet. Spoofing may be used to hide the original source of an attack or to work around network access control lists (ACLs) that are in place to limit host access based on source address rules.

Although carefully crafted spoofed packets may never be tracked to the original sender, a combination of filtering rules prevents spoofed packets from originating from your network, allowing you to block obviously spoofed packets.

Countermeasures to prevent spoofing include:

- Filter incoming packets that appear to come from an internal IP address at your perimeter.
- Filter outgoing packets that appear to originate from an invalid local IP address.

Session Hijacking

Also known as man in the middle attacks, session hijacking deceives a server or a client into accepting the upstream host as the actual legitimate host. Instead the upstream host is an attacker's host that is manipulating the network so the attacker's host appears to be the desired destination.

Countermeasures to help prevent session hijacking include:

- Use encrypted session negotiation.
- Use encrypted communication channels.
- Stay informed of platform patches to fix TCP/IP vulnerabilities, such as predictable packet sequences.

Denial of Service

Denial of service denies legitimate users access to a server or services. The SYN flood attack is a common example of a network level denial of service attack. It is easy to launch and difficult to track. The aim of the attack is to send more requests to a server than it can handle. The attack exploits a potential vulnerability in the TCP/IP connection establishment mechanism and floods the server's pending connection queue.

Countermeasures to prevent denial of service include:

- Apply the latest service packs.

- Harden the TCP/IP stack by applying the appropriate registry settings to increase the size of the TCP connection queue, decrease the connection establishment period, and employ dynamic backlog mechanisms to ensure that the connection queue is never exhausted.
- Use a network Intrusion Detection System (IDS) because these can automatically detect and respond to SYN attacks.

6

Legal Policies, Law and Cyber Crime

In its nascent stages, cyber crime enjoyed a special legal status that belied common practice used in adjudicating crimes. Hacking was commonly perceived as a prank perpetrated by teenagers. Later, the lone, highly skilled attacker working against a high value target was mythologised and revered in some ways. The media and movie industry continued to foster the notion, so that when Kevin Mitnick was arrested in 1995, there was a relative groundswell of support for his release, despite having broken into systems, stolen millions of dollars in proprietary software, "altered information, corrupted system software, and eavesdropped on users, sometimes prevented or impeded legitimate use." The idea that cyber crime was "different" from regular crime persisted into the dawn of the Internet age, helped along by an unwillingness among police to get involved in patrolling and investigating cyberspace.

Such reluctance may have been due to lack of reference points in law, low rates of successful prosecutions and international resistance to help track cross-border crimes. The perception that cyber criminals are different entities has now been thoroughly discouraged. Indeed, "prosecutors are starting to make aggressive use of the Computer Fraud and Abuse Act, which carries penalties of up to 20 years in prison. The lengthiest sentence so far has been nine years, issued in December." There is no longer any calls to be lenient on a those who use computers to exploit, steal and abuse privileges, such as the Californian software executive who conspired to steal trade secrets from a competitor by illegally accessing network and computer systems.

The change in these commonly held notions happened gradually, but importantly, there is now a strong sense of civic empowerment given to the government to apprehend cyber criminals, which when coupled with the renewed diligence attributed to preventing terrorism, has allowed legislation to evolve rapidly in the past few years. As computers have become more integral to daily life, allowing users to conduct higher value operations, they have naturally become targets for those imbued with the criminal tendency. Most users have recognised the threat and the need for protection, even if they ignore certain precautions, like maintaining the secrecy of passwords. If users notice that they can no longer effectively use their workstations, legislation has usually been proposed, albeit after a lengthy period of discussion.

For example, a few years ago, spam was threatening to overwhelm the usefulness of e-mail. Subsequently, congress passed the CAN-SPAM Act of 2003, which made certain practices, like harvesting e-mail addresses, illegal, while imposing maximum fines of up to one million dollars. Despite flaws that some detractors have brought up, such as continuing to allow e-mail addresses to be sold to third parties, the act has provided a legal threshold to base decisions upon and brought notoriously flagrant spammers to justice. In a broader sense, the government has reacted to the demand for better enforcement and the need to extend legal jurisdiction over crimes that may have not been crimes before. The Cyber Security Enchancement Act of 2002, which fell under the Homeland Security Act, and the USA PATRIOT Act both instituted changes to deal with cyber crime. Other, more comprehensive laws, like the Fraud and Related Activity in Connection with Computers, located in the the US Criminal Code and Unlawful Access to Store Communications have been codified for a longer period of time. The increase in awareness of cyber criminality has begun to manifest itself with the passage of laws, creation of organisations and advisory committees and powers granted to enforcement agencies. Their application to current cyber crime has found varying degrees of success. What needs to then be examined and discussed with the aforementioned issues in mind are the crafting of laws, enforcement and effectiveness. These have to be multiplexed across national and international settings, while being interpreted within a framework of technology and trends that are rapidly evolving. Only then can a broad understanding of the legal policies surrounding cyber crime be achieved.

International Cyber Crime

A significant problem that arises when working with cyber crime is that most crimes transit data through a multititude of international borders before reaching the final, intended target. Such circuitousness has a deleterious effect on investigating cyber crimes as well as the application of laws. An illustrative example of the legal hurdles faced with international incidents comes from the "Searching and Seizing Computers and Obtaining Electronic Evidence in Criminal Investigations" manual for the United State Department of Justice. The manual reports that when seeking assistance from ISPs overseas, officers must work "with the consent of that country," which means certain formalities need to be resolved before proceeding.

First, prior permission of the foreign government must be obtained. Next, approval from the Justice Department's Office of International Affairs, and finally a clear indication that the actions would not be objectionable in the foreign country. The process is long and unwieldy, especially since by the time the necessary paper work is filed, ISPs may have already deleted the information. Or in a worse case, after the information is obtained, it will then be discovered that the attacker went through another country, forcing the process to be repeated. Many developing countries are short on the resources and technical knowledge needed to expedite this process, causing the investigation to fail.

By 1997, the problem was being recognised internationally and the G-8 Justice and Interior Ministers noted that to be "consistent with the principles of sovereignty and the protection of human rights, nations must be able to collect and exchange information internationally, especially within the short time frame so often required when investigating international high-tech crimes." To aid this process they created a Point of Contact network which required participating countries to specify a specific group that could assist 24 hours a day, 7 days a week. By 2002, twenty countries were participating. These types of mutual legal assistance treaties (MLATs) have been effective where in the past law enforcement has been stymied. For example, in 1992, the US government required assistance from Switzerland regarding an attack in the U.S., but since Switzerland had no such laws regarding hacking on the books, they refused to help. In devising MLATs, a country can either create bilateral or multilateral relationships, each having its own benefits and drawbacks.

Traditionally, sovereign nations have entered bilateral agreements with countries that they trust and are willing to accept each other's legal characteristics. They are quicker to negotiate, produce more detailed documents, are easier to change and allow nations to feel more comfortable sharing sensitive information. In fact, after the 2001 terrorist attacks, the US was eager to more quickly establish such ties and has concluded over 45 such agreements. The drawbacks of course are that separate, and perhaps unequal, agreements must be reached, resulting in varying interpretations of crime and legal precedent. Multilateral pacts seem more suited to issues that are global in scale, much like cyber crime. Thus, it was with great fanfare that in November of 2001, thirty countries signed the Council of Europe's Convention on Cyber crime.

The convention had been five years in the making and represents the first truly multinational attempt at defining, regulating and providing a framework for the legal issues in relation to cyber crime. Briefly, it established conduct that is prohibited, identified required national legal processes and addressed international cooperation. At the U.S. Senate hearings on ratifying the treaty, Swartz noted "in the past, if an electronic transmission's trail led to another country, the chances were slim of successfully tracking the communication to its source or securing the evidence before deletion.

With the tools provided for under the Convention, however, the ability of U.S. law enforcement to obtain international cooperation in identifying major offenders and securing evidence of their crimes so that they can be brought to justice will be significantly enhanced." Although the Senate Foreign Relations Committee approved the treaty, it has stalled in the Senate for nearly two years, as certain groups have opposed it for reasons related to civil liberties. The current state of multinational legislation thus remains a patchwork of bilateral treaties put together piece by piece. Establishing transnational treaties is a difficult task and remains as an open policy debate. What can be agreed upon is that all nations need multilateral assistance in a global sense, not just a limited group, as cyber criminals can route through any country. Treaties, then, need to harmonise laws, while building capabilities.

Most importantly, such treaties should not be used to violate human rights, even though to do so may be legal in some countries. For example, with the current Convention on Cyber crime, China could ask the U.S. to assist in finding political dissidents and supporters of democracy and the U.S. would be obliged, under the terms of the Convention, to provide assistance. More often than not, even if a successful conviction can be obtained, extraditing a criminal is still a tough legal battle. For example, in October of 2001, a Pakistani man was charged with defacing an American-Israeli organisation's web site. The FBI, working with the U.S. Embassy in Pakistan, was able to identify the attacker and get a warrant issued for his arrest in Pakistan, yet three years later he is still at large. Clearly, there is a need for a more comprehensive international plan.

Future Trends in Legislation

The direction of legislation has slowly been proceeding to more severe and serious punishments for cyber crime. November 3 saw the first prosecution for owning and operating a botnet system. It seems probable as legislatures, federal and state, become aware of threat posed by botnets, and as methods become more advanced in discerning botcontrollers, legislation aimed at the problem will follow. Whether it will become an effective deterrent probably rests with the ability to investigate and prosecute.

Another area of concern is identity theft, a process facilitated to a large degree through the Internet. California has been the first to create legislation aimed at companies with lax security regarding the protection of personal information they may store. The California Security Breach Information Act (SB-1386), which went into effect in July of 2003, forces organisations to notify individuals if there is such a security breach. It has been a powerful method for not only making people aware of the issue, but also applying a force for change in policy within many organisations, lest they be branded as uncaring and incompetent. With more sensitive information being stored by a greater number of third parties, more states will come to the conclusion California has and indirectly apply pressure to organisations to reform. In another example, a recent piece of county legislation in Westchester, New York proposed to make it illegal for companies storing personal information to allow insecure access to their networks. In a sense, it would criminalise using a wireless network with no security measures.

Although, many have pointed out specific weaknesses in the bill, the idea has been praised as a step in the right direction and an important conduit for educating the public. Cyber crime presents a challenging position for lawmakers, as they struggle to keep up with changes in technology and in the methods used to exploit those technologies for maliciousness. Unfortunately, legal wrangling leaves the judicial system in a state that can be behind the times. It should be realised that in the end, laws can only do so much to regulate an activity. Proactive security, user education and vigilance, combined with effective forensics and enforcement remain the best remedies for combating cyber crime. Legislation still needs to enact appropriate punishments and establish frameworks, though and in that sense it has a crucial role to play in the mitigation of cyber crime.

THE FUTURE OF CYBER CRIME ACTIVITY

During an eight day period in August of 2003, three separate worms cost the U.S. economy close to two billion dollars in lost production. Later that summer, the east coast of the United States experienced a massive blackout that might have been exacerbated by a worm called Blaster. Robert Cringley believed that same year that "the cost to society of identity theft is in the range of $4-5 billion per year and may be even higher." With the convergence of organised crime and technically savvy cyber criminals, the growing fear of cyberterrorism, the inability to understand security from major software vendors and the slow footedness of the government, the future seems to point to an Internet that is not only vulnerable to major attacks, but also infested with scams, thieves, and ever increasing opportunities for exploitation. Although inherently difficult to predict trends within the field of technology, there are some eventualities that seem certain, like the growth of extortion and fraud though the Internet. These difficulties will of course result in new responses that better protect customers and force criminals into new realms. Although it is a hackneyed expression, the Internet is still in the Wild West stages. It is important to remember, though, that the Wild West eventually turned into suburbia after successful methods were found to control and police criminals, making their life extremely difficult. An examination of some of the potentialities will help to illustrate how the Internet and cyber crime can be envisioned, at least in the near term future.

Future Trends in Cyber crime Activity

The pace at which cyber crime is growing is one of the most disturbing trends. Valerie McNiven, a U.S. Treasury Advisor, has proclaimed "last year was the first year that proceeds from cyber crime were greater than proceeds from the sale of illegal drugs, and that was, I believe, over $105 billion." She further added that "cyber crime is moving at such a high speed that law enforcement cannot catch up with it." It seems clear that the issue will only become worse in the next few years, now that professionals have realised the potential windfalls if exploited properly. Recently, there has been significant discussion over the amalgamation of organised criminals and cyber crime. Such a pairing indeed forebodes an ill omen for the near term future.

With most of the criminal groups operating out of eastern Europe, Russia and Asia, where laws and enforcement are scanty, there seems little hope in containing and neutralising the threat through traditional means. Phil Williams, a visiting scientist at

CERT, summarised the issue succinctly. "The Internet provides both channels and targets for crime and enables them to be exploited for considerable gain with a very low level of risk. For organised crime it is difficult to ask for more." The result that can then be expected will be an increase in sophisticated phishing attacks and other means for identity theft that may be two pronged. For example, using call centers to notify "customers" ahead of time of some issue, and then following up with e-mails that request personal information. These types of social engineering attacks can be very damaging and have had a long history of success within cyber crime and fraud related transgressions.

The Internet makes it even easier since a degree of authority can be imparted with official looking e-mails and fraudulent web sites that mimic their legitimate counterparts exactly. In the past, such social engineering relied on interpersonal skills like gaining trust. Now, the same idea has been transferred to technology, which can be done with greater ease by a wider group of people. Another aspect of fraud will result from the aggregation of personal information in many third party data centers, making them valuable targets to infiltrate. It is not hard to imagine criminals using data mining techniques to find the most gullible consumers, or tailoring phishing e-mails for specific people based on their medical, financial or personal history. Identify theft will also move in more automated directions. For example, botnets will become vehicles not just for denial of service attacks and spam, but also as giant search platforms for finding personal information, like credit cards and social security numbers.

Controllers of the botnets will then receive payment to run queries on their "database." With professional criminals managing the money laundering and organisation of such schemes, it begs to ask where will all the technical know-how come from in order to perform cyber crime? Unfortunately, there are growing numbers of intelligent black-hats with university degrees spread around the globe, many of them operating in countries where legal employment does not pay as well and the chances of being caught are slim.

But more troublesome is that it has become easier than ever before to be a hacker capable of inflicting great harm on networks and committing cyber crime. The Internet has created a repository of knowledge where anyone is able to learn the fundamentals of subverting computer systems, with numerous tutorials available that spell out in nearly layman's terms how to perform a buffer overflow or a man in the middle attack. Interestingly, the greatest problem is not those who will take the time to learn and find new exploits. In fact this group will probably remain a small, highly intelligent network of researchers and security groups focused solely on finding holes in software. In this, it is preordained, that even if someone is motivated to learn how exploits work, finding a new exploit takes a degree of investigation, skill and diligence that most are not willing to invest.

The real threat comes from the profound ease at which anyone can run a programme like "MetaSploit," a framework for running exploits against targets that allows new modules to be imported and run automatically. The attacker literally needs to know nothing about how computers work, besides how to operate one. In fact, for almost all attacks, the hard work is done by a small group of people, and then released into the public domain, allowing almost anyone to just run the attack. Botnets are no longer handcrafted software made by one group who truly understood the fundamentals, but instead are opensource collaborative efforts that aim to make it as easy as possible to control remote computers, such as BotNET, eggheads and CSharpBot, all available from SourceForge. Thus, the barrier to entry to the field is so low that it allows almost anyone to experiment and join the swelling ranks of cyber criminals.

With the learning curve so low, it should prompt discussion on the need for a new paradigm of thought in how to pre-empt and deal with criminals, in a way that is no longer tied to traditional methods. For example, for someone to break into a house, not only do they need to plan the opportune moment, but they may also have to be aware of lock picking, security system evasion and possess a degree of gumption to overcome moral thresholds. In opposition, the ease of cyber crime seems inversely proportional to the lucrativeness that it bestows and moreover, these trends show signs of accelerating. Beyond the "who" and the "why" of future cyberattacks, the "how" will also change as operating systems become more secure and harder to exploit. With the damage that comes with each new security hole released, Microsoft, Apple and open source vendors have finally begun to seriously focus on security. Of course that hasn't stemmed the flow of vulnerabilities discovered, but techniques such as address space randomisation to stop buffer overflows, advanced and automatic code reviews and more training will reduce the ability to compromise a machine through operating system protocols over time. The real danger in the future lies with user applications, which are created by individuals or small groups without the knowledge or training required to implement security correctly.

Especially dangerous are web applications that can be installed on web servers. The traditional problem with these types of security vulnerabilities was finding susceptible hosts. But with Google, a programme can automatically search for sites with a specific version of a programme installed and then launch an attack. If remote code can be executed, the programme may not be able to take over the whole system, but it can run programmes as the user which may be enough to install bots and automatically replicate. The first instance of such an attack occurred in December of 2004 with the Santy worm that attacked a popular bulletin board system by searching through Google to find hosts with a specific file that was vulnerable. Such attacks aim their weapons at the least secure and vetted of software created. Although the installed base of such systems may be small, with "Google Hacking," they can still be quickly located and exploited.

Another avenue of attack that will open up will be through embedded systems, such as cell phones, mobile devices and other electronics that may connect to the Internet for the most mundane of purposes. Software is usually recreated for each iteration of a device as it is specifically designed for the hardware. This allows for security problems to creep back in over time that may have been eliminated before.

As these devices start to allow consumers to make purchases, while storing valuable information, they will become more attractive for criminals. The incentives now to do so are low, so security researchers have only seen "proof-of-concept" viruses, like the one that infected cellphones running a version of the Symbian OS that could spread automatically. It appears organised crime has not moved into this area due to the lack of research and understanding of how such attacks can be made profitable. Much as with the Internet, it will take time to exploit successfully. In the same vein, eventually automobiles, home electronics devices, refrigerators and almost all devices can and will use the Internet in order to perform maintenance, download upgrades or monitor performance.

These will present opportunities for maliciousness and blackmail that doesn't equate in the same way as the purely virtual environment of the Internet. If someone enters their car, controlled by a foreign agent that demands a wire transfer or else the car will be crashed at high speeds, a situation arises that people will no longer accept. Whether such a scenario will occur is debatable, but the possibility will certainly exist.

Mitigating Cyber crime Activity

Although it is inevitable that cyber crime will increase and continue to explore new vectors for undermining privacy, authentication and law enforcement, there will also be valid and useful attempts for mitigating the abilities of criminals, as well as the effects of cyber crime. These solutions will take form in better software, anti-spyware and anti-virus software integrated into operating systems and more user education regarding phishing and identify theft. These solutions will come primarily from software vendors themselves. On the other side, legislators will work with banks to reduce and prevent fraud, putting some of the liability with those most able to prevent it. Finally, advanced solutions coming out of research and academia will try to inhibit the inherently anonymous and insecure nature of the Internet.

With Microsoft's upcoming release of Vista, the latest version of their operating system, they'll have a new chance to focus on not only improving the general security of the system through fundamental changes, but also in providing methods for eliminating common problems, such as botnets, spyware and phishing attacks. In October of 2005, Microsoft began working together with the FTC to educate customers about botnets and the danger of allowing a computer to turn into a zombie. To deal with the problem of phishing, Microsoft released a programme in July of 2005 called the "Microsoft Phishing Filter," which aims to invalidate the ability of phishers to reach Microsoft customers by dynamically notifying them when there is a high chance that what is being viewed is a phishing attack. Finally, Microsoft released their "AntiSpyware" programme in January of 2005, to be included with Vista as well, that automatically scans your computer for programmes that match spyware signatures or that try to perform suspicious actions, like modifying system functionality or trying to run upon computer start up. If cyber crime continues to grow to epidemic proportions, as all indications seem to point to, legislation will invariably step in, but more importantly, those with the most to lose will become more involved.

This includes credit card companies, banks, lending operations and other organisations dealing with monetary transactions. While also serving as a bank in many capacities. With only an e-mail address and a password required to send money, this low hanging fruit has been one of the most heavily exploited realms for phishing attacks. In response, Paypal has offered at least a thousand dollars of purchase protection and a supposed one hundred per cent protection against unauthorised payments sent from an account. A fraud investigation team responds to queries and according to their web site, they have software that automatically monitors every transaction for inconsistencies.

This last measure used by Paypal has also become fertile ground for credit cards companies, as their systems have become powerful at identifying fraudulent purchases though the use of neural networks, a type of software emerging out of the field of artificial intelligence. In some cases, this software has been able to reduce fraud by thirty per cent or more. It's important to remember that the systems are not perfect solutions, but do address a large portion of illegal activity. Combined with other efforts, the goal is to reduce the effect of fraud, while making it more difficult to achieve. Legislation will attempt to do its part as well, even though it has moved notoriously slowly when dealing with cyberthreats. The past few years have seen laws specifically crafted for spam and dealing with attacks that threaten the integrity of the infrastructure of the Internet. If the botnet problem continues to grow, coupled with identify theft, surely more action will be taken. Although, it is still unclear how effective it will be without a significant contribution to cyberforensic development and funding for the various governmental enforcement agencies responsible for handling cyber crime matters.

Another issue discussed in the Legal Policies section is the need for more international cooperation in locating, extraditing and prosecuting foreign criminals when possible, as the current system leaves much to be desired. Finally, as with any dangerous and difficult problem, there will be new and inventive ways to handle security issues coming out of research. One contribution that has limited, but not eliminated many common security flaws that are exploited, is the use of randomisation in dealing with code, data and other programmatic necessities. By introducing a factor of unpredictability, it can make the work of a hacker much more difficult and prone to error, limiting the ability of those who do not posses the skill to effect a novel attack. Other interesting proposals have included trace back systems that can remove the anonymous identity of data traveling through the Internet, devising a system for fast and accurate discovery of the source of even one packet of data. Stopping distributed denial of service attacks and worm discovery has also been proposed as a method that can be automated and integrated into the backbone of the Internet, high speed routers.

By analysing similar patterns coming from separate locations, such detectors can realise an attack while it is in its infancy and isolate infected hosts. There is also still room for ISPs to actively monitor and discourage botnets, spam and DDoS attacks from occurring. As the first link in the chain for many zombie hosts, as well as attackers, they are in a prime position for stopping spam, either by blocking outgoing mail, which most users have no need for, or by identifying when one host is sending out a large amount of data that does not match expected behaviour. Additionally, if they noticed that a number of hosts were acting in concert, with regards to the data being disseminated from those machines, they may assume with likelihood that they are being controlled remotely. Consequently, the ISPs can examine logs to find who is sending the commands and initiate a complaint with the F.B.I. The problem holding back this kind of proactive approach has not been technical in nature, but rather legalistic, as it can be considered an invasion of privacy. Furthermore, such methods are being used to track down minor copyright violations, instead of focusing on more substantial problems, such as cyber crime and identify theft.

Looking Ahead

The future of the Internet is still up for grabs between criminals and normal users. Fears of a cyber-apocalypse still abound, while the potential extent of damage that can be caused by wide scale fraud is nearly unbounded. These anxieties should be rationally tempered with the knowledge that the problems are being addressed, although perhaps not fast enough. The usefulness of the Internet has proved itself in numerous and myriad ways that will hopefully be enough to ensure it does not become a wasteland of criminal activity and a bastion for the malicious. The government still has an important role to play, but most of the prevention needs to be done by commercial entities producing software and those with the ability to stop fraud. Relying on consumer education programmes will only affect a percentage of possible victims. The others need to be automatically protected through measures that do not stress and require considerable participation. Security needs to be easy and effective if it is do work. Whether cyber crime is still a pertinent issue ten years from now is unknowable in a sense, but if the Internet will continue to grow, it must be solved so that the realities of cyber crime will be proportional to real-world crimes, if not better.

CYBER LAWS AND LEGAL ISSUES

Cyberlaw is a term that encapsulates the legal issues related to use of communicative, transactional, and distributive aspects of networked information devices and technologies. It is less a distinct field of law in the way that property or contract are, as it is a domain covering many areas of law and regulation. Some leading topics include intellectual property, privacy, freedom of expression, and jurisdiction.

Jurisdiction and Sovereignty

Issues of jurisdiction and sovereignty have quickly come to the fore in the era of the Internet. The Internet does not tend to make geographical and jurisdictional boundaries clear, but Internet users remain in physical jurisdictions and are subject to laws independent of their presence on the Internet. As such, a single transaction may involve the laws of at least three jurisdictions: 1) the laws of the state/nation in which the user resides, 2) the laws of the state/nation that apply where the server hosting the transaction is located, and 3) the laws of the state/nation which apply to the person or business with whom the transaction takes place. So a user in one of the United States conducting a transaction with another user in Britain through a server in Canada could theoretically be subject to the laws of all three countries as they relate to the transaction at hand.

Jurisdiction is an aspect of state sovereignty and it refers to judicial, legislative and administrative competence. Although jurisdiction is an aspect of sovereignty, it is not coextensive with it. The laws of a nation may have extraterritorial impact extending the jurisdiction beyond the sovereign and territorial limits of that nation.

This is particularly problematic as the medium of the Internet does not explicitly recognize sovereignty and territorial limitations. There is no uniform, international jurisdictional law of universal application, and such questions are generally a matter of conflict of laws, particularly private international law. An example would be where the contents of a web site are legal in one country and illegal in another. In the absence of a uniform jurisdictional code, legal practitioners are generally left with a conflict of law issue.

Another major problem of cyberlaw lies in whether to treat the Internet as if it were physical space (and thus subject to a given jurisdiction's laws) or to act as if the Internet is a world unto itself (and therefore free of such restraints). Those who favour the latter view often feel that government should leave the Internet community to self-regulate. John Perry Barlow, for example, has addressed the governments of the world and stated, "Where there are real conflicts, where there are wrongs, we will identify them and address them by our means. We are forming our own Social Contract. This governance will arise according to the conditions of our world, not yours. Our world is different". A more balanced alternative is the Declaration of Cyber secession: "Human beings possess a mind, which they are absolutely free to inhabit with no legal constraints. Human civilization is developing its own (collective) mind. All we want is to be free to inhabit it with no legal constraints. Since you make sure we cannot harm you, you have no ethical right to intrude our lives. So stop intruding!" Other scholars argue for more of a compromise between the two notions, such as Lawrence Lessig's argument that "The problem for law is to work out how the norms of the two communities are to apply given that the subject to whom they apply may be in both places at once" (Lessig, Code 190).

Though rhetorically attractive, cyber secession initiatives have had little real impact on the Internet or the laws governing it. In practical terms, a user of the Internet is subject to the laws of the state or nation within which he or she goes online. Thus, in the U.S., Jake Baker faced criminal charges for his e-conduct, and numerous users of peer-to-peer file-sharing software were subject to civil lawsuits for copyright infringement. This system runs into conflicts, however, when these suits are international in nature. Simply put, legal conduct in one nation may be decidedly illegal in another. In fact, even different standards concerning the burden of proof in a civil case can cause jurisdictional problems. For example, an American celebrity, claiming to be insulted by an online American magazine, faces a difficult task of winning a lawsuit against that magazine for libel. But if the celebrity has ties, economic or otherwise, to England, he or she can sue for libel in the British court system, where the standard of "libelous speech" is far lower.

Net Neutrality

Another major area of interest is net neutrality, which affects the regulation of the infrastructure of the Internet. Though not obvious to most Internet users, every packet of data sent and received by every user on the Internet passes through routers and transmission infrastructure owned by a collection of private and public entities, including telecommunications companies, universities, and governments, suggesting that the Internet is not as independent as Barlow and others would like to believe. This is turning into one of the most critical aspects of cyberlaw and has immediate jurisdictional implications, as laws in force in one jurisdiction have the potential to have dramatic effects in other jurisdictions when host servers or telecommunications companies are affected.

Free Speech in Cyberspace

In comparison to traditional print-based media, the accessibility and relative anonymity of cyber space has torn down traditional barriers between an individual and his or her ability to publish.

Any person with an internet connection has the potential to reach an audience of millions with little-to-no distribution costs. Yet this new form of highly-accessible authorship in cyber space raises questions and perhaps magnifies legal complexities relating to the freedom and regulation of speech in cyberspace.

Recently, these complexities have taken many forms, three notable examples being the Jake Baker incident, in which the limits of obscene Internet postings were at issue, the controversial distribution of the DeCSS code, and Gutnick v Dow Jones, in which libel laws were considered in the context of online publishing. The last example was particularly significant because it epitomized the complexities inherent to applying one country's laws (nation-specific by definition) to the internet (international by nature). In 2003, Jonathan Zittrain considered this issue in his paper, "Be Careful What You Ask For: Reconciling a Global Internet and Local Law".

In many countries, speech through cyberspace has proven to be another means of communication which has been regulated by the government.

The Open Net Initiative, whose mission statement is "to investigate and challenge state filtration and surveillance practices" in order to "...generate a credible picture of these practices," has released numerous reports documenting the filtration of internet-speech in various countries. While China has thus far proven to be the most rigorous in its attempts to filter unwanted parts of the internet from its citizens, many other countries-including Australia, Singapore, Iran, Saudi Arabia, and Tunisia-have engaged in similar practices of internet censorship. In one of the most vivid examples of information-control, the Chinese government for a short time transparently forwarded requests to the Google search engine to its own, state-controlled search engines.

These examples of filtration bring to light many underlying questions concerning the freedom of speech, namely, does the government have a legitimate role in limiting access to information? And if so, what forms of regulation are acceptable? The recent blocking of "blogspot" and other websites in India failed to reconcile the conflicting interests of speech and expression on the one hand and legitimate government concerns on the other hand. In the UK the case of Keith-Smith v Williams confirmed that existing libel laws applied to internet discussions.

Governance

The unique structure of the Internet has raised several judicial concerns. While grounded in physical computers and other electronic devices, the Internet is independent of any geographic location. While real individuals connect to the Internet and interact with others, it is possible for them to withhold personal information and make their real identities anonymous. If there are laws that could govern the Internet, then it appears that such laws would be fundamentally different from laws that geographic nations use today.

In their essay "Law and Borders — The Rise of Law in Cyberspace", David Johnson and David Post offer a solution to the problem of Internet governance. Given the Internet's unique situation, with respect to geography and identity, Johnson and Post believe that it becomes necessary for the Internet to govern itself.

Instead of obeying the laws of a particular country, Internet citizens will obey the laws of electronic entities like service providers. Instead of identifying as a physical person, Internet citizens will be known by their usernames or email addresses. Since the Internet defies geographical boundaries, national laws will no longer apply. Instead, an entirely new set of laws will be created to address concerns like intellectual property and individual rights. In effect, the Internet will exist as its own sovereign nation.

Even if the Internet represents a legal paradigm shift, Johnson and Post do not make clear exactly how or by whom the law of the Internet will be enforced. Instead, the authors see market mechanisms, like those that Medieval merchants used, guiding Internet citizens' actions like Adam Smith's invisible hand. Yet, as more physical locations go online, the greater the potential for physical manifestation of electronic misdeeds. What do we do when someone electronically turns off the hospital lights?

However, there is also substantial literature and commentary that the internet is not only "regulable," but is already subject to substantial regulation, both public and private, by many parties and at many different levels. Leaving aside the most obvious examples of internet filtering in nations like China or Saudi Arabia or Iran (that monitor content), there are four primary modes of regulation of the internet described by Lawrence Lessig in his book, Code and Other Laws of Cyberspace:

1. Law: Standard East Coast Code, and the most self-evident of the four modes of regulation. As the numerous statutes, evolving case law and precedents make clear, many actions on the internet are already subject to conventional legislation (both with regard to transactions conducted on the internet and images posted). Areas like gambling, child pornography, and fraud are regulated in very similar ways online as off-line. While one of the most controversial and unclear areas of evolving laws is the determination of what forum has subject matter jurisdiction over activity (economic and other) conducted on the internet, particularly as cross border transactions affect local jurisdictions, it is certainly clear that substantial portions of internet activity are subject to traditional regulation, and that conduct that is unlawful off-line is presumptively

unlawful online, and subject to similar laws and regulations. Scandals with major corporations led to US legislation rethinking corporate governance regulations such as the Sarbanes-Oxley Act.

2. Architecture: West Coast Code: these mechanisms concern the parameters of how information can and cannot be transmitted across the internet. Everything from internet filtering software (which searches for keywords or specific URLs and blocks them before they can even appear on the computer requesting them), to encryption programs, to the very basic architecture of TCP/IP protocol, falls within this category of regulation. It is arguable that all other modes of regulation either rely on, or are significantly supported by, regulation via West Coast Code.
3. Norms: As in all other modes of social interaction, conduct is regulated by social norms and conventions in significant ways. While certain activities or kinds of conduct online may not be specifically prohibited by the code architecture of the internet, or expressly prohibited by applicable law, nevertheless these activities or conduct will be invisibly regulated by the inherent standards of the community, in this case the internet "users." And just as certain patterns of conduct will cause an individual to be ostracised from our real world society, so too certain actions will be censored or self-regulated by the norms of whatever community one chooses to associate with on the internet.
4. Markets: Closely allied with regulation by virtue of social norms, markets also regulate certain patterns of conduct on the internet. While economic markets will have limited influence over non-commercial portions of the internet, the internet also creates a virtual marketplace for information, and such information affects everything from the comparative valuation of services to the traditional valuation of stocks. In addition, the increase in popularity of the internet as a means for transacting all forms of commercial activity, and as a forum for advertisement, has brought the laws of supply and demand in cyberspace.

EMERGING LEGAL ISSUES

Ambiguity in Definition

While the Guidelines and Revised Licence discuss what services would amount to Internet Telephony for the Indian context, they have failed to define the term Internet telephony per se. The meaning given to the Internet telephony is a restrictive in nature, as it states what services would fall within and outside the purview of Internet telephony for the Indian ISPs.

In fact, many of the services, which are prohibited under the Revised licence amount to Internet telephony in the international context. For example, originating or terminating a voice communication service from / to a telephone in India would amount to Internet telephony in the international context, if the public Internet is used as the medium of communication.

The Guidelines and Licence do not lay down any clear parameters that need to be satisfied by any telecommunication service to be classified as Internet telephony. While this problem exists world over, and even at the ITU level, this ambiguity could lead to problems in the future when new forms of technology and modes of communication emerge.

At the earliest, as TRAI has suggested, there is a need to distinguish between Internet Telephony and VOIP. The Governments of different countries need to come together and resolve this issue at the earliest.

Meaning of PC and Telephone

The Revised Licence states that PC to PC Internet telephony is permitted in India. However, the Revised Licence does not clearly define a PC. Under the Information Technology Act, 2000 (ITA), a computer is defined as follows:

Computer means any electronic magnetic, optical or other high-speed data processing device or system which performs logical, arithmetic or memory functions by manipulations of electronic, magnetic or optical impulses, and includes all input, output, processing, storage, computer software, or communication facilities which are connected or related to the computer in a computer system or computer network. Thus the definition of a computer is extremely wide and is not merely restricted to a normal computer, which is used at home or in offices.

Moreover, while the Revised Licence states that the telephone call cannot be originated from or terminated on a telephone in India, it does not define the word telephone. Even the telecommunications laws in India have no clear definition of the term telephone.With the emergence of new technologies and products, the meaning of PC and telephone could be extended to also include personal digital assistants (PDA) (eg.palm pilots) and even mobile phones with computing power (like the Nokia 9110). Moreover, there is also a convergence between PDAs and telephones (like the TREO). If a call is made from such devices, it is uncertain whether the same would be legally permissible.

Another emerging legal issue is concerning IP phones. There exists some ambiguity as to whether IP phones can be freely used to provide Internet telephony services. While it is technically possible to originate calls from IP-based networks, it is uncommon to terminate calls from other networks onto an IP-based network (except in the case of IP PABX system). Since a call from to a number on the national numbering plan is prohibited, a call from an E.164 universal numbering plan may also not be allowed. However, the International Telecommunications Union is studying an option of assigning an E.164 numbering resource to an IP phone using the ENUM protocol. The ENUM protocol converts the E.164 number to an IP address, and a telephone user can call an IP phone by dialing the E.164 number. The perturbing question is whether this would be allowed under Indian laws as they stand right now.

Therefore, it would be necessary to determine and clarify the legitimacy of the type of instruments and the system being used while making an Internet telephone call in order to stay out of any legal problems.

Quality of Services

One of the major difficulties in Internet telephony is in achieving a similar standard of QOS for Internet telephony services as for normal telephony services. The difficulty could arise due nature of the IP network. The IP network uses packet mode of data transmission that can degrade the quality of the voice communication as the packets could get lost in transmission on the public Internet, there could be a delay in transmission, there could be a variation in the packet arrival or there could be an echo effect due to the delay between the transmission of a signal and its receipt.

Therefore, while determining what amounts to real time in the context of Internet telephony, it is necessary that the TRAI keeps in mind the recommendations of the ITU on Real Time . The ITU in its recommendation no. G.114 (2.96 revision) recommended certain limits for one-way transmission time for conditions with echo adequately controlled . According to Recommendation G.131 (Stability and Echo): 0 to 150 ms: Acceptable for most user applications .150 to 400 ms: Acceptable provided that Administrations are aware of the transmission time impact on the transmission quality of user applications .above 400 ms: Unacceptable for general network planning purposes; however, it is recognized that in some exceptional cases this limit will be exceeded.

Another practical difficulty that ISPs are facing is the lack of adequate co-operation from basic telephone operators. Unless the basic operators give better QOS in their agreements with ISPs, ISPs will not be able to provide better QOS to their subscribers. While last year, the TRAI released its recommendations for QOS for ISPs offering Internet Services, ISPs are unable to meet these QOS terms because of the lack of co-operation from basic operators. Therefore, the TRAI must keep in mind the existing competition and economic scenario while framing QOS for Internet telephony services.

Liability of the ISP

The ITA contains provisions dealing with the liability of Network Service Providers (NSPs). A NSP has been defined under the Act to mean "an intermediary". An "intermediary", with respect to any particular electronic message, means any person who on behalf of another person, receives, stores or transmits that message or provides any service with respect to that message. Thus an ISP would be an NSP as it receives, stores or transmits electronic messages over the Internet on behalf of its subscribers. The ITA stipulates that every NSP is given general immunity as regards any offence under or contravention of the Act or the provisions made thereunder, if such NSP proves that

(i) such offence or contravention was committed without its knowledge or

(ii) that it had exercised all due diligence to prevent the commission of such offence or contravention.

Under the ITA, publication or transmission or causing publication of any obscene information is an offence.

Therefore, if while using Internet telephony services, if the subscribers transmit any obscene information, the ISP could be held liable for such transmission. However, if the ISP can prove that it was not aware of such contravention or if it had taken reasonable steps to prevent such contravention, it may be immune from any penalty or liability. Therefore, ISPs must be careful to include appropriate terms in their subscriber agreements to preclude such liability.

Validity of Messenger Services

Off late, there has been some debate regarding voice chat facility which instant messenger services have been offering. There are various issues that arise in this context which need to be addressed in order to determine whether such a voice chat facility is legal. The first issue that arises is whether such services amount to Internet telephony. Under normal circumstances, they would amount to Internet telephony as the instant messengers use the public Internet as a means of transmitting voice between two or more users.

The second and more important issue is whether these messenger services are permitted to offer these services in India. As discussed above, in order to offer Internet telephony services, the service provider requires a license. Currently only ISPs and basic service operators (i.e.BSOs, NLDOs and ILDOs) are allowed to provide such services as per the provisions of their licence. Moreover, no interconnection is allowed between an ISP who has the Internet telephony licence and an ISP that does not. Therefore, in order to offer the voice chat facility using the public Internet, the messenger would have to obtain an ISP licence. Otherwise, the messenger may have to enter into an appropriate arrangement with the ISP wherein the voice chat facility is offered to the messenger users. However, the validity of such an arrangement is also unclear under the law (specially as ISPs are not allowed to assign or sublicense their services). The issue is further complicated if the ISP with w!hom the messenger has an arrangement does not possess the Revised ISP licence. It is essential that ISPs and the messenger services settle this problem at the earliest.

Blocking of Internet Telephony Websites

The ISP licence does not require that an ISP must provide Internet telephony services only to its Internet subscribers, nor does it mandate that Internet telephony and Internet services have to be provided together. However, news reports indicate that after April 1, 2002, some ISPs have started blocking access to websites of other rival ITSPs (including foreign ITSPs) . If so, do they have the authority to block the sites? Further, many ITSPs have tied up with international ITSPs to leverage their customer base. The viability of this option remains to be seen, as foreign ITSPs can set up 100% subsidiaries in India without the help of Indian ISPs. Infact, it may be economically advantageous for them to do so as they would already have their servers and networks established in foreign countries.

COMMUNICATIONS CONVERGENCE BILL, 2001

The Communications Convergence Bill, 2001 (Convergence Bill) aims at promoting, facilitating and developing the carriage and content of communications including broadcasting, telecommunication and multimedia in an orderly manner. It recognizes the coming together of voice, video and data, aims to set up a single super-regulator for the telecom, Internet and broadcasting sectors, to be called the Communications Commission of India (CCI). The Convergence Bill will replace the Indian Telegraph Act, 1885, the Indian Wireless Telegraphy Act, 1933, the Telegraph Wires (Unlawful Possession) Act, 1950, the Cable

Television Networks (Regulation) Act, 1995 and the TRAI Act, 1997. In the present scenario different services like basic telecom, cellular, Internet and satellite television have different licenses and are regulated by different agencies. The present situation does not allow bundling of services, like your cable operator cannot offer you telecommunication services, your ISP cannot carry voice etc.

The licensing regime that exists as of today service operator has to apply for licenses separately and are permitted based on the regulations governing service. This would change with the adoption of the Communication Convergence Bill, 2000.Recommendations of the Bill: The Convergence Bill proposes to have a single authority Communications Commission of India responsible for issuance of licenses and regulating the communications sector including the infrastructure and the content delivered through the infrastructure. The bill also proposes setting up Communications Appellate Tribunal. Any person aggrieved by any decision or order or penalty of the commission could appeal to the tribunal for speedy decision on the appeal. The commission and the appellate tribunal have been given power equivalent of a civil court. Responsibilities of the Commission.The commission would be responsible for providing licenses under four categories namely:

1. Network Infrastructure facilities (Infrastructure Service Provider)
2. Network Services (Network Service Providers)
3. Application Services (Application Service Providers)
4. Content application services (Content ASP).

The classification is technology neutral and service sector neutral. The segmentation of the market into the four different segments would be based on the services provided . Each layer is dependent on one or more of the earlier layers for the provision of services.The Act, it is hoped, shall usher in the era of convergent handling of communication medium in place, ie the Communication Commission of India shall be responsible of handling basic telephony, cellular service, cable, satellite channel and Internet service operators. The bill shall segment the market on the basis of the layers as illustrated above. This would enable operators to obtain licenses for the specific layer rather than for the service. For eg an operator could take license for offering only infrastructure facility with the services being offered by some other operator. Hughes Tele.com, the private basic service operator for Maharashtra would be able to offer services like telephony,Internet (it offers these even today), interactive content or any other service over the cable coming into your home.

The Convergent View "Convergence" refers to the fact that different kinds of communication services, whether in the form of voice, text or video, can be provided using the same basic infrastructural facility, and similarly, different kinds of infrastructural facilities can be utilised to provide the same service. For instance, share prices can be accessed via the Internet on a PC or through the wireless medium on a mobile phone. Perhaps the most significant aspect of the Bill lies in the name itself. It recognises the "blurring of borders between telecommunications, computing and media" . Further, it also acknowledges that "The continuous development of new technologies results in an inability to predict the future evolution of convergence viz. the development of new services like web-casting, Internet Telephony etc. resulting in the need for regulations which does (sic) not aim to predict the future, but aspires to be flexible enough to accommodate and propagate any permutation and combination of technologies and services." The Bill, smartly enough, has steered clear of burdening itself with technological details. The three key aspects in any communication are : The infrastructure facilities used, such as earth stations, satellites, cables, etc. The kind of service provided such as telephony, broadcast of cricket matches, etc. The technology used to provide the service The Convergence Bill does not concern itself with the third aspect above. It only seeks to regulate the communication sector based on the nature of infrastructural facility and the nature of service provided. The basic objectives Irrespective of the infrastructure or technology used, long distance communication is based on electromagnetic waves, of varying frequency. In order to ensure hassle-free communication, a proper allocation of frequency bands to various service providers is crucial . For this purpose, the Bill proposes the setting up of a Spectrum

Management Committee, which will earmark distinctfrequency bands for use in strategic and commercial purposes.

The Bill also envisages the setting up of the Communications Commission of India, which will be the regulatory agency on the communications sector. The Commission will be responsible for assigning the various frequencies (earmarked by the Spectrum Management Committee for commercial purposes) among the various users, and giving out licences to service providers. The objectives of the Commission, as listed in the draft Bill, are as follows: "The Communications Commission of India, while exercising its functions shall be guided by the following principles:

(i) that the communication sector is developed in a competitive environment and that market dominance in a converged environment is suitably regulated;

(ii) that communication services are made available at affordable cost to all uncovered areas including the rural, remote, hilly and tribal areas;

(iii) that there is increasing access to information for greater empowerment of citizens and towards economic development;

(iv) that quality, plurality, diversity and choice of services are promoted;

(v) that a modern and effective communication infrastructure is established taking into account the convergence of information technology, media, telecom and consumer electronics;

(vi) that defence and security interests of the country are fully protected;

(vii) that introduction of new technologies, investment in services and infrastructure, and maximization of communications facilities and services (including telephone density) are encouraged;

(viii) that equitable, non-discriminatory interconnection across various networks are promoted;

(ix) that licensing criteria are transparent and made known to the public;

(x) that an open licensing policy allowing any number of new entrants (except in specific cases constrained by limited resources such as the spectrum)is promoted; and

(xi) that the principle of a level playing field for all operators serving consumer interest, including existing operators on the date of commencement of the Act, is promoted."

Effects

With the bill adopted, service operators would be able to offer multiple services over the same network. This shall reduce the cost and other overheads for the operator. The bill defines the physical network, network services and the content delivered over them independently thus enabling the use of the same network to carry multitude of services. This shall help solve the anomaly of having a separate license and network for say offering Internet, telephony and cable services . The bill shall increase the value of companies in the communications business specially the businesses owning the last mile access like MTNL, Hughes Tele.com, BSNL etc. The cable operator in your colony would have the best of the world with his network. He could now also start bundling telephone services, Internet and other value added services than just the plain old un-interactive cable television.Licensing Regime under the Bill. The Convergence Bill also provides for a new licensing regime, with a limited number of five licenses, which include network infrastructure facilities, networking services, network application services, content application services and value-added network application services. While granting licences, the CCI may grant them either singly or jointly, depending upon the nature of services to be offered. Therefore, while providing Internet telephony services, the service provider would have to obtain the network application services licence and probably the value-added network application services licence under the Convergence Bill.

CYBER CRIME IN INDIA AND ITS LAWS

Cyber crime is a new term for most of the people in india. The laws are also new better say evolving. The sole purpose of this blog is to creat awareness among people and try to help them to understand the law by answaring their mails.

Cybercrime is more Effective than Drug Trading

Global cybercrime generated a higher turnover than drug trafficking in 2004 and is set to grow even further with the wider use of technology in developing countries. No country is immune from cybercrime, which includes corporate espionage, child pornography, stock manipulation, extortion and piracy.

"Last year was the first year that proceeds from cybercrime were greater than proceeds from the sale of illegal drugs, and that was, I believe, over $105 billion."

"Cybercrime is moving at such a high speed that law enforcement cannot catch up with it."

Cyber Evidence Collection..a Major Challenge to Law Enforcement in India

Whether in the case of a Cyber Crime pursued by the Police or a Computer Audit pursued by an auditor, "Evidence" plays a vital part in securing the interests of the Information Asset owner. Naavi discusses the legal requirements and the devices required for the purpose of collecting judicially acceptable Cyber Evidence. It is more than three years since law was passed in India to recognize electronic documents as admissible evidence in a Court of law. The necessary amendments were made to the Indian Evidence Act 1872 by the Information Technology Act 2000 (ITA-2000).

In the case of electronic documents produced as "Primary Evidence", the document itself must be produced to the Court. However, such electronic document obviously has to be carried on a media and can be read only with the assistance of an appropriate Computer with appropriate operating software and application software.

In many cases even in non-electronic documents, a document may be in a language other than the language of the Court in which case it needs to be translated and submitted for the understanding of the Court by an "Expert". Normally the person making submission of the document also submits the translation from one of the "Experts". If the counter party does not accept the "Expert's opinion", the court may have to listen to another "Expert" and his interpretation and come to its own conclusion of what is the correct interpretation of a document. In the case of the Electronic documents, under the same analogy, "Presentation" of document is the responsibility of the prosecution or the person making use of the document in support of his contention before the Court.

Based on his "Reading" of the documents, he submits his case. This may however be disputed by the counter party. In such a case, it becomes necessary for the Court to "Get the document Read by an expert" to its satisfaction. It is necessary to have some clarity on the legal aspects of such documents presented to the Court because most of the court battles are expected to revolve around "Proper Reading " of the documents and "Possible manipulation of the documents".

In making presentation of an "Electronic Document", the presentor may submit a readable form of the document in the form of a "Print Out". Question arises in such a case whether the print out is a "Primary Evidence" or a "Secondary Evidence".

According to Indian Evidence Act, section 65 refers to "Cases in which secondary evidence relating to documents may be given". However, the modifications made to this section by ITA-2000 have added Sections 65 A and Section 65 B.

Though these sections have been numbered as A and B of 65, these are not to be treated as sub sections of Section 65. As per schedule II to ITA-2000, serial number 9, it appears that 65A and 65B are to be treated as independent sections. According to Section 65 A therefore, " Contents of electronic records may be proved in accordance with the provisions of Section 65B".

Whether by design or otherwise, Section 65B clearly states that " Not withstanding anything contained in this (Ed:Indian Evidence Act) Act, any information contained in an electronic record which is printed on a paper, stored, recorded or copied in optical or magnetic media produced by a computer (herein after called the Computer Output) shall be deemed to be also a document...."

However, for the "Computer Output" to be considered as admissible evidence, the conditions mentioned in the Section 65 B (2) needs to be satisfied.

Section 65B(2) contains a series of certifications which is to be provided by the person who is having lawful control over the use of the Computer generating the said computer output and is not easy to be fulfilled without extreme care.

It is in this context that the responsibility of the Law Enforcement Authorities in India becomes onerous while collecting the evidence.

In a typical incident when a Cyber Crime is reported, the Police will have to quickly examine a large number of Computers and storage media and gather leads from which further investigations have to be made. Any delay may result in the evidence getting obliterated in the ordinary course of usage of the suspect hard disk or the media.

Any such investigation has to cover the following main aspects of Cyber Forensics, namely,

1. Collection of suspect evidence
2. Recovery of erased/hidden/encrypted data
3. Analysis of suspect evidence.

If the process of such collection, recovery and analysis is not undertaken properly, the evidence may be rejected in the Court of law as not satisfying the conditions of Section 65B of the Indian Evidence Act.

In the evolution of the Indian challenge to Cyber Crimes, it may be said that during the last three years, Police in different parts of the Country have been exposed to the reality of Cyber Crimes and more and more cases are being registered for investigation. However, if the Law enforcement does not focus on the technical aspects of evidence collection and management, they will soon find that they will be unable to prove any electronic document in a Court of Law.

Cyber Evidence Management

In the previous article, we had discussed the requirements of Indian Evidence Act for the admissibility of Electronic Evidence. In this article we shall discuss the hardware required for making copies of hard disks for further analysis. In most of the incidents of Cyber Crime investigation by the Police or suspected fraud in a Corporate network, it becomes necessary to seize the suspect Computer or its hard disk for a detailed examination.

Some times even in an "Intelligence gathering Mission" it may be necessary to subject a hard disk for a detailed examination. The practical problem in most such cases is that if the computer is seized immediately, it may disrupt the operations of the enterprise seriously. If the Police make this as a common practice, then no Company would be comfortable in preferring a complaint in case of a computer crime. A similar problem also arises in case of an auditor who suspects some fraud in a hard disk but needs access to the same for a prolonged time for further analysis.

It therefore becomes necessary for the investigator or the auditor to make a "Copy" of the original "Evidence" and carry on his investigations on the "Copy". The question then arises that if he stumbles upon some evidence during his examination and then comes back to seize the original hard disk, the data on the original hard disk may no longer contain the evidence he had unearthed during the investigation.

Even assuming that the "Original Hard Disk" itself had been seized and the investigations have unearthed some evidence, there would be a charge from the accused that the evidence was in the custody of the Police/Auditor and could have been tampered with. It becomes absolutely essential therefore for the investigator to preserve the original evidence and at the same time subject it to any type of analysis he may like besides not disrupting the regular user of the system and the hard disk.

A device required for this purpose is one which makes a "Bit Image Copy" of the suspect hard disk, creates a "hash code" for the "original" being copied so that the original can be preserved, the "Clone" can be subjected to analysis and in case of necessity prove with the hash code that the data as captured from the "Original" has not been tampered with during the process of "analysis".

Ineffective Law Enforcement, Bad Economy Fueling Cybercrime

Cyber-criminals operating worldwide are benefitting from ineffective law enforcement and a growing economic recession that could make jittery people more susceptible to cybercrime scams. So concludes security firm McAfee in its new report, "Virtual Criminology Report—Cybercrime vs. Cyberlaw." published Tuesday. The report pulls together the opinions of about two dozen legal experts, academic researchers and security-response professionals working as far afield as Britain, continental Europe, the Baltic countries, Brazil, India, Japan, Australia, New Zealand and North America.

"There have been a few cases where Cyber-criminals have been promptly arrested, but they're usually responsible for the small attacks," says Paulo Lima, a Brazilian lawyer specializing in computer-related crime. "Those responsible for the large operations have never been arrested. The public sector has usually acted in a mitigating manner, attacking the symptom and not the illness — there is an antiquated system and a completely unprepared law enforcement body."

Lima's sentiment is echoed in Britain, India and elsewhere by those involved in trying to combat a worldwide cybercrime spree that includes phishing, denial-of-service (DoS) extortion rackets, botnets, spam, cyber-espionage and national attacks of a political nature.

"Cybercrime has become a big problem in India this year," says Vijay Mukhi, president of the Foundation of Internet Security and Technology in India. "However, politicians and judges do not understand how to deal with it, and in fact few of them ever use the Internet. Police are reluctant to register cases because they prove too difficult to prosecute." The view among some in the United Kingdom is only slightly more optimistic. Peter Sommer, a British professor and consultant whose main research field is the reliability of digital evidence, says there's some progress being made in how the U.K. courts address technology-related crimes, but the computer forensics piece of the puzzle is not yet complete. "The Council for Registered Forensics Practitioners scheme to accredit experts is still not yet working," he adds.

Anther problem is talent: In many places around the world, private industry is siphoning the cybercrime fighting talent from government, offering them more money to work in the private sector. In addition, many worry that the growing economic recession and banking fiscal crisis is being exploited by Cyber-criminals to prey upon jittery consumers.

Politics is also an issue. China, Russia and Moldova are often blamed as international sources for all kinds of cybercrime, and the McAfee report takes up the issue of whether there are places around the world where prosecution of cybercrime is thought to be especially lax.

"Criminal behaviour is still receiving political cover," says Eugene Spafford, professor of computer sciences at Purdue University and executive director of the Center for Education and Research in Information Assurance and Security in the United States.

One example Spafford cites is the July cyberattack on Web sites protesting the Burmese military regime, in which the government in Myanmar was thought to have had a hand. "In the case of the Myanmar denial-of-service attacks, they took place with local Eastern European and Russian support," he says.

"Russia and China are especially reluctant to cooperate with foreign law enforcement bodies for reputation and intelligence reasons," Spafford adds.

Another contributor to the report, Dmitri Alperovitch, says he believes that Russian's President Vladimir Putin and political influence within the Federal Security Service (Russia's successor to the Soviet KGB) are hampering efforts to prosecute cyber-crimes, such as those related to the Storm botnet. Alperovitch is director of intelligence analysis and hosted security at Secure Computing (recently acquired by McAfee). McAfee says Russia is the predominant source of the most sophisticated, well-designed malware.

"The vast percentage of 'professional' malware we see today is, frankly, coming out of Russia," acknowledges Dave Marcus, director of security research and communication at McAfee Avert Labs. "We find it on Russian hosting sites and the read-me documents are in Russian."

National concerns about political uses of malware and denial-of-service attacks are growing, according to the McAfee report.

Estonia, which suffered massive and crippling DoS attacks in April 2007, this year established a "top-secret cyber security hub," which has been "operational as of August 2008 and backed by NATO and seven EU countries (Estonia, Germany, Italy, Latvia, Lithuania, Slovakia and Spain)," the McAfee report states.

Estonia also is said to have pledged 50,000 Euros to back the Council of Europe Convention on Cybercrime.

But while some countries end up as high-tech crime scapegoats, the report notes, in reality it's very difficult to precisely identify origination points.

"In fact, obfuscation seems to be the name of the game," says Alana Maurushat, acting director of the Cyberspace Law and Policy Centre of the University of New South Wales in Australia. "It is easy to make it appear as if malware or espionage activities are originating from a county other than the original source. There is considerable misdirection as to origin of attacks. Much traffic is misdirected as a decoy. The actual attack may originate in the same city as the target. This is often done with cases of country espionage and corporate espionage."

Those out on the Web front lines say they can only speak about what they witness daily.

"We're getting hacking attempts constantly," says Clay Hill, Web site manager at the libraries division at Mississippi State University, which allows authorized access to research. "And most of it is from China."

CYBER CRIME LAW IN INDIA

The general laws in India were drafted and enacted in the 19th century. Whilst each of the general laws have undergone modifications and amendments, the broad and underlying provisions have withstood the test of time, including unimaginable advancements in technology, which speaks to the dynamism of the General laws. The general laws referred to in this Article are the Indian Penal Code, 1860 ("IPC"), which is the general penal law of India and the Indian Evidence Act, 1872 ("Evidence Act"), the general law pertaining to admissibility of evidence in civil and criminal trials. The manner in which trial of criminal cases are to be conducted is dealt with under the Criminal Procedure Code, 1973 ("Cr. P. C"). India got its first codified Act in the Information Technology Act, 2000 ("IT Act), which fell far short of the Industry's requirements to meet global standards. The focus if the IT Act was however recognition of electronic records and facilitation of e - commerce. Barely ten sections were incorporated in the IT Act to deal with Cyber Crime. At the time when the IT Act was passed several acts deemed to be illegal in most jurisdictions including virus attacks, data theft, illegal access to data/ accessing and removal of data without the consent of the owner, etc., were listed as civil penalties under the IT Act. The IT Industry continued to rely on self –regulation and contractual undertakings to appease its global clients, as it had done before the passing of the IT Act.

The primary offences under the IT Act were:

- Tampering with source code;
- Deleting, destroying or altering any data on any computer resource with mala fide intent to cause wrongful loss or to diminish its value;
- Publishing or transmitting pornographic material through a computer resource;
- Provisions pertaining to encryption technology, the right of the Government authorities to intercept and decrypt such data and to call upon any entity or individual to decrypt such data were also included in the IT Act. Certain acts affecting the integrity and sovereignty of the nation were classified as offences.

The saving grace of the IT Act were the amendments carried out to the IPC and Evidence Act, which to some extent provided for prosecution of rampant offences like the Nigerian Scams, Phishing and other Banking frauds may be prosecuted.

Cyber Crime prosecution was however not resorted to in many instances due to lack of awareness (amongst both the victims and the enforcement authorities) about the applicability of such general Laws to cyber crimes (like Phishing). To add to this, administrative delegation of powers treated offences under the IT Act differently to those falling under general laws! Further, crimes like data theft; illegally accessing/ removal of data; virus attacks etc., could not be prosecuted due to the lack of relevant penal provisions.

S.66 of the Act misleadingly titled "hacking" is one of the most misused and abused provisions in India. Recently *i.e.*, in September 2009, the Delhi High Court has quashed the criminal proceedings initiated in or about July 2005, under S.66 of the IT Act by M/s. Parsec Technologies Ltd., against some of its former employees, who left and started their own Company, holding that the continuation of the proceedings would amount to abuse of process of law.

Likewise the IT Act did not provide sufficient recourse for women and child victims of cyber crimes like Cyber Stalking and paedophilia. Controversy has dogged the IT Act from its inception. The Ministry of Information Technology prepared and posted proposed draft amendments to the IT Act in 2005. In 2006, the IT Bill with substantial changes brought about as a result of the objections to the proposed amendments of 2005 was tabled before the Parliament. In December 2008 as a knee–jerk reaction to the November 2008 terror attacks in Mumbai, India, the Information Technology (Amendments) Act, 2008 ("ITA, 2008") was hastily tabled before the Parliament and was passed hastily and without any debate whatsoever. Unlike the IT Act of 2000, the focus of the new ITA 2008 is clearly on Cyber Terrorism and to a significant extent, Cyber Crime. This paper deals with some important provisions of ITA, 2008 relating to data protection, privacy, encryption and cyber crime and to what extent it arms one against emerging trends in Cyber Crime.

Definitions

The replacement of the word "Digital" with the word "Electronic", which makes the IT Act more technology neutral and expands its applicability beyond just the digital medium.

- Inclusion of cell phones, personal digital assistants and other such devices in the definition of "Communication Devices" broadens the scope of the statute.
- The modified definition of "Intermediary" includes all service providers in respect of electronic records again

broadens the applicability while inclusion of Cyber cafes in the definition of Intermediaries removes the need to interpret the statute.

The extensive definition of "cyber security" as including protection of both data and the equipment from unauthorised access, use, disclosure etc., is another vital inclusion that impacts the new Data Protection provisions included under the ITA, 2008. The relevance of these definitions, where applicable are set out below.

Data Protection

The IT industry has been lobbying for a law to protect Data and the new legislation has addressed the industry's demands to a certain extent particularly since Mphasis Limited, a Pune based Company suffered the notoriety of puncturing the Indian BPO fairy tale in April 2004, when some of its employees stole confidential credit card information of clients and used it to siphon substantial amounts. Apart from highlighting the security lapses within the Company, this case also brought to the limelight the lack of suitable Data Protection Laws in India. Several cases have now been reported where former employees are accused of data theft and misuse of Confidential and proprietary Information and data. In one instance, a BPO Company purportedly closed down due to rampant data theft.

The Indian Legislature's response to the hue and cry raised is the transposition of certain civil penalties into criminal offences and the addition of one section under civil penalties as set out hereunder:

- The only provision under the IT Act for data protection was S.43, which only imposed Civil Penalties in the event of the commission of certain acts without the permission of the owner or person in charge of the computer or computer systems such as:
  - Securing access (without permission);
  - Downloading or copying of data stored in a computer or computer system;
  - Introducing computer viruses;
  - Damaging computers and or data stored therein;

- Disrupting computers;
- Denial of access;
- Abetting such acts; or
- Illegal charging for services on another's account.

S.43A has now been added under the ITA 2008 to address the data protection requirements of the Industry. S.43A stipulates that any "Body Corporate" possessing, dealing with or handling any "sensitive personal data or information" in a computer resource it owns, controls or operates, is liable for negligence, if it fails to maintain "reasonable security practices and procedures" and thereby causes wrongful loss or wrongful gain to any person. What amounts to reasonable security practices and procedures remains to be finalised by the Central Government.

Apart from the above addition under Civil Penalties, the Civil wrongs set out under S.43 of the IT Act have now been qualified as criminal offences under the ITA 2008 under S. 66. A reverse transposition has further been carried out under the ITA 2008 of two criminal provisions from the IT Act (S.66 and S.65) as civil penalties under S.43 (i) & S.43 (j), respectively. Any act set out under S.43, if committed "dishonestly or fraudulently", would amount to a criminal offence, punishable with punishment of up to three years or fine of a maximum of Rupees Five Lakhs or both, under the ITA 2008.

Though S.66 of the IT Act has purportedly been deleted, the addition of S.43 (i) under the ITA 2008 has in effect resulted in the retention of the contentious S.66 of the IT Act. However retention of S.65 of the IT Act without any modification despite its transposition into S.43 appears to be a tautology, which could be due to oversight. S.66B inserted by the ITA, 2008 is on the lines of similar provisions in the Indian Penal Code ("IPC"), which provides for punishment of the receiver of stolen property. S.66B makes the receipt or retention of a stolen computer resource or communication device punishable with imprisonment up to three years or with fine up to Rupees One Lakh or both.

Whilst S.66B may seem to also apply to hardware, which is also covered under the IPC, the term "computer resource" is defined under the IT Act as a "Computer, computer system, computer network, data, computer database or software." The extension of the above provision to the receiver of stolen data, software etc., may prove to be substantially useful when faced with issues of Corporate Espionage.

Further Analysis of the Data Protection Legislation

Although the data protection provisions introduced by the ITA, 2008 may not comprehensively address the industry specific requirements applicable to data providers and handlers; nevertheless this is an important head start towards introduction of specific data protection legislation in India, which is absolutely essential in today's business environment. One of the important outcomes of the ITA, 2008 amendments is the clarity on whether Data theft is considered a criminal offence. Commission of acts provided in S.43 to 66 dishonestly or fraudulently, clearly implies "Data Theft" as an offence in such instances.

However these acts would amount to a punishable offence only if such data is "downloaded, copied or extracted" from a computer resource. Therefore it may be argued that the provisions of S.43 (b) are not inclusive, as they do not provide for removal of data through uploading. Criminal provisions give rise to liability only in cases of unambiguity.

If a provision has to be applied through interpretation, then such interpretation, which favours the Accused, would have to be applied. With the addition of S.43A by the ITA, 2008, the onus of implementing "Reasonable Security Practices" is on the business entity. Whilst this may be a known liability that parties agree upon, unsuspecting companies or firms may get mulcted with liability if duties and obligations are not specified, as the Central Government guidelines will then become applicable. As of now, violations under S.43 A are however not criminal offences.

Confidentiality and Privacy

India was shocked out of its complacent conservatism due to the widespread circulation of a MMS clip shot by a Delhi schoolboy. This case took an unexpected twist when this clip was circulated on Bazee.com and its Chief Executive Officer of American origin was arrested. S.66E has now been introduced under the ITA, 2008 for the protection of physical or personal privacy of an individual. This section makes intentional capturing of the images of a person's private parts without his or her consent in any medium and publishing or transmitting such images through electronic medium, a violation of such person's privacy punishable with imprisonment of up to three years or with fine up to Rupees Two Lakhs, or both. A case of posting of the personal information and obscene material on a Yahoo! Site was touted as the fastest trial and conviction of a cyber crime case in Chennai. It appears that this conviction has recently been reversed.

S.72 A of the ITA, 2008 now explicitly provides recourse against dissemination of personal information obtained without the individual's consent through an intermediary or under a services contract, with intent to cause wrongful loss or wrongful gain. The maximum punishment prescribed for this offence is three years imprisonment, or fine up to Rupees Five Lakhs or both. Service providers on the Internet, social networking sites, Companies, firms, individuals and other intermediaries ought to now be careful in the collection, retention and dissemination of personal data. Interactive websites and P2P site operators also have to be extremely careful to ensure that the provisions of S.66E and S.72 A are not violated.

Other Cyber Crimes Including Cyber Terrorism

Provisions to combat cyber frauds have now been introduced under the ITA 2008. However certain issues relating to protection against banking frauds such as Phishing, money transfers through online hacking, e-mail frauds and cyber squatting (including through wilfully misleading domain names) to name a few have not been addressed separately in the ITA, 2008, even though these are significantly increasing problems. S.66C inserted by the ITA, 2008 makes dishonest or fraudulent use of a person's electronic signature or identity, password or any other unique identification feature punishable as theft with imprisonment of up to three years and fine up to Rupees One Lakh.

S.66D inserted by the ITA, 2008 makes cheating by personating through a computer resource punishable with imprisonment of up to three years and fine up to One Lakh Rupees. It may be noted that S.419 of IPC already provides for punishment for cheating by personating but does not provide for the maximum fine imposable. In addition to S.67 of the IT Act, S.67A and S.67B have been included by the ITA, 2008 *inter alia* to combat child pornography. S.67A makes transmission of a sexually explicit act or conduct punishable and S.67B makes publishing and transmission of child pornography an offence, punishments for which range from five to seven years and fine.

Several exceptions have also been set out to S.67 and S.67A, including for depictions in any book, pamphlet, paper, writing, drawing, painting representation or figure in electronic form. Further, S.67C introduced by the ITA, 2008 imposes liability on Intermediaries for retention and production of information. However the duration, manner and formats of retention of such information are still subject to prescription by the Central Government. This section appears to be directed mainly against Cyber Cafes and has already been subject to dissension. Failure to comply with such requirements is punishable with imprisonment up to three years and also fine.

Observations on the Cyber Crime Provisions under the ITA, 2008

- S.43 was included in the IT Act, 2000 to address certain kinds of illegal acts. However, the Legislature has not looked beyond S.43 to address recent trends in Cyber Crimes and for dealing with such issues.
- S.66 of the IT Act, under the heading "Hacking" which was misleading was criticised for its ambiguity and for the possibility of abuse. However, whilst the proposed amendments sought for its deletion, this section has been transposed to not only being applicable as a civil penalty but is also retained as a criminal offence. With the retention of S.66 of the IT Act, one of the main issues that need to be addressed is the criminality of actions resulting in "diminishing of value" of any information residing in a computer resource. Even if the law – makers thought fit to retain this provision, its use and abuse Since, 2000 ought to have been evaluated when re-defining this provision.

- S.66C only addresses some kinds of cyber frauds and not all such frauds committed without using digital or electronic signatures. Further S.66D may be considered redundant in the light of the amendments made to the IPC after the enactment of the IT Act in 2000, save and except for the maximum fine imposable under the ITA, 2008.
- S.67A is a much – needed introduction to the IT Act and would help in combating the pernicious offences of child pornography as observed in some recent shocking incidents involving school children. Several new provisions have been introduced under the ITA 2008 to combat Cyber Terrorism. These provisions appear to be a necessary and welcome addition though there are apprehensions about their abuse and whether the Government authorities are well equipped to handle and protect the information, acquired by it in compliance with such provisions.
- S.66A inserted by the ITA, 2008 is an essential provision from the perspective of combating Cyber Terrorism and to address several instances of cyber stalking, cyber harassment, etc. However this provision can also be easily abused. S.66A provides for punishment of three years and fine against any person found guilty of: (i) sending information through a computer resource or devise, which is grossly offensive or of menacing character; (ii) false information intended to annoy, inconvenience, deceive or mislead the addressee or recipient about the origin of such message; or (iii) endanger, obstruct, insult, injure, intimidate or to cause enmity, hatred or ill will. This would not only help the police against anonymous and false messages etc., and harassed individuals, but also corporate bodies, which could rework their internal policies in consonance with this provision.
- S.66F directly addresses the issue of cyber terrorism. Acts intended to: (i) threaten the unity, integrity, security or sovereignty of India; (ii) to strike terror in the people or any section of the people by denial of access, hacking and virus attacks; and (iii) by such means does or may cause

death or injuries to persons or damage to property or disrupts supplies or services essential to the life of the community; or (iv) adversely affects the critical information infrastructure; is the commission of Cyber Terrorism, the punishment for which ranges from imprisonment from three years to life and fine depending upon the seriousness of the crime.

Encryption and Data Privacy

Mid 2008, customers in India thought twice about buying Blackberry phones – no reflection on the performance of the phones but due to a sudden conflict between the Department of Telecommunications of the Indian Government ("DoT") and Research in Motion ("RIM") Blackberry Services. DoT requested RIM to share its encryption codes with the department, stating security concerns over data transmitted through e-mail services on Blackberry phones or to set up servers in India and permit DoT to monitor such transmissions. After several rounds of talks the Government of India dropped its request reversing its stand on the issue of a security threat. The Indian Telegraph Act, 1885 vests extensive and absolute power on the DoT *inter alia* to deal with, monitor and regulate transmission of messages within India. These provisions therefore stand automatically extended to transmission of encrypted Data also.

The Guidelines issued by the DoT for transmission of encrypted data and the ISP license requirements permits transmission of encrypted data of 40 bit key length in RSA algorithms or its equivalent in other algorithms without having to obtain permission from the Telecom Authority. However, if encryption equipments higher than this limit are to be deployed (which would be the case for most encrypted data), individuals/groups/organizations require prior written permission of the DoT and may be further called upon to deposit the decryption key, split into two parts, with the DoT. These provisions appear to have prompted the Blackberry case. Now in addition to the above powers vested in the Telecom Authority of India, certain provisions have been added under the ITA 2008 (as set out hereunder), which further strengthens the hands of the Telecom Authority in India.

S.69 of the IT Act, which dealt with encrypted data has been replaced with a new S.69, which empowers the Central Government or a State Government through their authorised officers to intercept, monitor or decrypt any information generated, transmitted, received or stored in any computer resource. These powers may be exercised for reasons set out in S.69 including in the interest of the sovereignty or integrity of India, defence, security of the State, or even for preventing commission of any cognizable offence or for investigation of any offence.

The only restraint in exercising such powers is the necessity of maintaining written records of such actions. The additions to S.69 and inclusion of new provisions under S.69A to S.69C under the ITA 2008 may be subject to criticism and concern. S.69A empowers the Central Government or any of its authorised officers to block or cause to be blocked access by public of any information generated, transmitted, received, stored or hosted in any computer resource. Under S.69B, the Central Government may, through its authorised agency, monitor and collect traffic data or information generated, transmitted, received or stored in any computer resource for enhancing cyber security and for identification, analysis and prevention of intrusion or spread of virus in the country. Intermediaries have to provide such data and assistance as sought by the authorised agency and failure to extend such assistance is punishable with imprisonment up to three years and fine.

S.70A and S.70B provides for notification of any Government organization as the national nodal agency for Critical Information Infrastructure Protection and notification of any Government organization as the Indian Computer Emergency Response Team, respectively. S.84A gives extensive powers to the Central Government to prescribe encryption methods to ensure secure use of the electronic medium and for promotion of e-governance and e-commerce.

Other Relevant Provisions

S.77A of the ITA, 2008 provides for compounding of offences under this Act, other than:

- Offences punishable with life or imprisonment for a term exceeding three years;

- In cases of enhanced punishment;
- Those affecting the socio economic conditions of the country; or
- Offences against a child below the age of 18 years or a woman.

Whilst some of these exceptions appear to be precise and appropriate, certain others appear ambiguous *i.e.,* exception on the grounds of socio economic conditions.

S.77B makes all offences punishable with three years and above imprisonment cognizable and bailable, notwithstanding the provisions of the Indian Code of Criminal Procedure, 1973. With the increase in cyber crimes amounting to offences under the ITA, 2008, the power to investigate offences under this Act has been vested with an Inspector instead of the Deputy Superintendent of Police. This may reduce the confusion relating to jurisdiction for registering of offences. Further this would entail commencement of extensive and immediate cyber law awareness measures by the investigation agencies throughout India. There is however anxiety in the minds of the industry about the ability of the police official of such rank being able to handle such additional responsibility.

S.79 has been modified by the ITA, 2008 to restrict the liability of an Intermediary under this section to specific instances, *i.e.,* if he provides access to communication systems for transmission or temporary storage of third party information, data or communication links made available or hosted by him. The Intermediary should however observe due diligence and comply with the prescribed guidelines, while discharging his duties.

S.85 of the IT Act, which imputes vicarious liability in case of offences by companies, has been retained in its original form despite criticism by different industry sectors. As most of the offences under the IT Act have been made cognizable, and with the increase in the number of offences added under the ITA, 2008, this provision may be cause for concern.

Conclusion

Though the ITA 2008 has been passed by the parliament, the Amended Act is still not the law of the land. The ITA 2008 will come into effect only from the date notified by the Government of India, which still remains pending as on the date of publication of this paper.

Introduction of several provisions in the IT Act by the ITA, 2008, relating to data protection, are extremely essential in today's business environment as several Indian companies providing services to or in conjunction with foreign entities handle large amounts of data that are accessed and/or processed by their employees. Such cross border exchange/ transmission of Data further mandates compliance with the provisions of foreign enactments on Data Protection. The increased accountability of data handlers and data aggregators and the enhanced punitive measures, therefore meets such requirements to some extent. The existing provisions along with the additional/ revised provisions under the ITA, 2008 provide for criminal prosecution and stringent monetary penalties that are likely to act as effective deterrents. Whilst some inclusions in the ITA 2008 have been subject to criticism, the amendments and additions made to the IT Act are expedient and much awaited additions. Absence of effective provisions to combat offences like Cyber Stalking and cyber squatting are avoidable loopholes, which one hopes will soon be rectified. One could safely conclude that whilst the ITA 2008 is still work in progress, it is definitely headed in the right direction.

7

National Security and the Internet

In September of 1997, the President's Commission on Critical Infrastructure Protection released a preliminary report calling for a vast increase in funding to protect eight key elements of U.S. infrastructure: electric power distribution, telecommunication, banking and finance, water, transportation, oil and gas storage and transportation, emergency services and government services.

"These are the life support systems of the nation," said the Commission's chairman, retired Air Force General Robert T. Marsh. "They're vital, not only for day-to-day discourse, they're vital to national security. They're vital to our economic competitiveness world wide, they're vital to our very way of life." "The Internet provides an access point into all these infrastructures," said Marsh. Commission member John T. Davis, representing the National Security Agency, said the government should develop a secure "Next Generation Internet" for official use.

The commission recommended doubling the current federal R&D budget of $250 million for protecting these systems, with increases of $100 million each year after 1999 to $1 billion per year by 2004. In February, 1998, U.S. Attorney General Janet Reno unveiled a $64 million plan to build a new "command center" to fight "cyber attacks" against U.S. computer systems. This new "command center" is called the National Infrastructure Protection Center, a Justice Department response to the report from the President's Commission on Critical Infrastructure Protection. These are just some of the more recent and visible results of concern over "cyber war," "infowar," "cyberterrorism," and other, related threats now perceived by law enforcement personnel and national security officials as new and important terrain. And these authorities commonly view the Internet as the "highway" upon which these threats will be borne. The character of the Internet has been dramatically transformed over the past five years, as everyone knows. What began as a communications network for scientists, academics, engineers, and specialists is now a vast, global, communications medium that rivals the public telephone network, television broadcasting, and even radio. The Internet-using population, worldwide, is now over 60 million people, and Matrix Internet Data Services, an Internet demographic consulting company in Austin, Texas, has predicted that, by the year 2002, there could be more than 700 million people using the network.

Senior executives in large telecommunications companies, an industry which is now the largest in the world, routinely report that data traffic will soon surpass voice traffic, and that packet-switched networks, like the Internet, may eventually supersede the circuit-switched telephone network worldwide. The Internet "model," of packet-switching, distributed communication, and unmanned digital nodes, appears to be the bedrock for nearly all future communications. Of particular importance to those charged with national security is the fact that increasing levels of international commerce are conducted over the Internet, and also increasing levels of government service. International funds transfers, now surpassing over a trillion dollars a day, are carried by computer networks. Power grids, banks, government databases, large corporate enterprises, news networks, transportation facilities, and many other essential components of civilized life are increasingly "on the net," delivering services or conducting critical communications over the Internet.

Disruption of such services or communications could, someday it is feared, resemble or approach in severity an actual physical attack such as a military strike or a major terrorist incident. At present, the potential for a computer attack that would produce a major national calamity is controversial. Most computer attacks documented so far have been merely intrusions or annoyances. In many cases, vulnerability to computer attack is shrouded in secrecy or proprietary prudence. In other cases, vulnerability may be exaggerated to enhance the status and commercial value of computer security firms or to improve the negotiating position of government agencies that are seeking more funding or clout. What is important now, however, is that officials of the U.S. government and experts in the private sector are arguing, persistently, that the growth of the Internet, and its expanding capabilities, combined with the fact that it is increasingly embedded in "critical national infrastructures," makes protection of computers on the Internet a matter of national security. In other words, regardless of the current threat, the future indicates growing vulnerability and thus a growing urgency for protection and vigilance.

Jamie Gorelick, U.S. Deputy Attorney General, told the host of TV's "Nightline" news talk show, Forrest Sawyer, in December of 1997, "My own assessment, Forrest, is that we have a couple of years before there is a really serious threat. We have seen indications in criminal activity, in the plans of foreign nations, in the plans of terrorist groups that lead us to believe that we should be about the process of hardening our computers against attack". In yet another irony, what may contribute to the threat of computer attack in the U.S. is the country's unrivaled military superiority. General Marsh said on the same "Nightline" programme, "Nobody around the world today would attempt to defeat us on the battlefield. Instead, they will be seeking means to find vulnerabilities in our systems that they can exploit and do serious harm without having to confront us in the conventional armed way of the past."

If the Internet does prove to be a viable means for nations to attack one another, nations capable of such threats will be able to afford a credible threatening status far more cheaply than if they needed vast arsenals of missiles and tanks. A relatively modest investment in the skills of a handful of network trespassers and hackers would become a substitute for immense investments in weaponry. As such, the sources of credible threats could proliferate. This "new terrain" of computer warfare or cyberterrorism poses some serious and unfamiliar challenges to national security authorities. First, all forms of warfare in the past have involved a threat to geographically specific assets by equally geographically specific threats — such as massed armies or ballistic missiles. One of the chief characteristics about computer attacks is their ambiguity in nearly every dimension: it's difficult to ascertain where the attack is coming from, who is behind it, what the motive is, whether it is the work of a determined enemy or merely a curious trespasser, etc. Penetrations that come from trespassers inside the U.S. may not be benign or "domestic."

Before the war in the Persian Gulf, for example, there was a report of a U.S. hacker breaking into Pentagon computers and then offering to sell the information to Saddam Hussein (who didn't buy it because he didn't believe it was genuine). It's not even clear what the term "cyberwar" describes. If it means an organised and coordinated attack on computer systems by another state government, that may be too high a threshold; it's unlikely we'll see an unequivocal example of this soon, except perhaps by the U.S. attacking an enemy's computers. "Cyberterrorism" may be more likely, but, as in the distinction between war and terrorism by other means, this prospect might call for solutions different than protection from "cyberwar." If a computer attack were to occur in the midst of some other crisis of national security, says Roger Molander, an expert now at the RAND Corporation, the very ambiguity of the attack may complicate decision-making tremendously.

This is a murky world for national security officials. Second, the United States has historically avoided major military attacks because of its relative isolation from belligerents, a kind of "continental defence." Most of the country's history in military strategy has been to keep conflict as far from the U.S. mainland as possible. But the Internet poses a new dilemma: its global character, and the way it works, allows easy access to almost any networked computer inside the United States, including those running critical systems, from nearly anywhere else in the world. For a determined adversary, there are now millions of entry points to the U.S. heartland, and requiring no logistical effort, in contrast to the obstacles facing adversaries in the past. Third, because of the fact that computer attacks can come from both inside and outside the U.S., and the fact that the origins of such attacks are difficult to identify promptly, jurisdictional controversies and overlap among law enforcement and national security agencies are already rampant. The U.S. has had a long tradition, for fifty years at least, of separating the jurisdictions of agencies responsible for domestic threats from those responsible for foreign threats.

If the Internet is factored into their responsibilities, these jurisdictional boundaries are rendered exceedingly vague and arbitrary, leading to confusion and conflicting interests. Finally, the biggest issue of all: for the most part, in the past, the U.S. military and its national security allies, such as intelligence agencies, have been charged with protecting military assets first, and using these as offensive weapons or deterrents against enemies. In a "cyberwar" scenario, however, conventional military assets will be useless, and there may be no appropriate offensive weapons available. The military and law enforcement and national security agencies are increasingly faced with protecting private assets, such as corporate computer systems, or other information systems far outside the jurisdiction of the federal government. Given the nature of U.S. democracy, the federal government's powers for forcing protection schemes on private companies or other governmental entities are limited. And, as demonstrated by the ongoing debate over encryption restrictions, the government may have interests quite different from those of private companies, especially those that compete in the global marketplace.

Indeed, given the evolving nature of global enterprise, it's commonly unclear where a U.S. company stops and a foreign counterpart or partner begins. The Internet does tend to erase national borders, as does global commerce. The U.S. defence establishment has traditionally been able to circumscribe what constitutes a "national asset," but this is getting more and more difficult to do. For all these reasons, many of which have emerged only in the past half decade, the Internet is a new factor in national security assessment. And, given the significant influence of national security agencies in setting national political agendas, and in shaping technological trends, this new friction between the Internet and national security is likely to affect the way the Internet develops for the foreseeable future. At stake is whether the Internet can retain its democratic, global, and egalitarian features, or whether it will be absorbed into older patterns of national competition for power and status.

THE INTERNET AND NATIONAL SECURITY AGENCIES

By now, nearly every federal agency within the U.S. government has some department or division responsible for computer security. But the pre-eminent agencies of the field are still the agencies charged with national security, such as the National Security Agency, the Central Intelligence Agency, the Federal Bureau of Investigation, and, to a lesser extent, the Justice Department and the Secret Service within the Treasury Department. It is important to acknowledge that it is the character of these agencies, their histories and their other responsibilities that give the subject of computer security in the United States a particular kind of atmosphere, largely that of the military and national security community itself.

Thus, the "command and control" model of computer security has tended to dominate the U.S. government's approach. In 1987, the Computer Security Act of the U.S. Congress apportioned responsibilities for computer security to the National Institute of Standards and Technology (NIST), of the U.S. Department of Commerce, for non-classified computer systems; and to the National Security Agency (NSA) for classified systems. This law was the result of a certain level of alarm, on the part of Congress and civil libertarians, during the Reagan administration because of a pair of White House national security directives that pointed towards NSA control over all computers in the U.S. The Computer Security Act was an attempt to mark a boundary for civilian control of unclassified information systems. However, since the Computer Security Act the U.S. National Security Agency has worked diligently to regain and secure its supremacy over computer security policy.

A 1989 "Memorandum of Understanding" between NSA and NIST shifted power back to NSA, and in 1994 President Clinton issued Presidential Decision Directive 29, which set up the Security Policy Board, which has recommended that all computer security functions for the government be merged under NSA control. At the same time that NSA has attempted to impose its own standards on computer security in the U.S., the Justice Department's Federal Bureau of Investigation has tended to extend its responsibilities beyond domestic law enforcement to international crime, counter-terrorism, and counter-intelligence. While officials of the NSA are largely unknown to the public, FBI Director Louis Freeh is a common face in the news, often called upon to testify and make the government's case for control over encryption and computer security in the name of national security.

The 1993 bombing of the World Trade Center in New York City, which was apparently connected to a foreign conspiracy in the Middle East, strengthened the FBI's role in monitoring international terrorism immeasurably. Freeh also points to international drug cartels, new foreign sources of organised crime, the international terrorist activities of so-called "rogue states," the frightening potential for the uncontrolled proliferation of small nuclear weapons, and other threats to make the case that the FBI now has a host of new targets. These two phenomena of recent years have tended to blur the line between domestic security and national security, a blurring that has produced crises of constitutional protections in the past. But Congress has been persuaded by the federal law enforcement and national agencies.

The Intelligence Authorisation Act of 1997 states:

- ... elements of the Intelligence Community may, upon the request of a United States law enforcement agency collect information outside the United States about individuals who are not United States persons. Such elements may collect such information notwithstanding that the law enforcement agency intends to use the information collected for purposes of a law enforcement investigation or counterintelligence investigation.

Whitfield Diffie, the co-inventor of public key encryption, and his co-author Susan Landau, in their 1998 book Privacy on the Line, comment: "This wording carefully steers clear of permitting the intelligence community to spy on Americans directly, but opens the way for unprecedented collaboration between the intelligence and law enforcement communities". The boundary-free character of the Internet will likely intensify the merging of conventional law enforcement activities inside the U.S. and the activities of national security agencies. The front line in the debate about this trend is encryption policy. In September of 1997, the U.S. Congress' House National Security Committee voted to strengthen controls on the export of digital encryption, reversing a trend towards relaxing such controls, one of the chief goals of the high tech industry. Committee members cited the warnings they received in "classified briefings" as the main reason for their vote.

Congressman Mike Oxley, a Republican of Ohio, told The New York Times, "I would find it difficult to believe that a member who heard the briefing could walk away not committed to addressing security issues. Frankly, I wish everyone interested in this issue could have heard for themselves the alarming briefing that members of our committee heard". Constraints of space prevent a comprehensive or even adequate review of the encryption debate here. In summary, the U.S. government's position is that law enforcement and national security authorities need to retain the ability to intercept and interpret communications, including digital data, in order to fulfill their responsibilities to protect the United States from crime and foreign threats. As such, the federal government has proposed a series of arrangements that have all included the concept of "escrowed keys," meaning the ability of authorised officials to acquire an encryption key to unlock scrambled data. Opponents of this scheme, which is the traditional approach in military cryptography, argue that public key encryption, without escrowed keys, is the only safeguard for privacy and authenticated electronic commerce.

These opponents also argue that criminals and foreign adversaries will have no incentive to use encryption with escrowed keys — *i.e.*, the "key escrow" approach will provide keys to the communications of people who obey the law, while others will have easy access to unbreakable encryption algorithms. The ready availability of public key encryption, argue government critics, means that "the horse is out of the barn" already. Moreover, they point out, the task of security in the computer age is for each person, or each computer administrator, to be responsible for computer security, because the task is too immense and complex for bureaucratic oversight. The argument has been framed as one in which the protective schemes are characterised as a choice between armies or locks, and each of these has its attendant interest group. While the Congress has been largely sympathetic to and supportive of the federal law enforcement and national security agencies, another front has opened up in the U.S. courts.

In early 1997, in a case heard before the United States District Court for the Northern District of California, Bernstein v. United States Department of State, U.S. District Court Judge Marilyn Hall Patel ruled that national security considerations cannot be used to censor cryptographic schemes on the Internet. Daniel Bernstein, a graduate student, created an encryption algorithm called "Snuffle." After four years of correspondence with the U.S. State Department, Bernstein learned that his source code and all other material about "Snuffle" except a research paper were in violation of export control laws and could not be posted to the Internet. Bernstein sued the State Department, claiming that this ban violated his First Amendment rights. Judge Patel agreed with Bernstein, and wrote a stinging rebuke of the government's position. Patel ruled that computer source code is protected as free speech by the First Amendment, and that the government's attempt to ban such speech amounted to "prior restraint," which is unconstitutional. Judge Patel specifically prevented the U.S. government from using claims of a breach of national security to impose prior restraint on the distribution of encryption source code.

The U.S. government has appealed the Bernstein decision to the U.S. Supreme Court, and it is there that a final ruling is expected. If the Supreme Court upholds Judge Patel's ruling, this may close the encryption debate for the foreseeable future; after such a ruling, all encryption source code could be posted to the Internet without intervention by national security or law enforcement agencies. This would effectively kill the means by which such agencies now control the distribution of non-escrow encryption algorithms. On the other hand, if the Supreme Court overturns the Bernstein decision, this will reinforce the role of national security agencies in shaping the future of the Internet. Because of this, the Bernstein case is being watched very closely by both sides of the encryption debate.

The dispute over encryption has put into stark relief the dual nature of the national security mission: the responsibility of such agencies to protect national technological assets and also retain the ability to intercept and interpret digital communications. In the era of the Internet, these two responsibilities are in conflict with each other, thus posing significant dilemmas to national security officials. On the one hand, these agencies are urging businesses, other government agencies, and individuals to protect their computer data from attack.

On the other hand, these agencies seek to control the way these people protect such data in order to protect law enforcement and national security agency access to this data. Not surprisingly, both businesses and individuals are hesitant to implement encryption schemes that require turning over keys to people they don't know or whose motives they don't fully comprehend. Because of this hesitancy, the first mission of the security agencies, that of increasing protection for U.S. computer systems, is stymied. General Marsh, the chairman of the President's Commission on Critical Infrastructure Protection, has told the press he hopes the dispute about encryption policy is resolved soon, because he believes, with justification, that this ongoing dispute is obstructing the implementation of greater security for computer systems. Members of the commission have hinted at their support for a loosening of encryption controls, but have also leaked the information, to The New York Times, that "they are under fairly strict orders' to fall in line with the FBI's push for key recovery". Business executives are understandably reluctant to invest in security systems that may be superseded by other technologies or blocked by court rulings.

The U.S. federal government's rapid transition from one policy recommendation to another — such as from DES to the "Clipper chip" to key escrow to "key recovery — has not helped foster confidence in the business community. And of course, some influential business organisations, such as the Business Software Alliance are allied with civil libertarians and other opponents of U.S. government policy in the case of encryption standards. Despite the hopes of General Marsh and others, at present the encryption debate in the United States is so polarised that compromise solutions are not visible nor likely to emerge soon. This polarisation has been exacerbated by some ideological and political trends in the U.S. Republican conservatives who now control the U.S. Congress are more sympathetic to law enforcement and national security arguments than was true of the Congress just a few years ago.

For example, for many years the U.S. House Subcommittee on Civil and Constitutional Rights was chaired by Rep. Don Edwards, a Democrat and a former FBI agent who was highly critical of any law enforcement encroachment on civil liberties. But Congressman Edwards has retired, and conservative Republicans have taken his place as committee chairmen. Another new phenomenon is the emergence of a new breed of "cyberlibertarians — typically young, talented technologists who reject most of the assumptions of the national security establishment. Some of the more radical of these ideologues have argued that the Internet is the beginning of the end of the nation-state, let alone the end of the national security state. This perspective is not just an isolated intellectual discourse, either: the "cypherpunk" movement, for example, has complex and extensive ties to outlaw hackers, most of them young men, some of whom have adopted the intellectual framework of "cyberlibertarianism" as an ideological justification for criminal penetrations of government computers — casting themselves as "Thomas Paines" of the digital revolution. Such "counterculture" attitudes are widely shared by educated young people all over the world, perhaps a natural attitude of young people rebelling against authority.

But when this attitude is combined with the fact that these same people are the most technically adept in the world, and a number of them are affluent or even wealthy because of this skill — once again, national security officials are confronting a new and alien environment, one dramatically different from eras of the past, when business leaders and skilled technologists were typically undisturbed by the alleged imperatives of national security. Now, when confronting young leaders of the digital revolution, national security authorities are in hostile territory. The end of the Cold War has given new impetus to calls for a dismantling of national security institutions, and the Internet, with its idealistic potential for global communications between planetary citizens, has come along at just the right time to fuel such ideas. Widespread use of phrases like "the digital revolution" and "Third Wave civilization" reinforce the popular notion that the "information age" entails an overturning of old regimes, including, perhaps, the centuries-old competition between nation states.

For these reasons, in addition to the prosaic clash of interests between the government and pragmatic corporations that are part of a global marketplace, the encryption debate is the leading edge of a much larger philosophical debate about the role of the state in the information age. It is unfair, of course, to characterise national security authorities as "dinosaurs" due for extinction, the way they are characterised by some of the "cyberlibertarians" — even a small dose of the daily news is enough to convince most people that there are in fact real threats that continue to justify the need for some national security protections. On the other hand, there is no compelling reason to assume that the missions and structures and traditions and size of national security institutions created during the decades of the Cold War need persist into eternity. Many critics of national security agencies argue reasonably and persuasively that the Cold War should be regarded as an anomaly in U.S. history, a struggle that imposed sacrifices in democratic values that need not be sustained or repeated in the absence of a threat equivalent to the Soviet Union.

These critics have quite rightly put on the table for debate the question of whether the "national security state" is an essential or necessary political form for nations in the 21st century, particularly in an era in which the Internet is challenging many assumptions and norms inherited from a pre-Internet period, that of World War II and the decades of the Cold War. It may seem grandiose to suggest that complex technical debates such as those surrounding digital encryption or the prospect of "cyberwar" are the most important political debates of our time. But this is in fact the case. This is not actually all that surprising, when one considers the catalyst of such debates: the Internet itself, one of the most remarkable, promising, and at the same time vexing creations of human enterprise in the history of the world.

NETWAR AND THREATS TO NATIONS

How big a threat to national security is the Internet? While the question is obvious, the answer, unfortunately, is not. While advancing technology has made assessing all threats to national security increasingly difficult, assessments of the threat of "cyberwar" or "cyberterrorism" via the Internet may be the most difficult of all, for a variety of reasons. First, of course, the Internet is constantly changing. Indeed, it may be the most rapidly evolving entity in human history. It is difficult, if not impossible, to fix a "moment" on the Internet to make an assessment that would last more than a few weeks, at most. This is very different than assessing other kinds of vulnerabilities or threats, which change or accumulate much more slowly. During the Cold War, U.S. intelligence sources had a reasonably good idea of the capabilities of the Soviet Union, at least in terms of the raw numbers of its military assets.

It's difficult to imagine how the same sources could "count" the threat of Russian hackers, for example, some of whom have penetrated deep into the computers of U.S.-based banks, such as CitiCorp in New York. The Internet has also extended and deepened its reach so broadly over the past few years that it's almost certainly impossible for anyone, or any group of people, to "know" everything it touches at any given time. Not only is the system vast, involving tens of millions of computers, but it is characterised by rapid change, contingency, complexity, innovation, and constant "churn," or the birth and death of new features almost overnight. This is, in short, a risk assessment team's worst nightmare.

Next, even if one were able to narrow one's focus to "critical" systems connected to the Internet, there are no public or even readily available data on how vulnerable such systems might be. Defence computers are buried under layers of secrecy and classification, and private companies are not likely to volunteer such information. We typically only hear about computer vulnerabilities after a break-in, and even then we learn little about the incident, and sometimes the descriptions of break-ins are not accurate, either. A New Jersey State Trooper once told the press that a teenage hacker he had arrested was altering the orbital paths of U.S. defence satellites, which was not only untrue but absurd.

People who reveal computer break-ins often have ancillary reasons for such revelations. Responding to a recent rash of reported break-ins in Pentagon computers, Peter Neumann, one of the world's leading computer security experts, told HotWired News, "Perhaps this is a con game....You put out a system with miserable protection and hope that someone breaks it," he said. "Then you can ask for millions of dollars more to perform further palliative protections, rather than getting to the core of the problem — significantly ratcheting up the security of the infrastructure". When officials like General Robert Marsh tell the press that the Internet provides access to many, if not all, of the critical infrastructure systems of the United States, it's difficult to assess this claim, except to suspect that he's right. The nature of the problem is one in which it's unlikely that we'll see detailed government reports on the levels and sources of current risks. Accumulating evidence based on anecdotal reports is likely to be the only information available.

Because of the paucity of hard data, and the difficulty of assessing what computer systems are vulnerable because of being connected to the Internet, it is ipso facto difficult to assess whether there is in fact an Internet-related threat that compares to other kinds of threats. Kevin Poulsen, who appeared on the "Nightline" TV programme mentioned earlier, and who was described on that programme as a "former computer hacker," said, "I've heard so much talk about the coming info war. I'll be more worried when somebody can actually show me a single case of a hacker doing something that malicious. So far they haven't." He went on, "The most heinous, coordinated, planned-out, conspiratorial, hacker attack imaginable wouldn't come close to a single bombing of a building. Nobody's ever going to die from anything that happens electronically. The government has held me up as an example of a hacker that had reached the very top. If I wasn't anywhere near having that kind of capability, then what reason is there to think that anybody is?" Most examples of computer break-ins have been annoyances and cause for alarm, not serious threats to critical systems.

Gene Spafford, another computer security expert, likened hacker break-ins to "being pecked to death by ducks. No one of these instances is really serious.... But if you've got 10,000 people doing that, its a huge problem". There have been some worrisome computer attacks, such as the attempt by German hackers to secure classified information and sell it to the Soviets, chronicled in Clifford Stoll's book *The Cuckoo's Egg*. There is some evidence that there was an attempt to disable Croatian computers during its war with Serbia, and Croatian security experts suspected Serbian programmers for the attacks, although there was no definitive evidence. The 1989 Morris "worm" that brought down thousands of Internet computers, and the 1998 virus that affected Windows computers on the net, highlighted the vulnerability of the system as a whole.

The Pentagon has admitted that its computers have been penetrated hundreds of thousands of times. Federal officials have hinted, in press briefings, that they have classified information about far more serious hacking attempts, successes, or penetration capabilities in other countries. And, of course, the Pentagon is busy building an offensive "info-war" capability of its own. But the overall problem facing national security authorities is that this threat of Internet-based terrorism or attack, however grave it might be, is to date not at all tangible to the average citizen, nor is it likely to become more so in the near future unless a catastrophe occurs for "demo" purposes. Their current strategy is to request vast sums of money to prevent something from occuring, not unlike the Year 2000 problem, which the public also barely understands, if at all.

This is, again, far different from the world of the recent past, in which the threat of Hiroshima in the United States was lodged quite vividly in the minds of most citizens. It's considerably more difficult to persuade the public that there is a large potential for threat to the nation via the Internet, when the entire country is on a big campaign to get everyone online, especially schoolchildren, and there is no obvious way to quantify or even nail down the full nature of the threat. Once again, this is "new terrain" for national security advisors. As everyone knows, "national security" is largely a game of perceptions, a combination of both real and imagined threats and assets. Even during the Cold War, it was controversial how big a threat the Soviet Union was to the U.S.; this controversy continues even today, nearly ten years after the end of that conflict.

So it's not surprising that it is controversial whether there is a national security threat posed by the Internet or whether this is a paranoid frame of mind; or, cynically, whether this is related primarily to institutions hoping to increase their budgets and their longevity. This controversy is fueled by the sparse information available about the true level of risk at hand, especially with respect to "critical" systems. Because we can expect that this dearth of information will continue, the controversy about the nature of the threat will no doubt extend far into the future as well. In the digital era, the very nature of the technology paradoxically makes perceptions more important, because tangible facts are harder to come by. What do we know? When computer security experts are asked whether Internet-networked computers are secure, their answers are almost always along the lines of "not enough," or "not yet."

One might discount such answers as self-interest and still conclude that more needs to be done about computer security. The explanation given by security experts about why we don't do more is that the public has not yet demanded more security for computers, and, without significant public demand, companies are not providing it. It's also expensive and sometimes troublesome to secure a computer and to keep it secure, imposing discipline on users and system administrators who would rather not be disciplined. It is common to hear of people learning about computer security the hard way, in a "trial by fire," absorbing a lesson after something nasty has occurred. Obviously if there is a real threat to national security via the Internet, such lessons are not an adequate substitute for prudent policymaking. It is the job of national security officials to prevent catastrophes, not to say "I told you so." The vexing issue is how we might feel safer without seriously compromising the best features of the Internet, trampling on democracy, or turning into a surveillance society.

These are not new concerns; they were not introduced into public debate by the appearance of the Internet. But they have been made rather dramatically more complicated by the first truly significant supra-national sphere of discourse and politics. They are further complicated by the dual role of national security agencies, which is to both protect national assets and to penetrate the defences of enemies. It is this dual role, embedded in the traditions and histories of national security agencies, which is at the heart of the intense debates about a possible solution to computer-based threats: widespread digital encryption.

THE POSITIVE ASPECTS OF INTERNET SURVEILLANCE

Millions of people around the world use the Internet. With the infinite knowledge and possibilities it provides, the Internet can definitely be utilised to connect people to one another and/or make everyday tasks easier. However, many people are unaware of the prospective perils the Internet has. "The rise of the Internet, with e-mail, instant messages, and more, has opened gigantic pipelines for all to use, including criminals". These criminals view the internet as the perfect way to commit crimes, to con individuals, or to affect millions of people through cyber-terrorism. Criminals also use e-mail to spread information to other criminals since, the process is convenient and fast.

This is where the Carnivore system comes in: it keeps an eye on these hazardous people to put a stop to their evil intentions. That in itself, Carnivore is a form of passive hacking used to detect the "real" illegal hackings and other wrongdoings. Carnivore is used by the FBI in five areas: cyber-terrorism, information warfare, child pornography, fraud, and virus writing. Terrorism is a great threat throughout the world. Particularly in the United States, cyber-terrorism can be devastating because of the society's reliance on computers. Cyber-terrorists have the capability to shut down national infrastructures like energy usage, transportation, water, and telecommunications as a means to intimidate and harm the society.

Carnivore attempts to stop or hinder terrorism by monitoring and supervising the Internet activities of known terrorist groups, with procedures equivalent to tapping phones lines. While testifying on the worldwide threat of terrorism, George Tenet, the Director of Central Intelligence, states that "terrorist groups, including Hizbollah, HAMAS, the Abu Nidal organisation, and Bin Laden's al Qu'ida organisation, are using computerised files, e-mail, and encryption to support their operations". These organisations have yet to succeed terrorising America through cyber terrorism; however, the potential threat is still greatly present. This is the very reason the FBI sees Carnivore as a necessity, because the system makes it possible for officials to monitor activity and prevent any catastrophic tragedies from occurring.

There have already been early signs of promise, such as when the FBI discovered that e-mail was a major method used for communication for a terrorist group. Thus, the FBI was able to stop this group from stealing explosives from National Guard Armories in several southern states. It was also discovered that this same terrorist group used the Internet to download information on Ricin, the 3rd deadliest toxin in the world. In instances like this, Carnivore can follow the steps of terrorists and stop them before they strike. Next, Carnivore is helpful when tracking down those individuals that intend to use information warfare against the United States.

Information warfare is a subcategory of cyber-terrorism. Since, many nations cannot measure up to America's power in terms of military strength, they seek information warfare as retaliation. "This type of war attempts to exploit our 'Achilles heel,' a national dependence on information technology in government, commercial, and private operations." A book published by two Chinese military officials explains that the use of unconventional techniques, such as spreading computer viruses, is the only way to neutralise the United States. Moreover, the Russian government has been known to think along the same lines.

Russian government officials acknowledge that attacking America's computer infrastructure could lead to the same result as using weapons of mass destruction; either way hurts the United States immensely. Another crime that Carnivore prevents is child pornography. Even though this is not a national security threat, it is destructive to communities and society. The offenders may download graphics from child pornography web sites and/or use the Internet as a device to arrange meetings between themselves and young children. This can lead to violent and sometimes deadly consequences. "Between 1995 and 2001, the FBI investigated over 800 cases involving offenders crossing state lines to carry out an illegal sexual relationship and more than 1,800 cases involving the exchange of child pornography over the Internet".

It is vital to track these people because they have the tendency to victimise repeatedly. Studies have shown that a child molester typically abuses approximately 70 children in his or her lifetime. With the help of Carnivore, the FBI devised a plan to capture these sexual predators through processes such as "Innocent Images." This site is intended to capture those who distribute child pornography with the Internet. A FBI agent will go undercover as a child over the internet and lure sex offenders to meet with them, allowing the agent to arrest and prosecute the criminal. Fraud is an issue that countless Americans have encountered. The Internet is ideal for fraud for three reasons.

First, people can be easily targeted with the amount of features that it offers, such as chat rooms, instant messages, e-mails, and forums. A person can look up names, addresses, and e-mail addresses through a directory and start sending out spam e-mails.

Secondly, individuals can remain anonymous. When a person creates a web site selling defective materials that do not actually work, he or she may experience fewer, if any, consequences because his or her real identity is kept secret. It is difficult to trace the real identity of the creators of millions upon millions of web sites that can be found. "The critical difference in fraud committed over the

Internet is that the perpetrator can 'virtually' vanish, leaving consumers wondering to whom or where to turn to for help".

Thirdly, those that commit fraud do not face expenses with obtaining a toll-free number, mail, and/or hiring people to maintain the mail. Since, they can sign up for free e-mail with companies like Yahoo and Hotmail and obtain a screen name for instant messages with AIM, these previous expenses are no longer necessary. According to the North American Association, Internet related fraud estimates to be about $10 billion per year. In one meticulous case in 2000, 19 individuals implemented an insider trading scheme, where a person with stock information passed along tips to firms through chat rooms.

These 19 people were accused of fraud and discovered to have pocketed several million dollars worth of illegal money. Had Carnivore been in place at the time of this occurrence, they may have been caught sooner than through traditional methods. Finally, the spreading of computer viruses is becoming increasingly perilous. Viruses can be detrimental to company and government computer systems, hurting individuals who simply open an e-mail. Viruses such as the Melissa Macro Virus and the Explore.Zip worm have destroyed individuals' computer files and programmes around the world. They can entirely shut down e-mail systems and delay communications. For example, in some incidents, Microsoft had to put a halt to all outgoing e-mails throughout the company.

A hacker can also spread a virus to a company to destroy its database, which often holds immeasurable valuable information. This can be costly and some of the data lost may never be recovered. All things considered, this new programme will eventually be able to do exactly what it was invented to do: monitor, track, and prevent criminals from breaking the law; protect potential victims from facing harmful consequences, and give society assurance that the world is safer place. Even with the loopholes found in Carnivore currently, the overall benefits this plan offers can outweigh its negative aspects. Since, this programme has recently been revealed and is relatively new, the public will have to wait and see if the FBI and government officials can keep their word on its potentials.

THE NEGATIVE ASPECTS OF INTERNET SURVEILLANCE

Evidence suggests that Carnivore may be powerful, but it still has several shortcomings. At the first glance, the name "Carnivore" alone suggests a negative connotation. The fact that Carnivore is for wiretapping and spying on citizens raises the public's concern. It has drawn significant criticism from civil rights groups. The main critics of Carnivore are the Electronic Privacy Information Center (EPIC) and the American Civil Liberties Union (ACLU), two public interest groups devoted to civil liberties issues.

On July 11, 2000, EPIC sued the FBI under the Freedom of Information Act (FOIA). It pursued the public release of Carnivore's background information, source code, technical details, and the potential privacy issues of the technology. The group was able to obtain some information and records, although the FBI still refused to turn over Carnivore's source code and some of its inner workings. The secrecy surrounding exactly how Carnivore operates causes the public, IT managers, and ISPs to feel ambiguous about its implementation. The public is also generally unclear the activities between the intelligence agencies and law enforcement. Many people have confused the Carnivore system with the "Echelon" system, a global mass surveillance system used by intelligence agencies. Hence, EPIC's general counsel David Sobel argues that "Carnivore's use should be suspended until the questions surrounding it finally can be resolved. There's a great deal about Carnivore that we still don't know". The main privacy concern is that the government and the FBI can misuse Carnivore by examining more data than their court orders permit. In other words, it can do a broad sweep and spy on all individuals' Internet traffic and e-mails. Carnivore's intended function is to track and record E-mail subject headers, URLs, and IP addresses, but not the actual contents of an E-mail. Donald Kerr's statement to the U.S., House of Representatives is that Carnivore "does not search through the contents of every message and collect those that contain certain key words like 'bomb' or 'drugs'".

EPIC's legislative counsel Chris Hoofnagle says that although the government claims to only monitor data traffic's subject headers, the real interceptions often include more substance. The FBI moves beyond the scope of a search warrant because it also has access to other information such as message size, time of transmission, the number of jumps that a message takes to reach its destination, and other valuable data that can be extracted. Although the FBI states that Carnivore does not have the capacity to monitor every single individual's e-mails and that the monitoring is only restricted within the court's terms, the public has no actual way of knowing whether the FBI will misuse their power or exactly what Carnivore is capable of. Carnivore's intended function is to filter the data traffic and only retains the relevant data.

The system should have the ability to distinguish between communications that have or have not been authorised for interception. For instance, Carnivore can be configured to intercept e-mail but not online shopping records. However, the software does not always work correctly. In some circumstances, the system picks up both the authorised and unauthorised interceptions. The reason that the system is not as selective with the data captured as the FBI has claimed is due to several imprecise technical functionalities. The controversy over Carnivore comes from the fact that communications through the Internet and the phone are different.

In phone communications, a direct connection exists between two parties. However, Internet communication is broken up into tiny packets, which mixes together pieces of many different conversations. Consequently, extracting one person's data often involves inspecting the data of many others as well. Overall, there is not enough confidence to ensure that Carnivore will only pick up the intended traffic. The intercepted data may be misinterpreted if a single packet is dropped, repeated, or miscategorised. Dynamic IP addresses also make it difficult to identify which computer the data is coming from.

Additionally, since, ISPs vary in their architecture, the system's components may work in one system's architecture but fail in others. ISPs and IT managers are also concerned that the system may damage the company's technology infrastructure. Lastly, the possibility of hacking exists since, Carnivore is controlled remotely and has open security holes. Since, the Carnivore system also intercepts unnecessary non-targeted content, it may have blocked the actual targeted criminal investigations. The unauthorised interceptions not only violate an individual's privacy, but also disrupt or delay anti-terror investigations.

For example, in March 2000 the system was unable to perform effectively under the FBI's International Terrorism Operations Section (ITOS) called "UBL Unit," which refers to the government's official designation of Osama Bin Laden. The Carnivore system was turned on, but it blocked the actual surveillance of the target by also picking up electronic communications of on non-targeted individuals. By this, critics have argued that the FBI is unable to effectively manage foreign intelligence surveillance activities. Privacy advocates are also concerned that Carnivore violates the Fourth Amendment of the Constitution.

The central purpose of the Fourth Amendment is to protect the public's privacy and security from the government's unreasonable invasion. Law enforcement must obtain warrants of probable cause or suspicion in order to conduct searches and seizures. However, law enforcement is allowed to conduct searches without these warrants under limited circumstances, such as those involving government issues. In other words, the government's interest can outweigh an individual's expectation of privacy.

An example is the pen-trap order, in which a probable cause is not needed to obtain a suspect's information. In criminal cases, a court order allows the interception and collection suspects' Internet transmissions without the suspects' knowledge or consent. However, at the same time, the system is given access to the data of those individuals that are not suspects. In the case that the system does capture the data of someone's illegal activity, to a certain extent that information may still be used as evidence in prosecution. Furthermore, an issue concerning property arises in regards to who has the ultimate control of the system.

Responsibility may be divided between the government that uses the system for surveillance, and the technical agents that install and operate the system. In this case, the technical agents are the ones that must configure the system properly so it does not collect data beyond what is permissible by the laws and court orders. The downside is that Carnivore does not have an auditing function to keep track of individual users' identities.

The system logs all users on as 'administrator' and gives everyone full access to all resources. In other words, if an agent changes the settings of Carnivore, it would be difficult to determine the actual person guilty of violating the restrictions. Whether the deed is intentional or due to error, the result is an over-collection of data instead of just the restricted data. The system still needs improvement with stricter controls and independent monitoring, where individual users can be held responsible for their actions within the system.

ETHICAL ANALYSIS AND THE FUTURE

Internet technology has grown tremendously over the past decade, and the same growth will continue to persist into the future. Cyberspace is accessible to a wide range of members in society, including those with criminal intents. With this growth, the United States government has placed more limits on individuals' privacy and promoted the more extensive use of electronic surveillance. Furthermore, the September 11th terrorist attacks have rapidly increased the pace of security measures all around the world. In the United States, law enforcement officials are given even greater power to conduct communications interceptions. The Patriot Act allows the use of Carnivore Internet surveillance technology without a judicial warrant but only a court order.

The warrant requirements needed for monitoring have been reduced, allowing government officials easier access to individuals' records. In addition, the government is promoting policies that require developing communication technologies to have built in surveillance capabilities, and is also seeking limits on devices that provide encryption. The Carnivore system's primary intention is seemingly a responsible and necessary approach to assist the law enforcement in capturing criminals. However, while it can protect the citizens' security, the government must also consider its ability to invade on the citizens' privacy.

Many people believe that electronic surveillance must be limited to only unusual circumstances, since, they are a highly intrusive form of monitoring. The controversial aspect of this issue is that governmental actions can never be equally supported by all viewpoints. When an investigative method such as Carnivore is used, privacy advocates criticise the government for invading the public's privacy rights. On the other hand, when there is a failure to eliminate a potential criminal threat, crime control advocates criticise that the government for being negligent in its regulation of social welfare. As technology advances, the government can no longer use existing standards to manage the surveillance of communications.

Due to the changing disposition and sensitivity of personal information, it is important to provide protection for individuals' privacy and human rights. Consequently, the government must be able to effectively apply new laws, policies, and standards to keep up with the changing technologies. The government has to decide the most appropriate method to increase the nation's security while maintaining a level of freedom and privacy for individuals. The Electronic Communications Privacy Act (ECPA) clarifies how existing wiretap laws can be applied to Internet surveillance and sets boundaries on how much the government can invade the citizens' online privacy.

As long as the Carnivore system is used within the constraints and guidelines of ECPA, it has the potential to be a useful weapon against criminal and national security threats. Due to the new anti-terrorism and security legislations, the level of Internet monitoring by the government will probably not decrease. Several methods can be used to protect the security and privacy concerns of individuals that are monitored by this Carnivore system surveillance. First, technical changes must be considered to address the problem. Improvement of Carnivore's configuration is needed so that it only extracts the intended data traffic.

This will reduce the system's possibility of invading into non-targeted individuals' privacy, and not jeopardise other important investigations, such as those involving terrorism. Second, specific identifications are needed to distinguish FBI agents operating on the system. This way, agents are responsible for any mishaps, such as the change of control settings to collect more data than the system is intended for. Third, many countries now require the public information reporting about the use of surveillances by the government agencies.

The FBI should disclose more about the systems' internal workings so there is not such a secrecy surrounding exactly how it operates. This way, the public can alleviate their security and privacy concerns once they become more aware about the functions of the Carnivore system.

CONCLUSION

The explosion of the Internet and computer networks allows individuals, businesses, and governments to find and store valuable information, communicate to one another, and enjoy the unique methods of making their lives easier. However, this also makes it possible for anyone to perform illegal actions and misuse the powerful technology through a variety of means. The changing nature of technology and the sensitivity of information raise the standards needed to protect the privacy and security of individuals. These standards include greater security consciousness among all computer system users, as well as tougher security measures and more stringent laws.

The outcome of Internet hacking and surveillance may seemingly appear negative, but these methods also consist of positive aspects that are beneficial towards society. Businesses can benefit from ethical hacking, which uses simulations to purposely attack the systems in order to test the security of networks, servers, and applications. This process tests the strength and vulnerability of Internet security measures and prevents the time and monetary costs used to fix the incurred damage. Additionally, law enforcement officials can benefit from the skills and knowledge of convicted hackers.

The previous offenders can assist companies and law enforcers in the fight against other dangerous offenders, and may help advance society's knowledge of technology. Finally, the U.S., government can benefit from the Carnivore passive hacking, since, it functions to capture criminals that conduct their plans over the Internet. The reduction of privacy for the sake of greater security remains a controversial topic. The opinion and morality of the subject depends on an individual's personal judgement and stems from his or her own culture. From one perspective, it may be reasonable for the government to restrict society's freedom and privacy in order to protect its citizens. From another perspective, hacking and surveillances remain an intrusion of individuals' privacy. As a result, individuals and businesses lose their sense of confidentiality and feel the need to heighten their sense of protection towards their personal information.

If one believes that hacking and surveillances should be allowed, questions arise as to what level it must reach before it is considered unethical. In regards to the principles of decision-making, an endsbased thinking may be applicable if the consequence is the greatest good for the greatest number. The assistance from ethical hacking and Carnivore Internet surveillance may very well outweigh the costs of many crimes. If the benefit is greater than the cost, then the processes can be successfully utilised in a more productive manner. However, all else technology should only be applied with strict regards to maintaining the public's privacy and security. In the end, it is up to the society to consider the social and ethical standards to apply to the everchanging technology, so valuable information does not fall into the wrong hands for the wrong purposes.

8

Cyber, Internet and Network Security

The world is becoming more interconnected with the advent of the Internet and new networking technology. There is a large amount of personal, commercial, military, and government information on networking infrastructures worldwide. Network security is becoming of great importance because of intellectual property that can be easily acquired through the internet.

There are currently two fundamentally different networks, data networks and synchronous network comprised of switches. The internet is considered a data network. Since the current data network consists of computer-based routers, information can be obtained by special programmes, such as "Trojan horses," planted in the routers. The synchronous network that consists of switches does not buffer data and therefore are not threatened by attackers. That is why security is emphasized in data networks, such as the internet, and other networks that link to the internet.

The vast topic of network security is analysed by researching the following:

- History of security in networks
- Internet architecture and vulnerable security aspects of the Internet
- Types of internet attacks and security methods
- Security for networks with internet access
- Current development in network security hardware and software.

Based on this research, the future of network security is forecasted. New trends that are emerging will also be considered to understand where network security is heading.

BRIEF HISTORY OF INTERNET

The birth of the interne takes place in 1969 when Advanced Research Projects Agency Network (ARPANet) is commissioned by the department of defence (DOD) for research in networking.

The ARPANET is a success from the very beginning. Although originally designed to allow scientists to share data and access remote computers, e-mail quickly becomes the most popular application. The ARPANET becomes a high-speed digital post office as people use it to collaborate on research projects and discuss topics of various interests. The InterNetworking Working Group becomes the first of several standards-setting entities to govern the growing network. Vinton Cerf is elected the first chairman of the INWG, and later becomes known as a "Father of the Internet."

In the 1980s, Bob Kahn and Vinton Cerf are key members of a team that create TCP/IP, the common language of all Internet computers. For the first time the loose collection of networks which made up the ARPANET is seen as an "Internet", and the Internet as we know it today is born. The mid-80s marks a boom in the personal computer and super-minicomputer industries. The combination of inexpensive desktop machines and powerful, network-ready servers allows many companies to join the Internet for the first time. Corporations begin to use the Internet to communicate with each other and with their customers.

In the 1990s, the internet began to become available to the public. The World Wide Web was born. Netscape and Microsoft were both competing on developing a browser for the internet. Internet continues to grow and surfing the internet has become equivalent to TV viewing for many users.

Security Timeline

Several key events contributed to the birth and evolution of computer and network security. The timeline can be started as far back as the 1930s. Polish cryptographers created an enigma machine in 1918 that converted plain messages to encrypted text. In 1930, Alan Turing, a brilliant mathematician broke the code for the Enigma. Securing communications was essential in World War II.

In the 1960s, the term "hacker" is coined by a couple of Massachusetts Institute of Technology (MIT) students. The Department of Defense began the ARPANet, which gains popularity as a conduit for the electronic exchange of data and information. This paves the way for the creation of the carrier network known today as the Internet. During the 1970s, the Telnet protocol was developed. This opened the door for public use of data networks that were originally restricted to government contractors and academic researchers.

During the 1980s, the hackers and crimes relating to computers were beginning to emerge. The 414 gang are raided by authorities after a nine-day cracking spree where they break into top-secret systems. The Computer Fraud and Abuse Act of 1986 was created because of Ian Murphy's crime of stealing information from military computers. A graduate student, Robert Morris, was convicted for unleashing the Morris Worm to over 6,000 vulnerable computers connected to the Internet. Based on concerns that the Morris Worm ordeal could be replicated, the Computer Emergency Response Team (CERT) was created to alert computer users of network security issues.

In the 1990s, Internet became public and the security concerns increased tremendously. Approximately 950 million people use the internet today worldwide. On any day, there are approximately 225 major incidences of a security breach. These security breaches could also result in monetary losses of a large degree. Investment in proper security should be a priority for large organizations as well as common users.

AN INTRODUCTION TO THE INTERNET

The Internet has become the greatest market place ever established by man. Businesses must decide the form of access they will have to the Internet and also the form of presence. Most companies have email facilities and many have an Internet presence using access providers but could successfully use other features and forms of access of this global market. Businesses using the Internet will make mistakes, misjudge the market or project the wrong products and services as has been seen with the 'Dot Com' collapse of 1999–2000. Typical reasons for this are given by Allis [Allis 2001] as:

- Their business plans, while often 'inspiring' or 'revolutionary', they were never profitable;
- They spent other people's money unchecked in an effort to gain market share as soon as possible;
- They had inexperienced teams whose only goal was the fastest possible growth of their company, not long term success;
- Their company may have made it in the end, but because of the failure of so many others their investor capital was pulled.

These risks are no different to any other business start-up risks, but were made in the public scrutiny of the Internet business boom of the late 1990's.

The change from the original lockup shop selling wares to the public who must enter the shop has dramatically changed to an 'open all hours' virtual shop that anyone in the world can enter with access to the Internet. It is also possible, given the Internet and email, to extend the reach of selling into the home and office of anyone connected to the Internet [Sherwood 1997]. This will further increase as the Internet becomes available through the television.

Forrester [Forrester 1998] estimated that worldwide Internet commerce would reach as high as $3.2 Trillion in 2003[1]. InfoTech Trends [InfoTech Trends 2000] produced a new estimate that the worldwide Internet commerce market will exceed $1.2 trillion. Other research organisations have produced different figures, but all of them are estimates and are subject to rapid change after events such as the 'Dot Com' crash. Whilst there have been long-term Internet survivors, such as *lastminute.com*, one of the first to turn a profit (May 2002) as reported in the press newmediazero [newmediazero 2002], there have been many high profile failures.

There are two different economies represented on the Internet, much the same as the real life 'economy'. One that pays tax and is law abiding, and the 'black economy' that seeks to avoid tax and is typically illegal either in trade or in tax evasion.

THE 'UPSIDE' OF THE INTERNET

Note that the figures included in the diagrams below are only up to 2002. This is because this is that last year that there are complete figures available. If full details were used with differing end dates then it would not be possible to compare 'like with like'

A Short History of the Internet

By the year 2010, it is estimated that 80% of the planet will be connected to the Internet [Slater 2002]. Email is expected to grow to the point where more than 75% of business to business correspondence will take place by email.

A brief history of the development of the Internet is shown below:

- 1969. A group of DoD researchers linked four computers at UCLA, SRI, University of Utah and the UCSB. They created a network to communicate with one another about government projects. The network was part of the DoD's Advanced Research Project Agency, and was dubbed ARPAnet;
- 1972. More than 50 universities and military agencies were linked together on the network. For a short period of time it was a top secret defence project, ensuring that computers could talk to each other in the event of a nuclear attack. The communication system between the sites was called email and was invented by Ray Tomlinson of Bolt, Berank and Newman;
- 1973. The links were extended to Norway and England;
- 1974. Transmission Control Protocol (TCP) was published and the military and educational links diverged. Organisations like NASA began to experiment with computer networks, and the networks began to interconnect and the name Internet was coined;

- 1976. The Queen sends an email from RSRE Malvern.
- 1983. TCP/IP become the protocol standard for ARPAnet. Scott Fahlman invents the smiley to convey emotions in email;
- 1984. In the US, the NSF built high speed, long distance lines that connected supercomputer sites across the USA. These eventually replaced the original ARPAnet. In time, NSFnet was joined by other networks at dozens of universities, research laboratories and high-tech companies. The system for assigning names to computers on the network was introduced–DNS. JANet was launched to connect British Universities;
- 1986. The NSF established its own faster network NSFnet and Network News Transfer Protocol (NNTP) was introduced making on-line interactive discussion a reality. Backbone speed was 56 Kbps;
- 1987. 1000th RFC and 10,000th host;
- 1988. Robert Tappan Morris releases the first Internet Worm and CERT was set up in response to this. Backbone speed upgraded to 1.544Mbps. IRC developed;
- 1989. 100,000th host. Cuckoo's Egg released by Cliff Stoll telling true story of East German cracker accessing US installations;
- 1990. ARPAnet ceased to exist and the Internet effectively took its role;
- 1991. Gopher, a software program for retrieving information from servers on the Internet was made available by the University o f Minnesota. The US Government announced that it no longer intended to restrict activity on the Internet to research. This policy shift was sufficient for 12 companies to co-operate and produce CIX. Phil Zimmerman released PGP. Backbone speed upgraded to 44.736 Mbps;
- 1992. The World Wide Web became a possibility after CERN, in Switzerland, released hypertext. 1,000,000th Host. The author gets his first dialup email account with Demon Internet (November 1992);

- 1993. Mosaic, a software program to browse Web sites written by Marc Andreesen, was released followed by Netscape;
- 1994. Shopping Malls arrive on the Internet. The UK Treasury goes on line and the first cyberbank opens. The first banner adverts appeared for Zima (a drink) and AT&T;
- 1995. Traditional dialup services (AOL, CompuServe etc) start to provide dialup services. The Vatican goes on line. A number of Internet companies go public. Netscape leads the field with the largest ever IPO on NASDAQ. DEC launches AltaVista, which claims to index every HTML page there is. Jeff Bezos launches Amazon.com. eBay is launched;
- 1996. 9,272 organizations find themselves unlisted after the InterNIC drops their name service as a result of not having paid their domain name fee. Various ISPs suffer extended service outages, bringing into question whether they will be able to handle the growing number of users. AOL (19 hours), Netcom (13 hours), AT&T WorldNet (28 hours–email only). China requires users of the Internet to register with the Police. Saudi Arabia restricts use to Universities and Hospitals. Domain name *tv.com* sold to CNET for US$15,000. Backbone speed upgraded to 622 Mbps;
- 1997. 2000th RFC. 16 Million hosts. 1,000,000th Domain name registered (March 6th for Bonny View Cottage Furniture Company);
- 1998. 3,000,000th Domain name registered. US Postal authorities allow purchase of postage stamps on line for downloading and printing. Gigabit Ethernet standard ratified. Google is launched;
- 1999. First full service bank opens on the Internet (First Internet Bank of Indiana). First forged web page, looking like Bloomberg, raises the shares of a small company by 31% (7th April). Melissa strikes. 5,000,000th Domain name registered. First Cyberwar starts between Serbia and Kosovo. Shawn Fanning Launches Napster–record labels are furious;

- 2000. 10,000,000th Domain name registered. French Courts require that 'hate' memorabilia for sale on Yahoo's auction site must be removed. Gnutella is launched. ICANN selects new top level domains. Backbone is upgraded to IPv6;
- 2001. Forwarding email becomes illegal in Australia (Digital Agenda Act). Napster forced to suspend service after legal action. Taliban bans the Internet in Afghanistan. Nimda released on the Internet;
- 2002. Distributed denial of Service attack hits 13 DNS root servers, causing national security concerns;
- 2003. The first official Swiss online election takes place in Anières (7 Jan), SQL Slammer (goes round the world in 10 minutes and takes out 3 of the 13 DNS Servers). Followed by SoBig.F (19 Aug) and Blaster (11 Aug);
- 2004. Lycos Europe releases a screen saver to help fight spam by keeping spam servers busy with requests (1 Dec). The service is discontinued within a few days after backbone providers block access to the download site and the service causes some servers to crash.

Internet Usage Growth

From a commercial standpoint it was the invention of the World Wide Web in 1992 by Tim Berners-Lee, a clever interface using words, pictures and sound (WWW or the Web), that made the Internet accessible and interesting. This, coupled with faster connectivity and security programs, opened new business and marketing possibilities. A further boost came as home users flocked to join, and coupled with the rate of use by the young and affluent, whole new markets were opened up. It should be noted that many of the figures given below are estimates and that different sources may have different figures, but they are all expected to be of the same order of magnitude.

Cost of Connection

The initial cost of the Internet connectivity to the individual user was made up of three components:

- Hardware (i.e. a modem) and software to run it;

- Phone call cost (where appropriate);
- Service provider cost.

In the early days of the Web, access in the UK was limited to 9,600 baud modems, which were very slow and page refreshing was a long and tedious process.

BT charged for calls at different rates during the day, there was a cheap rate after 18:00 and on weekends, a not so cheap rate after 13:00 until 18:00 and an expensive rate from 08:30 to 13:00. Service providers charged more or less what they wanted to meet market rates. This made the cost and accessibility of the Internet, and the Web specifically, an expensive hobby in the UK. Long downloads (i.e. Large files) were fraught with problems as line noise and line drop were constant concerns. In America, local calls were free which stimulated rapid growth of Internet use. Various other countries had different charging structures and so there is no real way of determining the true cost of connectivity over the period with any degree of accuracy.

Connection Speed

During the period 1992–2002 there has been a dramatic increase of high speed lines giving access to the Internet. In 1992 the highest speed available was a dial-up 14.4 Kbps modem, today high end home use is ADSL which provides the fastest access for most home users at 1,544 Kbps. With the advent of fast Internet connections there has been a massive increase in take-up of ADSL where available. The major restricting factor to more take-up is the physical infrastructure needed to run the cabling over, but alternatives such as satellite download and landline upload are available in some places–but at a cost.

Usage Summary

There is a lack of available data for much of the early period of the Internet and there are differences between the different sources quoted–presumably on account of the methods used to quantify figures. Additionally, there are, in some cases, problems in finding up to date figures and forecasts. Given these shortfalls it is still possible to see that the growth in number of users, hosts, and web sites has grown in an almost exponential manner between

1995 and 2006. Predictions are that the US has a steadily growing number of Internet users between 1995 and 2006 and this looks set to continue until the market finally becomes saturated. With both of these figures there will come a levelling off, as the exponential growth in users is constrained by the world population and the growth in use in America is likewise constrained by the US population reaching saturation.

In 2001, 80% of all UK businesses had websites; this was up from 66% in 2000. At the same time the amount of UK SMEs on line was 1.9 million, up from 1.7 million the year before [DTI 2001].' At the same time as this level of growth of usage, the cost of connection has dropped as there are more users using the service. At the same time of lowered costs, there has been an increase in the speed of connection to the Internet from dial-up 9,600 Kbps modems in 1992 to xDSL and cable in the UK in 2002 and T1 and T2 line in other parts of the world. The level of users accessing the Internet by broadband in the OECD is showing increase, especially in Korea and America. Given these statistics, it is a reasonable assertion to make that there are increasing numbers of people in the world that can access the Internet in faster and cheaper access channels as time and maturity of the Internet increase.

THE 'DOWNSIDE' OF THE INTERNET

As digital technology has advanced over the past 50-odd years with a force unprecedented in history, governments, businesses and people around the world have been affected immeasurably. This has been exacerbated over the last ten years by the introduction of the Internet. It is axiomatic that the changes have included substantial benefits. However, such fundamental restructuring in society also results in certain disadvantages, on all levels. There are increased possibilities of vulnerabilities in the infrastructure that is being relied upon and the human nature of distrust of new technologies. Vulnerability increases with the perceived value of and reliance on this technology. This increases the opportunities for the industrious to be more productive but also allows the criminals new avenues for crime.

Infrastructural Issues

The original CERT was set up in 1988 as a direct response to the 'Morris' worm of that year. Since then, the CERT has issued a constant stream of advice and monitored infrastructure issues on the Internet. CERT publishes an annual report and these figures have been used as consistent indicators of infrastructural issues of the Internet. Many countries now have their own CERTs, but CERT's figures have been used as they are the most complete.

There are a number of CERTs in the UK, each specialising in their own specific areas (e.g. UNIRAS for Government, Government contractors and CNI and JANet for Academia). UNIRAS was set up in 1992 and was a classified Government service until 2000 at which time it expanded its user base to include strategic Government partners and produced its first annual report in 2001.

Security Vulnerabilities

Security vulnerabilities have been measured by referring to the vulnerabilities reported to CERT for the years 1995 to 2006. Some of these are not specifically vulnerabilities for Internet infrastructure devices but are on the end users desktop or server (e.g. IIS vulnerabilities on customer servers). These vulnerabilities, however, contribute to the ability for financial crime to be carried out.

Incidents

An incident, as defined by CERT, may cover more than one site–in fact they could cover hundreds, thousands or even tens of thousands of sites. An incident may also be an ongoing case for a considerable time. Given this, the incidents reported may be considered as under-reporting the true extent of the problem. A vulnerability within a system may lead to a person (malicious or not) exploiting this and this could lead to an incident.

Many of the weaknesses identified could be linked to a later incident. The most famous of these is arguable the 'Morris' worm of 1988 that exploited a weakness in *sendmail* and other programs. Whilst this was a well known and publicised event, there were a number of installations that still had the relevant version *sendmail* in place for a considerable time after the 'worm' was released with all associated press coverage.

It is therefore reasonable to conclude that a number of the CERT incidents, if not the majority, are malicious.

Malicious Acts by Humans

At the same time as these increases in Internet use and users are seen, then the opportunity for any potential financial (or other) crime that can be perpetrated using the Internet as a medium will also be increasing so long as there is a motive. As with almost all crime there is the need for:

- Motive;
- Means;
- Opportunity.

The Internet can provide the latter two so long as the motive exists.

For the sake of simplicity and specifically for the purpose of this dissertation, there are two different categories of case examined here:

- *Direct Losses*
- *Indirect Losses.*

Direct Losses

Computer crimes are increasingly in the news. When Willie Sutton was asked why he robbed banks, he famously replied, "Because that's where the money is." Today, criminals have learned where the money is. Instead of settling for a few thousand dollars in a bank robbery, those with enough expertise can walk away from a computer crime with many millions.

Discussion with the Law Enforcement Agencies in the UK indicates that there are no overall statistics for Internet crime collated and published by any one organisation. There are a number of organisations in the UK that monitor specific trends of Internet use but they are all limited by:

- Being trusted by the respondents;
- Scope of survey;

- Size of population and sample;
- Skewing by the reporting organisations for a variety of reasons.
- Truthfulness of the respondents.

It is for this reason that specific results recorded in the US and generic reports from the US and UK are used for quantification purposes.

Internet Fraud Watch

One of the many threats facing consumers today is fraud. Criminals attempt to raid the pockets of consumers over the phone, through the mail, in person or over the Internet. To fight this growing threat, the National Consumers League (NCL) founded the NFIC in 1992. NFIC was designed to fight telemarketing fraud through prevention and by improving the enforcement capabilities of federal and state agencies.

In March 1996, the NCL launched the Internet Fraud Watch (IFW). IFW produces statistics of Internet fraud reported in the US but which may be perpetrated in other parts of the world.

These reports refer to reported domestic complaints only and so those not reported or outside the US are not included, but they do include cases reported where the victim was in the US even if the perpetrator was outside the US.

Reported Complaints to the IFCC

The Internet Fraud Complaint Centre (IFCC) was set up as a joint effort between the Federal Bureau of Investigation (FBI) and the National White Collar Crime Centre (NW3C). This has now become the Internet Crime Complaint Centre (IC3) IFCC's mission is to address fraud carried out over the Internet.

IFCC defines Internet fraud as any fraudulent scheme in which one or more components of the Internet, such as Web sites, chat rooms, and Email, play a significant role in offering nonexistent goods or services to consumers, communicating false or fraudulent representations about the schemes to consumers, or transmitting victims' funds, access devices, or other items of value to the control of the scheme's perpetrators. The frauds range from simple geometric progression schemes to complex frauds. The Internet appears to be a perfect manner to locate victims and provides an environment where the victims don't see or speak to the fraudsters.

Other Crime Statistics

There are a number of sources of Internet crime statistics and just two have been shown below with their sources. These both show 'direct' as well as 'indirect' losses.

WebSense: [2002 WebSense]:

- U.S. businesses spent $2.6 billion to clean up the Code Red virus alone [Source: Computerworld];
- In a study commissioned by the FBI, 78% of surveyed companies reported that employees had abused Internet privileges, such as downloading pornography or pirated software [Source: Computerworld];
- A report by the National Research Council estimates that there are between 2 million and 8 million subscribers to pornography Web sites, and that they paid between $40 and $100 for a year, for a total of approximately $800 million in 2002 [Source: CBS MarketWatch];
- A survey conducted on behalf of start-up Open Orchard, funded by British Telecom, found that Internet misuse is costing Britain's small businesses almost £1.5 billion per year [Source: BBC News];
- Jupiter Media Metrix estimates that online pornography revenues in the US will grow from $230 million in 2001 to $400 million by 2006 [Source: eMarketer];
- By 2006, Jupiter Media Metrix predicts that revenues from online music, games and audio-visual entertainment will far outweigh revenue from online porn [Source: eMarketer];
- The research group Datamonitor forecasts that the online gaming market will grow from $670 million in 2002 to $2.9 billion in 2005. While the largest market for online gaming is currently South Korea, the United States will bring in the most online gaming revenue by 2005 [Source: NUA Internet Surveys];

- A research report published by the Informa Media Group estimates that worldwide revenue from e-gambling will climb to $14.5 billion by 2006 [Source: eMarketer];
- Online shopping is dominated by Amazon.com and eBay both at home and at the office. Only 5.7 million workers visit eBay, compared with 21.5 million for the most-visited site, Yahoo. But eBay visitors stay at the auction site the longest, almost three hours [Source: Nielsen/Net Ratings].

Cerbian [2002 Cerbian]

- 82% of U.S. business executives surveyed by the consulting firm Dataquest (a division of the Gartner Group) believe Internet use should be monitored at their companies [Source: InformationWeek Online];
- 56.5% of employees feel that surfing the Net or sending non-work-related Emails decreases productivity, and 31% of employers said that they restrict employee Internet/ Email usage [Source: Vault.com survey];
- In 2001, 60.7% of employees surveyed said they visit Web sites or surf for personal use at work (up from 50.7% in 2000) [Source: UCLA study on Internet/Email use];
- 70% of all Internet porn traffic occurs during the nine-to-five workday [Source: SexTracker];
- 32% of those who have Internet access at work used the Internet while on the job to buy holiday gifts, while only 24% of Internet users as a whole purchased gifts online. This suggests that people are taking advantage of fast connections at work [Source: Pew Internet & American Life Project];
- In a survey of Internet sites, the majority reported that traffic to their site is heaviest during work hours. 14% reported that traffic was highest from 7am to 10am, 24% stated it was highest from 10 am to 2pm, 24% from 2pm to 5 pm, 20% from 5pm to 8pm, and 18% from 8pm to 7am [Source: Jupiter Communications];
- Finance sites reached over 30 percent more work users who spent nearly double the amount of time — an average

of 33 minutes per month — online than home users [Source: NielsenNetRatings, as reported by Reuters];

- Thirty-two percent of those who bought holiday gifts online in 2001 did at least some of their holiday shopping from work, up from 26% in 2000 [Source: Pew Internet & American Life];
- Popular sites that are not always work-related attract many visitors during the work hours. Expedia.com gets 47% of its traffic during the workday, while Travelocity, MSNBC, iWon, and Weather.com reported receiving 46%, 42%, 42%, and 41% of their total visits during working hours [Source: Jupiter Communications];
- 31.2% of employees feel it is appropriate to surf non-work-related sites up to 30 minutes a day, 14.8% said up to one hour is appropriate, and 9% said over an hour, while only 26.6% of employers feel it is appropriate for employees to surf non-work-related sites up to 30 minutes, 8.6% said up to one hour, and 4.2% said over an hour [Source: Vault.com survey];
- Web users at the office take advantage of high-speed connections to access broadband entertainment sites such as Broadcast.com and MP3 more frequently than at home [Source: NielsenNet Ratings];
- In a recent study conducted by Net Value, 27.5% of the younger population in the U.S. (age 17 and under) had visited an adult web site [Source: Net Value];
- 53% of teens have encountered offensive Web sites that include pornography, hate or violence. Of these, 91% unintentionally found the offensive sites while searching the Web. [Source: The Safe America Foundation]
- 37.1% of employees said they surf the Web constantly at work, 31.9% said a few times a day, 21.3% said a few times a week, and only 9.7% said never [Source: Vault.com survey];
- Shopping sites reached 18% more Internet users within the workplace than at home [Source: NielsenNet Ratings];

- During work hours 9% of employees earning under $35K surf the Net for a new job, while 11% of workers earning $75K to $100K do the same [Source: Greenfield Online];
- 28.83% said that their employer had caught them surfing non-work-related sites, although 54% of employers said that they have caught an employee surfing non-work-related sites at work [Source: Vault.com survey];
- Americans are spending more time surfing at work and less time surfing at home. In a typical day in 2001, 54% of adults went online only from home, down from 59% in 2000. But the percentage that goes online only from work increased in the same time period from 18% to 21% [Source: Pew Internet & American Life];
- A research report published by the Informa Media Group estimates that worldwide revenue from E-gambling will climb to $14.5 billion by 2006 [Source: eMarketer];
- Secret monitoring by the U.S. Treasury Department of Internet use among Internal Revenue Service employees found that activities such as personal Email, online chats, shopping and checking personal finances and stocks accounted for 51 percent of employees' time spent online. The top non-work Web activity favoured by IRS employees was going to financial sites. Chat and Email ran a close second, followed by miscellaneous activities (which included visiting adult sites), search requests, and looking at or downloading streaming media [Source: Chicago Tribune and Business 2.0];
- Napster music swapping software was found on about 20% of over 15,000 work PCs examined [Source: eMarketer.com];
- One in five men and one in eight women admitted using their work computers as their primary lifeline to access sexual explicit material online [Source: MSNBC];
- According to a recent report from comScore Networks, people shopping online from work spent more money in 2001 than those who bought online from home or from college. At-work buyers spent an average of $229 per month

in 2001 whereas at-home buyers spent $165 and college buyers spent $146 [Source: comScore Networks];

- An American Management Association survey this year found that 38 percent of the major U.S. companies polled check their employees' Email and 54 percent monitor Internet connections [Source: AMA];
- 28% of those who made gift purchases did so from their offices or cubicles [Source: Pew Internet & American Life Project];
- The No. 1 search term used at search engine sites is the word 'sex', according to Alexa Research. Users searched for 'sex' more than other terms such as 'games', 'travel', 'music', 'jokes', 'cars', 'weather', 'health' and 'jobs' combined. The study also found that 'pornography/porno' was the fourth-most searched for subject;
- Users of online auctioneer eBay Inc. at work spent 157 minutes at the site in January compared with 126 minutes while at home. Long a favourite among at-work surfers, eBay ranked 7th among the most-visited sites for at-work surfers. However, eBay ranks first in terms of average pages per person and time spent per month, at almost 300 pages and two hours per person. [Source: NielsenNetRatings, as reported by Reuters and Business 2.0];
- According to a survey of 2,100 firms by the American Management Association, 17 percent have fired employees for misusing the Internet. 26 percent have given workers formal reprimands and 20 percent have issued informal warnings [Source: AMA];
- The top 3 word searches on the Internet: 1) sex; 2) mp3; 3) hotmail [Source: Wordtracker.com].

Indirect Losses

Indirect losses are outside the scope of this peper. If they were included they would cover such costs as:

- Cost of investigation;
- Cost of lost sales;

- Cost of recovery (hardware, software and personnel);
- Cost of reputational damage (corporate an personal);
- Impact on personnel and morale (inside and outside work).

Summary of Growth in Internet Problems

There are always sensationalistic reports in the press of increasing problems with Internet crimes being on the increase, typical headlines read:

- 'Internet Crime Statistics up Again' [PC Direct][i];
- 'Financial Losses Due to Internet Intrusions, Trade Secret Theft, and Other Cyber Crimes Soar' [CSI];
- 'High Tech Crime is increasing Significantly' [NHTCU];
- 'Hackers turn UK into Cyber-Crime Central' [KPMG].

Other countries are also seeing a substantial increase in various categories of Internet fraud. In December 2000, the ICC's Commercial Crime Services (CCS) Division reported that Internet fraud in 2000 was 'rising dramatically', accounting for more than two-thirds (2,776) of the 4,139 cases that its business partners referred. This was stated to represent a 100% increase on the figures reported in 1999. Noteworthy attacks over recent years include such cases as the MCI Communications switch and credit card penetration resulted in a $50 million loss and the Russian Organized Crime Electronic Funds Transfer (EFT) attack on Citibank resulted in a $12 million loss in Aug 1994 [Cigital Labs 2002].

The fundamental problem in assessing and quantifying the cost of financial crime on the Internet revolves around disclosure. Currently the US leads the way in this area and the UK has no such mature process. Many UK organisations and Government are talking about addressing this issue but these talks have not produced a working process or system that can record and report crime statistics for the Internet. A meaningful overall estimate for losses due to financial crime on the Internet is almost impossible to establish, but in October 2000 the German Foreign Minister Joschka Fisher reported that G8 losses due to computer crime stood at $Bn 42.9 a year [IAAC 2001]. This did not identify specifically losses due to financial crime on the Internet.

In the UK in 2002 the NHTCU surveyed 105 organisations who reported 3000 incidents for the year [NHTCU 2002-1]. Of the 105, only 3 believed that their companies had not experienced any computer related crimes in the previous 12 months. It is noted that NHTCU has been subsumed into SOCA and has lost its original role.

PRIVACY THROUGH INTERNET

An electronic communications network that connects computer networks and organizational computer facilities around the world, the Internet has led to significant changes within our society. An infinite amount of information can be easily obtained and through the development of technology, has become more accessible. The introduction of the Internet into our daily activities has transitioned our society into a technology dependent era. The Internet has become an increasingly popular source for gathering information and a frequent form of communication. Privacy focuses on the control over information about oneself, and is argued vital for human dignity and intimacy. The Internet increased the availability of personal information that can be tracked, recorded, and accessed. The personal invasion of privacy due to Internet monitoring has become more of an ethical concern and looking at aspects from the business world we can better determine how the evolution of the Internet has shaped our lives.

Thesis : Issue of Privacy

The issue of privacy and ones right to privacy while at work or on the Internet has become increasingly an important issue companys deal with everyday. Companies have to spend time and money to write policies to cover these issues to protect themselves as well as the well being of their employees. They need to monitor their employees to ensure productivity and to make sure they are not doing anything illegal at work that could hurt the company. How far these companies can go to protect these things is what makes such an interesting issue. A person has a right to privacy and what they do on their break or outside of the office should be their business, but more and more companies are tapping into this to monitor them. A company can only go as far as to monitor them while they are working or doing work related activities anything outside of this realm in their private lives and e-mails should not be exploited.

Utilitarianism

Ethics has become a major concern within our society, especially within the business world. It is important to conduct business in an appropriate manner, monitoring productivity, and profit, while maintaining employee satisfaction. There are two fundamental ideas that underlie utilitarianism; first, that the results of our actions are the key to their moral evaluation, and second, that the one should assess and compare those results in terms of the happiness or unhappiness they cause "or, more broadly, in terms of their impact on peoples wellbeing." It is important to install morals into all aspects of business, including competitors, customers and employees. It is important to keep a sense of well being in order to provide a trustworthy service. Utilitarianisms guiding impulse is simple and transparent, and many people have found it attractive: human well-being or happiness is what really matters and, accordingly the promotion of well being is what morality is, or ought to be, all about." From a utilitarian perspective employees should be provided with a well being that satisfies each ones personal goals.

The Right of Privacy

The right of privacy has become a controversial issue. While there is no fundamental law or amendment that states ones right to privacy; however it has been implied by the Supreme Court in the United States Amendments and is considered ethically correct in our society. There is no specific law that governs ones right to privacy and this has resulted in a fine line between what is deemed acceptable and what information can be revealed to the public. This has resulted in various court cases in which citizens have tried to determine their own right to privacy. There have been numerous cases over the past century where the Supreme Court has had to determine whether a citizens privacy rights have been violated. This dates back to May 25, 1891 in the Union Pacific Railway Co. v. Botsfold, where it was decided that the plaintiff did not have to submit to physical examination as „no right is held more sacred, or is more carefully guarded, by the common law, than the right of every individual to the possession and control of his own person, free from all restraint or interference of others".

The Evolution of the Internet in the Workplace

The evolution of the Internet has shaped the way that companies conduct business. This has led to a dramatic change within the workplace and the responsibilities of employees. It is an employers responsibility to monitor employees and assess the quality and quantity of work that is being achieved. In the past, employers have done this by monitoring punch cards, productivity reports, profits and consumer satisfaction. The increase in technology and development of computers and the Internet has changed the security and supervision of daily business activities. Companies have a variety of reasons to maintain surveillance within the workplace. There are concerns for employees well being, competitors obstruction, and the productivity and profits of the business. These concerns are all relevant; however, the use of technology has made it easier for employers to snoop on their employees.

Employers have the ability to intercept electronic communication and access the information that has been stored on the companys computers. The easy access that employers have to this information raises the question of whether employers can ethically monitor employees. It has become Employees are expected to conduct business productively and to complete their job under the expectations that they were hired for. The Internet has made it easier for employees to be distracted from their tasks. Personal e-mailing and browsing the Internet has become a major concern within corporations, leading to the increase in electronic monitoring.

Right of Employers to Keep Work Place Efficient

Employers use electronic monitoring for two basic functions: providing feedback and implementing control. Providing feedback is an essential aspect in conducting business. Employees are monitored in order to provide performance-related feedback and suggestions for improvement, such as with recording a receptionists typing speed or accuracy of data entry clerks. This form of monitoring is understandable and an efficient way to conduct business. The type of monitoring that implements control is more harming to the business environment and calls into question the ethics of the company. The competitiveness of industries in todays business society has led to an increase in security and the need to monitor efficiency within the workplace. This has increased the level of acceptance of employee monitoring, especially through electronic measures. The increase of use of the Internet and its ease, has led to a dependency of many businesses using this form of a communication for all their business transactions. The security that each business requires, also involves the monitoring of their employees online activity in order to ensure there are no security breaches. This form of monitoring is vital in order to maintain the success of the business; however there is a fine line between monitoring electronic activity for the security of the business and monitoring to spy on employees.

Right of Employees Privacy

It is customary for every business to install a code of ethics, setting the standards for employee behaviour, standard of practice and it can also be used as a benchmark of evaluation. "The need for special ethical principles in a scientific society is the same as the need for ethical principles in society as a whole. They are mutually beneficial. They help make our relationships mutually pleasant and productive. A professional society is a voluntary, cooperative organization, and those who must conform to its rules are also those who benefit from the conformity of others. Each has a stake in maintaining general compliance.

" It is important for both employers and employees to follow these ethical guidelines. Employers create codes in order to provide standards to which employees should obey; however employers also have to maintain an ethical stance, ensuring the well being and utilitarian rights of their employees. Employees are often unaware of the control that their supervisors have and the intrusion that this can have on their personal life. In the historic case Smyth vs. The Pillsbury Company, Smyth sent inappropriate e-mails from his home computer to the Pillsbury system. At a later date the company intercepted these e-mail messages and terminated Smyths employment based upon their content. There had been a prior promise of confidentiality within the company; however, this did not protect Smyths rights to privacy.

Employees should be able to work in a trusting environment where they are respected. The Fourth Amendment states the public has the constitutional right to privacy. This is a fundamental right that is upheld within the United States; however, the increase in technology and the ability to observe others has weakened this imperative right. "The computers eye is unblinking and ever present. Sophisticated software allows every minute of every day to be recorded and evaluated". The introduction of the Internet to the workplace has made it easier for employers to observe what employees are doing at every moment. It is an employees utilitarian ethical right to receive privacy and to be treated in a manner that will result in happiness for the entire staff. They have the ethical right to dutiful respect and the right of common good, which contributes most to the achievement of quality of life. It is under these ethics that employees should be made aware of the surveillance within their workplace and the duties that are expected of them.

Right of Employers to Keep the Workplace Safe

The Internet has led to an increase in pornography, racist jokes, and inappropriate forms of electronic communication. The government has condoned the use of electronic monitoring to ensure the safety of employees and uphold civil rights. Under Title VII of the Civil Rights Act, an employers inefficient monitoring of the Internet and e-mail use and abuse may allow racial offensive or sexually explicit material to pervade the work environment and create or contribute to a hostile environment. Employers are expected to monitor their employees activities online to ensure civil rights are not violated and that employees receive the fundamental rights they are entitled to. This has been an effective form of detection within the workplace. In Strauss vs. Microsoft Corporation, the court held that among other remarks several jokes and parodies of a sexual nature e-mailed by a supervisor to employees were administered and relevant evidence of sexual harassment. The government has approved online regulation however no standards have been introduced that respect the well being of the employees or considers the effects that these actions cause. The ethical values of employees have been discarded.

THE ALREADY BIG THING ON THE INTERNET: SPYING ON USERS

In 1993, the dawn of the Internet age, the liberating anonymity of the online world was captured in a well-known New Yorker cartoon. One dog, sitting at a computer, tells another: "On the Internet, nobody knows you're a dog." Fifteen years later, that anonymity is gone.

It's not paranoia: they really are spying on you. Technology companies have long used "cookies," little bits of tracking software slipped onto your computer, and other means, to record the Web sites you visit, the ads you click on, even the words you enter in search engines — information that some hold onto forever. They're not telling you they're doing it, and they're not asking permission. Internet service providers are now getting into the act. Because they control your connection, they can keep track of everything you do online, and there have been reports that I.S.P.'s may have started to sell the information they collect.

The driving force behind this prying is commerce. The big growth area in online advertising right now is "behavioural targeting." Web sites can charge a premium if they are able to tell the maker of an expensive sports car that its ads will appear on Web pages clicked on by upper-income, middle-aged men.

The information, however, gets a lot more specific than age and gender — and more sensitive. Tech companies can keep track of when a particular Internet user looks up Alcoholics Anonymous meetings, visits adult Web sites, buys cancer drugs online or participates in anti-government discussion groups.

Serving up ads based on behavioural targeting can itself be an invasion of privacy, especially when the information used is personal.

The bigger issue is the digital dossiers that tech companies can compile. Some companies have promised to keep data confidential, or to obscure it so it cannot be traced back to individuals. But it's hard to know what a particular company's policy is, and there are too many to keep track of. And privacy policies can be changed at any time.

There is also no guarantee that the information will stay with the company that collected it. It can be sold to employers or insurance companies, which have financial motives for wanting to know if their workers and policyholders are alcoholics or have AIDS.

It could also end up with the government, which needs only to serve a subpoena to get it (and these days that formality might be ignored).

If George Orwell had lived in the Internet age, he could have painted a grim picture of how Web monitoring could be used to promote authoritarianism. There is no need for neighbourhood informants and paper dossiers if the government can see citizens' every Web site visit, e-mail and text message.

The public has been slow to express outrage — not, as tech companies like to claim, because they don't care about privacy, but simply because few people know all that is going on. That is changing. "A lot of people are creeped-out by this," says Ari Schwartz, a vice president of the Centre for Democracy and Technology. He says the government is under increasing pressure to act.

The Federal Trade Commission has proposed self-regulatory guidelines for companies that do behavioural targeting. Anything that highlights the problem is good, but self-regulation is not enough. One idea starting to gain traction in Congress is a do-not-track list, similar to the federal do-not-call list, which would allow Internet users to opt out of being spied on. That would be a clear improvement over the status quo, but the operating principle should be "opt in" — companies should not be allowed to track Internet activities unless they get the user's expressed consent.

The founders wrote the Fourth Amendment — guaranteeing protection against illegal search and seizure — at a time when people were most concerned about protecting the privacy of their homes and bodies. The amendment, and more recent federal laws, have been extended to cover telephone communications. Now work has to be done to give Internet activities the same level of privacy protection.

NETWORK SECURITY

System and network technology is a key technology for a wide variety of applications. Security is crucial to networks and applications. Although, network security is a critical requirement in emerging networks, there is a significant lack of security methods that can be easily implemented. There exists a "communication gap" between the developers of security technology and developers of networks. Network design is a well-developed process that is based on the Open Systems Interface (OSI) model. The OSI model has several advantages when designing networks. It offers modularity, flexibility, ease-of-use, and standardization of protocols. The protocols of different layers can be easily combined to create stacks which allow modular development. The implementation of individual layers can be changed later without making other adjustments, allowing flexibility in development. In contrast to network design, secure network design is not a well-developed process. There isn't a methodology to manage the complexity of security requirements. Secure network design does not contain the same advantages as network design.

When considering network security, it must be emphasized that the whole network is secure. Network security does not only concern the security in the computers at each end of the communication chain. When transmitting data the communication channel should not be vulnerable to attack. A possible hacker could target the communication channel, obtain the data, decrypt it and re-insert a false message. Securing the network is just as important as securing the computers and encrypting the message.

When developing a secure network, the following need to be considered:

- Access–authorized users are provided the means to communicate to and from a particular network

- Confidentiality–Information in the network remains private
- Authentication–Ensure the users of the network are who they say they are
- Integrity–Ensure the message has not been modified in transit
- Non-repudiation–Ensure the user does not refute that he used the network

An effective network security plan is developed with the understanding of security issues, potential attackers, needed level of security, and factors that make a network vulnerable to attack. The steps involved in understanding the composition of a secure network, internet or otherwise, is followed throughout this research endeavour. To lessen the vulnerability of the computer to the network there are many products available. These tools are encryption, authentication mechanisms, intrusion-detection, security management and firewalls. Businesses throughout the world are using a combination of some of these tools. "Intranets" are both connected to the internet and reasonably protected from it. The internet architecture itself leads to vulnerabilities in the network. Understanding the security issues of the internet greatly assists in developing new security technologies and approaches for networks with internet access and internet security itself.

The types of attacks through the internet need to also be studied to be able to detect and guard against them. Intrusion detection systems are established based on the types of attacks most commonly used.

Network intrusions consist of packets that are introduced to cause problems for the following reasons:

- To consume resources uselessly
- To interfere with any system resource's intended function
- To gain system knowledge that can be exploited in later attacks.

The last reason for a network intrusion is most commonly guarded against and considered by most as the only intrusion motive. The other reasons mentioned need to be thwarted as well.

Typical security currently exists on the computers connected to the network. Security protocols sometimes usually appear as part of a single layer of the OSI network reference model. Current work is being performed in using a layered approach to secure network design. The layers of the security model correspond to the OSI model layers. This security approach leads to an effective and efficient design which circumvents some of the common security problems.

Differentiating Data Security and Network Security

Data security is the aspect of security that allows a client's data to be transformed into unintelligible data for transmission. Even if this unintelligible data is intercepted, a key is needed to decode the message. This method of security is effective to a certain degree. Strong cryptography in the past can be easily broken today. Cryptographic methods have to continue to advance due to the advancement of the hackers as well.

When transferring ciphertext over a network, it is helpful to have a secure network. This will allow for the ciphertext to be protected, so that it is less likely for many people to even attempt to break the code. A secure network will also prevent someone from inserting unauthorized messages into the network. Therefore, hard ciphers are needed as well as attack-hard networks.

The relationship of network security and data security to the OSI model. It can be seen that the cryptography occurs at the application layer; therefore the application writers are aware of its existence. The user can possibly choose different methods of data security.

Network security is mostly contained within the physical layer. Layers above the physical layer are also used to accomplish the network security required. Authentication is performed on a layer above the physical layer. Network security in the physical layer requires failure detection, attack detection mechanisms, and intelligent countermeasure strategies.

HISTORY OF NETWORK SECURITY

Recent interest in security was fuelled by the crime committed by Kevin Mitnick. Kevin Mitnick committed the largest computer-related crime in U.S. history. The losses were eighty million dollars in U.S. intellectual property and source code from a variety of companies. Since then, information security came into the spotlight. Public networks are being relied upon to deliver financial and personal information. Due to the evolution of information that is made available through the internet, information security is also required to evolve. Due to Kevin Mitnick's offence, companies are emphasizing security for the intellectual property. Internet has been a driving force for data security improvement.

Internet protocols in the past were not developed to secure themselves. Within the TCP/IP communication stack, security protocols are not implemented. This leaves the internet open to attacks. Modern developments in the internet architecture have made communication more secure.

THE FIGHT AGAINST CRIMINAL CYBER NETWORKS

Security firms have battled botnets for many years, but only in the last 18 months, with takedowns of rogue ISPs (especially McColo), has the security community been more aware of opportunities to disrupt botnets, and grown more confident that this online menace can be successfully fought.

Botnets are distributed networks of 'zombie' or 'bot' PCs, infected by malware which enables them to be marshalled by cyber criminals primarily to distribute enormous volumes of spam and other malware and launch phishing attacks via e-mail.

Botnets have been around for years. Back in 2003–ancient history in internet terms–security firms often saw thousands of PCs infected with the Sobig mass-mailing virus, and later in that same year, when the Fizzer malware logged thousands of computers into internet relay chat (IRC) rooms.

At that time this was perceived only as a problem for IRC admins. In fact, the infected PCs were being connected to chat rooms by their human bot-masters, waiting to receive command and control (C&C) instructions. It was only when MessageLabs Intelligence correlated the malware and spam traffic from each spam sending IP address, that the bigger picture was later revealed.

Over the years security firms kept botnets under observation, doing their best to inhibit their ever-increasing output of spam, but not knowing how to tackle their C&C infrastructure. Then in October 2008, the security community stepped up efforts to disrupt the botnets and start to pursue the ISPs that hosted them.

The first high profile ISP to go at the end of September 2008 was Intercage (aka Atrivo), linked to the infamous Russian Business Network. However, the most widely publicised was McColo, a San Jose-based ISP, which was found to deal almost exclusively with cyber gangs. McColo, set up by a 19 year-old Russian, was host to a botnet called Srizbi controlling 1.3 million IP addresses, as well as the Mega-D, Rustock, Asprox, Bobax and Gheg botnets.

In November 2008, community action resulted in McColo's peering ISPs disconnecting it from the internet, largely because of an article written by Brian Krebs in the Washington Post [blog.washingtonpost.com/securityfix]. Taking down McColo came as a shock to the botnet gangs and spam levels dropped instantly by as much as 80 per cent, which represented an enormous victory against the spammers.

Srizbi was crippled, never to return and the other botnets were badly disrupted. Over the following two months, spam gradually recovered to previous levels, as the surviving botnets relocated their command and control channels, the criminals spawned several new botnets as well.

The operations behind many of these botnets were forced to re-evaluate how they functioned and sought to put more protection in place to prevent a repeat of the huge disruption caused by the take-down of a single ISP. Take-downs like McColo must cost bot herders and spammers hundreds of thousands of dollars-perhaps millions-in lost revenues.

When Srizbi disappeared, activity from the surviving botnets increased dramatically, seeking to fill the huge gap in the market left behind. At that time, Srizbi had been responsible for as much as 50 percent of all spam. After losing their botnet of choice, spammers rented capacity from other botnet operators in order to keep up their spam campaigns.

However, when the next major take-down of a dubious ISP took place, it was clear that the cyber criminals had already learned from the strike against McColo.

This time the security community's target was another California-based ISP called 3FN (aka APS Telecom and Pricewert) which was hosting command and control channels for Cutwail (aka Pandex), one of the oldest botnets which had been spewing out malware since January 2007. By June 2009 Cutwail had swollen to more than 1.5 million active IP addresses in an aggressive recruitment drive.

3FN was put under a preliminary injunction by the FTC on Friday 5 June 2009 and Cutwail went with it. But within a couple of days, by Monday morning, Cutwail was back online and as strong as before.

Botnet gangs had made many refinements to their creations in the six months since the McColo take-down. Thus the organisations behind Cutwail were able to quickly reorganise after losing an important part of their botnet infrastructure. The fact that the technology was now much more flexible and robust allowed them to review the status of the botnet and return to business as usual in just a few days. It was clear that botnets now had a business continuity or disaster recovery plan of their own.

The botnet C&C mechanisms had shifted away from IRC towards HTTP. Instead of receiving instructions from one place, algorithms were built into the bots so they would look for random-looking domain names, which are purchased by the botnet gang each day, and from which the bots receive their commands. This ensures that the botnets aren't so reliant on one ISP.

But as the botnet controllers evolved their tactics, so did the security firms. One botnet in particular had grown significantly in the wake of the McColo take-down; a botnet called Mega-D (aka Ozdok). By November 2009, the algorithms behind the C&C mechanism used to issue the botnet with new instructions were broken by FireEye, a security company that specializes in combating botnets. It was now possible to predict which domain names were to be used by the botnet and to register them in advance of the botnet controllers. It was almost like cracking the Enigma code;

and for the first time it was possible to know the botnet's next move and to register these domains faster than the botnet controllers.

Mega-D appeared to be crippled, its spam-sending days seemed to be over, until a few days later, MessageLabs Intelligence identified large volumes of Mega-D spam being distributed from IP addresses that had not been used to send spam previously. This suggested that the botnet controllers had enacted their business continuity plan, seemingly with inactive sleeper bots or perhaps even a whole parallel backup botnet.

Disaster Recovery isn't the only tenet that botnet controllers have borrowed from the world of corporate IT; they also use a technique called "fast-flux" hosting, which dynamically distributes resources across a number of continually changing IP addresses using a form of "round-robin" DNS. In the hands of a botnet controller, fast-flux can hide the true location of websites used to host malware, spam and phishing content, by hiding them behind the IP addresses of compromised, botnet-controlled computers, each acting as a web server or proxy.

Another technique that botnet controllers use to hide their botnets from the prying eyes of security firms is to expose only a small proportion of their zombies at any one time, cycling their use over a period of several days and limiting the amount of spam sent from each to minimise the risk of them appearing in backlists of known spam-sending IP addresses.

Until recently, botnet controllers had to recruit one PC at a time. But with the advent of "generic droppers" like Bredolab, and perhaps Conficker, larger botnets can be assembled to order, whether for a spam campaign or something even more sinister.

Cyber criminals can now purchase the control of thousands– even tens of thousands-of ready-compromised PCs, recruited en masse to their own botnet. For example, cyber criminals may pay for malware, spyware or botnet Trojans to be installed by the Bredolab operators who would then instruct the Bredolab botnet to "drop" the malware onto however many computers were needed, using computers that were already under their control. This takes botnet recruitment from a random, scattergun approach where PCs are infected at random, to a more commoditized recruitment campaign. The only limitation to the size of the botnet is how much the criminals are prepared to spend.

Now cyber criminals with enough cash can set up a botnet operation and be in business virtually overnight.

As botnets grow in sophistication and number, there is a danger of them becoming an extension of the hidden world of international and industrial espionage. The authorities in many countries are now concerned that attacks on government and business resources will become the next battleground in cyber warfare. The botnet could become the weapon of choice to disrupt infrastructure, and a lot less expensive-or traceable-than a ballistic missile.

The Resources Exist for States to be Attacked from the Inside

More concerning perhaps is that such an attack could come from within a country's own borders and as such would be difficult to prevent. In an average week in the UK the UK Messagelabs Intelligence tracks at least 16,000 active spam sending bots. The actual number of active bots in the UK is likely to be much larger than this. One way to look at this is as a potentially massive sleeper cell. It would take hundreds rather than thousands of zombie PCs to launch a successful DDoS attack against a typical web server; however, cyber criminals often prefer to spread the workload across sever thousand computers to better avoid detection.

The zombie PCs that make up botnets are recruited largely from inadequately protected domestic PCs, but there are also numerous compromised business networks too. Conventional firewalls that don't inspect HTTP streams –the preferred C&C mechanism for many contemporary botnets-are not sufficient protection, nor is conventional antivirus software on its own.

Businesses should minimise the risk of becoming part of a botnet by ensuring that they are protected by filtering internet traffic for spam and other malicious or harmful content before it reaches their corporate network. Many ISPs provide such value-add services now, as more pressure is brought to bear on the industry to tackle this problem as close to the source as possible.

Service Level Agreements (SLAs) are also critical here, for example, during a major spam run, how many false positives does the SLA allow for before too much genuine mail is be quarantined along with all of the spam?

All eyes are now on the cloud, whether private or public, to fight the spammers. Traditional desktop appliances are no longer flexible or strong enough to keep defences running around the clock, 365 days of the year, which is what is now required from businesses and individuals. Botnets are essentially 'private clouds' working together, distributing the infected software to PCs. Botnet operators are like SaaS providers, with all the will in the world it will be almost impossible to fully eradicate the problem using technology alone. The most effective way to alleviate the botnet burden is by turning the Internet against them using the fabric of the cloud as a catalyst to kill the botnets, making the internet a safer neighbourhood to stroll once again.

9

Challenge for Cyber Intelligence

There are many forms of threats which are the big challenges for the cyber intelligence deal with and try to make the internet technology secure by clearing or removing their effects. There are much type of cyber threats that take part on the challenging side of cyber intelligence such as cyber terrorism, identity theft, and different type of viruses or spywares that are used to steal the personal information of the users without its permission and many more. One of the big challenges for the cyber intelligence is that such crimes are not only or the personal computers but the hackers also destroy the governmental media and their important information. Cyber intelligence also finds the way to stop the hacking and stealing of the different secrets of the Government and also trying to prevent the leaking of some country secrets to terrorist.

WORKING OF CYBER INTELLIGENCE

Cyber intelligence has many works to do that are related to the security of the internet technology. There are different type of hackers are terrorist that are used to break the security of the technology but cyber intelligence play its vital role to save the technology and the personal information of the users as well. One of the major works that is part of the architecture of the cyber intelligence is to defend the digital media from hacklers and as well as provide high security to them. They also suggest different type of antivirus softwares to the users to save the data. First of all cyber intelligence analyse the threat and rescue the hacker then try to take some steps to retrieve the data that has been stolen earlier. Daily check up of the technology is there with the help of firewalls and different type of softwares. Analysing aspects of the cyber intelligence is completely based on the old methods of collecting the information about the hackers and threats and then suggest solution.

Another important and the final aspect of the cyber intelligence are to fight against the threats. For this purpose special training has been given to the people who are the member of the community of the cyber intelligence. They can track those hackers of all ages and the people also that can break the security with the different laws.

PERSPECTIVES OF CYBER INTELLIGENCE

Today cyber intelligence is working brilliantly in defending the internet technology and its architecture from the different types of criminal people and processes used by them to steal the personal information of the users and the government sector as well. But in the present era there are some problems related to such security problems remain there which have no solution but the cyber intelligence take the challenge and trying to find the solution in the future to provide the complete security to the customers.

SPYWARE IN COMPUTER SOFTWARE

Spyware, is a computer software programme or hardware device that enables an unauthorized person (such as an abuser) to secretly monitor and gather information about your computer use. There are many types of computer software programmes and hardware devices that can be installed to monitor your computer activities. They can be installed on your computer without your knowledge, and the person installing them doesn't even need to have physical access to your computer. Whether computer monitoring is legal or illegal depends on the state you live in, and the context in which it is installed and used. Regardless of the legality, Spyware is invasive, intrusive, and may put victims in grave danger.

Spyware programmes are sometimes marketed as ways to monitor your children or your employees. As an employer, it is always best to have your employees read and sign a "Technology Use Policy." This policy should explain allowable uses of company property, expectations of online behaviour, and TELL employees if their computer will be monitored. Additionally, choose a software package that displays an icon to remind your employees that they're being monitored.

There are some similarities and differences between Spyware and its close relatives.. For example:

- *Adware*: These are hidden marketing programmes that deliver advertising to consumers, and might also profile users' Internet surfing & shopping habits. Adware is often bundled or hidden in something else a user downloads. Most average computer users are infected with adware fairly regularly, and common symptoms include a sluggish system and lots of advertising pop-ups.
- *Malware*: This is any programme that tries to install itself or damage a computer system without the owner's consent. Malware includes viruses, worms, spyware and adware.

Spyware Work

Spyware can keep track of every keystroke you type, every software application you use, every website you visit, every chat or instant message you send, every document you open, and everything you print. Some spyware gives the abuser the ability to freeze, shutdown or restart your computer. Some versions even allow the abuser to remotely turn on your webcam or make your computer talk.

Once Spyware is installed, it can run in stealth mode and is difficult to detect or uninstall. If the person who installed it has physical access to your computer, he or she can use a special key combination that will cause a log-in screen to pop-up. After entering the password, an options screen will pop up that allows the installer to view all of the computer activity since their last login, including e-mails you sent, documents printed, websites visited, and more. Perpetrators without physical access to your computer can set the spyware to take pictures of the computer screen (screen shots) every few seconds and have these pictures sent to them over the Internet without a victim's knowledge.

How Does It Get On My Computer?

Abusers can install Spyware on your computer if they have physical or Internet access to your computer or handheld device. Some abusers might hack into your computer from another location via the Internet. Some might send spyware to you as an attached file that automatically installs itself when you open the e-mail or when you initially view it in a preview window. Others may e-mail or instant message a greeting card, computer game, or other ruse in order to entice you or your children to open an attachment or click on a link. Once opened, the programme automatically installs spyware on the victim's computer, in stealth mode without notification or consent, and can then send electronic reports to the perpetrator via the Internet. While most spyware is software based (a programme that can be installed on your computer), there are also some hardware-based spyware devices called keystroke loggers. These tiny keylogging devices may appear to be a normal computer part. However, once the keylogger is plugged into your computer, it can record every key typed, capturing all passwords, personal identification numbers (PIN), websites visited, and any e-mails sent onto its small hard drive. Additionally, there are keyboards with keystroke logging capabilities built-in.

OVERVIEW OF SPYWARE

Spyware is one type of malicious software (malware) that collects information from a computing system without your consent. Spyware can capture keystrokes, screenshots, authentication credentials, personal e-mail addresses, web form data, internet usage habits, and other personal information. The data is often delivered to online attackers who sell it to others or use it themselves for marketing or spam or to execute financial crimes or identity theft. Software installed after the user has read and agreed to a clear privacy policy or to an End-User License Agreement (EULA) that describes the software's data collection activities does not meet the definition of spyware. It is your responsibility to carefully read such polices and agreements to make sure you understand and agree with their terms.

ONLINE ATTACKERS

Online attackers' primary interest in spyware is using it to steal personal information for financial crimes such as carding (illicit trafficking in stolen credit card and credit card information) and identity theft, or to sell that information to someone else who then executes more traditional financial crimes.

Marketing Organizations

Marketing organizations are interested in personal information such as e-mail addresses, online shopping and browsing habits, keywords in search queries, and other personal and trend-related information that can be used to execute marketing campaigns like spam, spim (unsolicited messages received via instant messaging systems), browser popups, home page hijacking (changing the default web address for a user's browser), and more.

Spying by a Trusted Insider Trusted insiders include those who have physical access to computer systems for legitimate purposes. Some examples are employees, contractors, temporary workers, and cleaning crews. A trusted insider might be, for example, an employee who uses spyware to collect corporate information that can be sold in the underground economy, used for blackmail, or used to gain access to more valuable information at some later time. Another example of the trusted insider group includes family members or close relations such as spouses or significant others trying to catch inappropriate behaviour or infidelity.

Data Gathered by Spyware

Spyware can monitor nearly any activity or data related to your computing environment. This is not limited to files on your hard drives but can also include temporary data such as screen shots, keystrokes, and data packets on connected networks.

How Spyware Operates

Spyware tracks online activity looking for web sites visited, financial data or identity data such as credit card numbers on screen or entered into form fields, browsing and online purchasing habits, and authentication credentials. When keywords of interest like names of banks, online payment systems, or pornographic web sites are observed, the spyware starts its data collection process.

Email Addresses

Email addresses can be harvested from an infected user's computer and marketed for use in spam mailing lists. Common techniques for harvesting e-mail addresses and other contact information includes enumerating e-mail applications' address books, monitoring incoming and outgoing network packets related to e-mail, and scanning files on the system's disks for strings that match the format of an e-mail address.

Windows Protected Store Windows contains a service called the Protected Store. Its purpose is to provide encrypted storage for sensitive data.

The following are some examples of data that might be in the PStore:

- Outlook passwords
- Passwords for web sites
- MSN Explorer passwords
- IE AutoComplete passwords
- IE AutoComplete fields
- Digital certificates.

Even though the PStore is encrypted, access to it is indirectly controlled by the data owner's login credentials. Since most spyware runs under the security profile of the user who is logged on, spyware can harvest this information.

Clipboard Content

The system clipboard often contains sensitive information. Some common examples include product registration codes and user credentials that are copied and pasted into login forms. Other information that might be found in the system clipboard buffer includes sections of potentially sensitive data from recently modified documents or personal information about you or your associates that could be used in crimes related to identity theft.

The Keys You Press

Key logging is one of the first spyware techniques used to capture sensitive data from a system. Both hardware and software key loggers exist. Hardware devices usually slip inline between the keyboard cable and computer. Modern key logging hardware is small and unobtrusive and has even been hidden inside the physical keyboard casing, making it almost impossible to detect. One limitation of hardware-based keylogger units is the need for physical access to install and retrieve the device and its data. A more common alternative, and the type present in spyware, is the software key logger. Software key loggers capture keyboard events and record the keystroke data before it is sent to the intended application for processing. Like most other spyware capture technologies, software based keyloggers can turn their capture on or off based on keywords or events. For example, many keyloggers target instant messaging clients, e-mail applications, and web browsers but might ignore other applications that don't provide the kind of data the attacker is targeting for harvest.

Network Traffic

Network traffic is another valuable source of data. Data commonly extracted from network captures includes user names, passwords, e-mail messages, and web content. In some cases, entire files can be extracted and reconstructed from the captured streams.

Impact of Spyware

Spyware can cause people to lose trust in the reliability of online business transactions. Similar to the problem of counterfeit currency in the physical world, spyware undermines confidence in online economic activity. Consumers' willingness to participate in online monetary transactions decreases for fear of personal financial loss. Vendors lose confidence that the person making the purchase is who they say they are and not actually a criminal using a stolen identity or illicit funds. In efforts to manage the risk, vendors and financial institutions often implement additional verification and other loss prevention programmes at increased operational cost. Even when financial organizations cover an individual's loss from online fraud, these costs plus the overhead required to administer loss prevention programmes are eventually passed back to consumers in the form of higher service fees, interest rates, or other price increases on the goods and services consumed. As a result, growth rates in commerce are slowed, costs increase, and demand shrinks.

Impact to Computers

By monitoring and reporting user activity, spyware consumes system resources as well as network bandwidth. Depending on the number of spyware components loaded on a system and their functionality, users may experience significant performance degradation. Because spyware is not always carefully written and tested, systems infected by it are often found to have reliability problems. Affected applications may crash more frequently or the entire system may become unstable, resulting in potential productivity and data loss. Often, spyware is difficult to remove without detailed knowledge of how it works or by taking drastic measures such as wiping the system clean and starting over. In many cases, verifying the integrity of the system requires the operating system, patches, and applications to be reinstalled. These difficulties, combined with the efforts necessary to recover user data, can take a lot of time.

Risk of Future Security Incidents

The sensitive information collected by spyware often includes authentication credentials that may be used for future access to the infected system. People often use the same username and password for many different systems, so these stolen credentials may be used to access other systems not yet infected. Once access is gained, additional information theft or malware installation can take place. Another way spyware puts systems at future risk is by installing backdoor access mechanisms. These backdoors give the malware operator access to control the system or to command the system to download and run arbitrary applications. Attackers can build vast collections of compromised systems without originally compromising a single system.

COMMON SPYWARE FORMS

There are thousands of instances of malware. Many forms of malware act primarily as spyware, while other malware programmes contain spyware features.

Browser session hijacking

This class of spyware attempts to modify the user's browser settings. Hijacking spyware can be installed in various ways, but the intent is to modify the behaviour of the browser so the user is directed to sites of the malware author's choice instead of sites the user might have reached normally. These redirects often lead users to advertisements that earn the hijackers commissions when they are visited.

Browser Helper Objects

Browser Helper Objects (BHOs) are a feature of Internet Explorer that can be exploited by spyware. They are not always easy to detect. BHOs can access files, network resources, and anything else the user who launched Internet Explorer can access.

Malicious BHOs can be installed via stand-alone dropper malware but are also often installed using the "drive-by install" technique, in which code is installed or requested to be installed simply by the action of a user visiting a malicious or compromised web site. One technology often used in this type of installation is the ActiveX functionality present in Internet Explorer. Depending on system and browser configuration, the installation may take place automatically and be carried out without prompting the user. In cases where there is prompting, information necessary to make an informed decision can be covered with popup windows or other obfuscation techniques such as naming the control "Click yes to download ringtone."

Another effective social engineering technique is inundating the user with repeated popup requests to install the software that only end when the user leaves the site or finally agrees and installs the component. Once the component is installed, it can operate independently, download and install further malware, and even modify browser settings that allow malware to be downloaded with no user notification or interaction.

Cookies and Web Bugs

Cookies are small pieces of information stored on a user's system by a web server. During subsequent visits, the web server can retrieve these cookies. Often, cookies are used for storing user authentication, preferences, and other types of user state information. They can be used to track a user across multiple web sites. Using correlation and techniques such as "web bugs," over time they can be used to build profiles of individual users. Web bugs are HTML elements, often in the form of image tags, that retrieve information from a remote web site. While the image may not be visible to the user, the act of making the request can provide information about the user. Web bugs are often embedded in web pages and HTMLenabled e-mail messages. Links are used to track access using previously set cookies or with unique strings embedded in the URL. A typical use of this is to log the successful delivery of messages to a unique e-mail address (a common technique for spammers). Once a user has accessed the image, a cookie can also be set and associated with their e-mail address as the beginning of a profile. The cookies can then be used to track portions of the user's browsing habits.

False Antispyware Tools

Applications available on some internet sites advertise themselves as spyware detection or removal tools when in fact they themselves are spyware.

Autonomous Spyware

As a class, autonomous spyware operates as a separate process or injects itself into other processes running on your system. This type of spyware often starts up when you log onto your computer and can frequently access anything on your system. Because autonomous spyware is simply a malicious application, it can be designed to perform almost any type of spying function. Spyware in this class often includes keyloggers, bots, e-mail and web monitoring tools, packet sniffers, and mechanisms that permit the intruder to remotely access and control an infected system.

Bots

A special class of malware known as a bot or zombie is one of the largest malware problems. Bots are remote control agents installed on your system. Bots are often controlled remotely via Internet Relay Chat (IRC). Once a system is infected with a bot, it becomes part of a bot network (botnet) and is used in conjunction with other botnet members to carry out the wishes of the bot owner or bot herder. Bots can scan networks for vulnerabilities, install various distributed denial of service (DDoS) tools, capture network packets, or download and execute arbitrary programmes. Often bots will contain additional spyware or install it. Computers or systems infected with bots can be used to distribute spam to make it harder to track and prosecute the spammers.

Antivirus and Antispyware Tools

Installing trusted antivirus and antispyware tools and keeping them and their signatures current is an important part of defensive computer security.

Browser Settings

Configuring your browser to block active content like ActiveX, Java, scripting, pop-ups, images, and other potentially harmful content can increase online security. While disabling active content features can stop many threats, it also has a tendency to break many modern web sites and applications. At the very least, the richness of the browsing experience will be reduced. One browser configuration strategy to manage the risk associated with active content while still enabling trusted sites is the use of Internet Explorer security zones. Using security zones, you can choose preset levels of security.

Email Configuration

If you use an e-mail programme, you can configure it to send and display e-mail using plain text instead of HTML. This can eliminate most of the risks from embedded script, web bugs, and other HTML-enabled techniques used by attackers. But just as disabling active content in web browsers reduces the functionality of some features, using plain text can reduce the usability of some features. Also, many e-mail clients are now offering the ability to disable scripting and block images until a user takes some action to display them.

Starting your Computer Safely

Almost all spyware needs a way to start itself when you are using your computer. Spyware often starts in conjunction with system startup, user login, or when certain applications like an internet browser or other software is launched.

Not all applications that automatically start are malicious, but it is good to know which software is legitimate. One good method to find and disable spyware on your system is to examine the software installed on your computer and determine whether it starts up automatically or not. You can find this out by looking in the system registry, startup folder, and services control panel.

10

Database Security

Database security concerns the use of a broad range of information security controls to protect databases (potentially including the data, the database applications or stored functions, the database systems, the database servers and the associated network links) against compromises of their confidentiality, integrity and availability. It involves various types or categories of controls, such as technical, procedural/administrative and physical. *Database security* is a specialist topic within the broader realms of computer security, information security and risk management. Security risks to database systems include, for example:

- Unauthorized or unintended activity or misuse by authorized database users, database administrators, or network/systems managers, or by unauthorized users or hackers (e.g. inappropriate access to sensitive data, metadata or functions within databases, or inappropriate changes to the database programmes, structures or security configurations);
- Malware infections causing incidents such as unauthorized access, leakage or disclosure of personal or proprietary data, deletion of or damage to the data or programmes, interruption or denial of authorized access to the database, attacks on other systems and the unanticipated failure of database services;
- Overloads, performance constraints and capacity issues resulting in the inability of authorized users to use databases as intended;

- Physical damage to database servers caused by computer room fires or floods, overheating, lightning, accidental liquid spills, static discharge, electronic breakdowns/ equipment failures and obsolescence;
- Design flaws and programming bugs in databases and the associated programmes and systems, creating various security vulnerabilities (e.g. unauthorized privilege escalation), data loss/corruption, performance degradation etc.;
- Data corruption and/or loss caused by the entry of invalid data or commands, mistakes in database or system administration processes, sabotage/criminal damage etc.

Many layers and types of information security control are appropriate to databases, including:

- Access control
- Auditing
- Authentication
- Encryption
- Integrity controls
- Backups
- Application security.

Traditionally databases have been largely secured against hackers through network security measures such as firewalls, and network-based intrusion detection systems. While network security controls remain valuable in this regard, securing the database systems themselves, and the programmes/functions and data within them, has arguably become more critical as networks are increasingly opened to wider access, in particular access from the Internet.

Furthermore, system, programme, function and data access controls, along with the associated user identification, authentication and rights management functions, have always been important to limit and in some cases log the activities of authorized users and administrators. In other words, these are complementary approaches to database security, working from both the outside-in and the inside-out as it were. Many organizations develop their own "baseline" security standards and designs detailing basic security control measures for their database systems.

These may reflect general information security requirements or obligations imposed by corporate information security policies and applicable laws and regulations (e.g. concerning privacy, financial management and reporting systems), along with generally-accepted good database security practices (such as appropriate hardening of the underlying systems) and perhaps security recommendations from the relevant database system and software vendors.

The security designs for specific database systems typically specify further security administration and management functions (such as administration and reporting of user access rights, log management and analysis, database replication/synchronization and backups) along with various business-driven information security controls within the database programmes and functions (e.g. data entry validation and audit trails). Furthermore, various security-related activities (manual controls) are normally incorporated into the procedures, guidelines etc. relating to the design, development, configuration, use, management and maintenance of databases.

Vulnerability Assessments and Compliance

One technique for evaluating database security involves performing vulnerability assessments or penetration tests against the database. Testers attempt to find security vulnerabilities that could be used to defeat or bypass security controls, break into the database, compromise the system etc. Database administrators or information security administrators may for example use automated vulnerability scans to search out misconfiguration of controls within the layers mentioned above along with known vulnerabilities within the database software.

The results of such scans are used to harden the database (improve the security controls) and close off the specific vulnerabilities identified, but unfortunately other vulnerabilities typically remain unrecognized and unaddressed. A programme of continual monitoring for compliance with database security standards is another important task for mission critical database environments. Two crucial aspects of database security compliance include patch management and the review and management of permissions (especially public) granted to objects within the database. Database objects may include table or other objects listed in the Table link.

The permissions granted for SQL language commands on objects are considered in this process. One should note that compliance monitoring is similar to vulnerability assessment with the key difference that the results of vulnerability assessments generally drive the security standards that lead to the continuous monitoring programme. Essentially, vulnerability assessment is a preliminary procedure to determine risk where a compliance programme is the process of on-going risk assessment. The compliance programme should take into consideration any dependencies at the application software level as changes at the database level may have effects on the application software or the application server. In direct relation to this topic is that of application security.

Abstraction

Application level authentication and authorization mechanisms should be considered as an effective means of providing abstraction from the database layer. The primary benefit of abstraction is that of a single sign-on capability across multiple databases and database platforms. A Single sign-on system should store the database user's credentials (login id and password), and authenticate to the database on behalf of the user.

Database Activity Monitoring (DAM)

Another security layer of a more sophisticated nature includes real-time database activity monitoring, either by analyzing protocol traffic (SQL) over the network, or by observing local database activity on each server using software agents, or both.

Use of agents or native logging is required to capture activities executed on the database server, which typically include the activities of the database administrator. Agents allow this information to be captured in a fashion that can not be disabled by the database administrator, who has the ability to disable or modify native audit logs. Analysis can be performed to identify known exploits or policy breaches, or baselines can be captured over time to build a normal pattern used for detection of anomalous activity that could be indicative of intrusion.

These systems can provide a comprehensive Database audit trail in addition to the intrusion detection mechanisms, and some systems can also provide protection by terminating user sessions and/or quarantining users demonstrating suspicious behaviour.

Some systems are designed to support separation of duties (SOD), which is a typical requirement of auditors. SOD requires that the database administrators who are typically monitored as part of the DAM, not be able to disable or alter the DAM functionality. This requires the DAM audit trail to be securely stored in a separate system not administered by the database administration group.

Native Audit

In addition to using external tools for monitoring or auditing, native database audit capabilities are also available for many database platforms. The native audit trails are extracted on a regular basis and transferred to a designated security system where the database administrators do not have access. This ensures a certain level of segregation of duties that may provide evidence the native audit trails were not modified by authenticated administrators. Turning on native impacts the performance of the server. Generally, the native audit trails of databases do not provide sufficient controls to enforce separation of duties; therefore, the network and/or kernel module level host based monitoring capabilities provides a higher degree of confidence for forsenics and preservation of evidence.

Process and Procedures

A *database security* programme should include the regular review of permissions granted to individually owned accounts and accounts used by automated processes. The accounts used by automated processes should have appropriate controls around password storage such as sufficient encryption and access controls to reduce the risk of compromise.

For individual accounts, a two-factor authentication system should be considered in a database environment where the risk is commensurate with the expenditure for such an authentication system. In conjunction with a sound *database security* programme, an appropriate disaster recovery programme should exist to ensure that service is not interrupted during a security incident or any other incident that results in an outage of the primary database environment. An example is that of replication for the primary databases to sites located in different geographical regions. After an incident occurs, the usage of database forensics should be employed to determine the scope of the breach, and to identify appropriate changes to systems and/or processes to prevent similar incidents in the future.

DATA SAFETY AND PRIVACY PROTECTION

As the situation now warranty legislation of data protection in India, visitors to any website want reassurances that privacy rights will be respected when they engage in eCommerce. It is part of the confidence-creating role that successful eCommerce businesses have to convey to the consumer. If industry doesn't make sure it's guarding the privacy of the data it collects, it will be the responsibility of the government and it's their obligation to enact legislation. The problem that arises in eCommerce is that the Internet is in itself global. Generally the actions in regulating by the Indian Govt will have very little impact unless they are part of a larger international setting.

The protection of personal data has never been a purely national problem; it was always a global issue. Here we are trying no to not deal with privacy issues relating to internal use by employees, sending personal data or using the employers Internet for personal purposes. It is to focus on issues relating to the collection, storage, accuracy and use of data provided by Net users in the use of the World Wide Web

Information that could be collected by Operating Websites and what way it can be Used? The type of information that could be collected and can be classified as either individually identifiable information or Mass undisclosed information.

Individually Identifiable Information

Individually identifiable information can be defined as information that can be used to identify an individual, that consist of information like name, address, telephone number, credit card number, or email address And other consumer specific information.

This information is linked with identifiable information from other sources, or from which other personally identifiable information can easily be found, including, but not limited to, name, address, phone number, fax number, email address, financial profiles, credit card information. And also IP address is associated with Personally Identifiable Information, unless you have affirmatively disclosed this information. The Internet generates an elaborate trail of data every stop a person makes. Pentium III processor identifier chip called Processor Serial Number or PSN, It is a number tied to the individual and used to validate one's identity through a range of interactions with any organization or demographic.

Mass Undisclosed Information

Mass undisclosed information" can be defined as information that: a website or third party on its behalf aggregates and categorizes by established geographical areas, such as postal codes and contains non-consumer specific information created from anonymous transactions for use by merchants in better managing their businesses and conducting mass media advertising.

There is a abundant of technologies that are utilized to collect both Classes of information on consumers. One of these tools are called "Cookies" Which is simply a piece of information [computer code] that is saved on your own Computer or your browser. It contains information as to the personal preferences exhibited when visiting a website. As it is impossible to differentiate between Visitors to a Web site, the server will somehow mark the visitor by storing information on them.

While Cookies themselves are not gathering the data, they are used as tracking devices to help people who are collecting information.

Any information gathered is associated with the value they keep in any Cookie. A Cookie cannot read hard drive to find out who they are, or there incomes or place of residence, However, that information could end up in a Cookie if you provided it to a site and that site saved it in a Cookie.

Policies to Protect Privacy

Accountability by organizations for information within their possession Limit the collection of the information.Revelation of personal data to the declared purpose except with the consent of the individual. Organization should retain information only as long as necessary. Information in possession of an organization should be accurate and up-to-date Security should be the Priority Organizations collecting should be transparent in their policy and practice Organizations should allow individuals access and the ability to rectify errors.

Fair information practices: Web sites would be required to provide consumers notice of what information they collect and how they use it. Web sites would be required to offer consumers choices as to how that information is to be used beyond the use for which the information was provided.

Web sites would be required to offer consumers reasonable access to that information and an opportunity to correct inaccuracies. Web sites would be required to take reasonable steps to protect the security and integrity of that information. Websites that collect personal identifying information from children 12 and under need to provide actual notice to the parent and obtain parental consent as follows.

The agency should issue interpretive rules defining fair information practices with greater specificity, taking into account industry-specific differences.

The purpose is to prevent violations of fundamental human rights such as unlawful storage of personal data, or the abuse or unauthorized disclosure of such data.

NETWORK SECURITY CONCEPTS

Network security starts from authenticating the user, commonly with a username and a password. Since this requires just one thing besides the user name, i.e. the password which is something you 'know', this is sometimes termed one factor authentication.

With two factor authentication something you 'have' is also used (e.g. a security token or 'dongle', an ATM card, or your mobile phone), or with three factor authentication something you 'are' is also used (e.g. a fingerprint or retinal scan). Once authenticated, a firewall enforces access policies such as what services are allowed to be accessed by the network users. Though effective to prevent unauthorized access, this component may fail to check potentially harmful content such as computer worms or Trojans being transmitted over the network. Anti-virus software or an intrusion prevention system (IPS) help detect and inhibit the action of such malware.

An anomaly-based intrusion detection system may also monitor the network and traffic for unexpected (i.e. suspicious) content or behaviour and other anomalies to protect resources, e.g. from denial of service attacks or an employee accessing files at strange times. Individual events occurring on the network may be logged for audit purposes and for later high level analysis.

Communication between two hosts using a network could be encrypted to maintain privacy. *Honeypots*, essentially decoy network-accessible resources, could be deployed in a network as surveillance and early-warning tools as the honeypot will not normally be accessed. Techniques used by the attackers that attempt to compromise these decoy resources are studied during and after an attack to keep an eye on new exploitation techniques. Such analysis could be used to further tighten security of the actual network being protected by the honeypot.

Security Management

Security Management for networks is different for all kinds of situations. A small home or an office would only require basic security while large businesses will require high maintenance and advanced software and hardware to prevent malicious attacks from hacking and spamming.

Small Homes

- A basic firewall or a unified threat management system.
- For Windows users, basic Antivirus software. An anti-spyware programme would also be a good idea. There are many other types of antivirus or anti-spyware programmes out there to be considered.
- When using a wireless connection, use a robust password. Also try to use the strongest security supported by your wireless devices, such as WPA2 with AES encryption.
- If using Wireless: Change the default SSID network name, also disable SSID Broadcast; as this function is unnecessary for home use. (However, many security experts consider this to be relatively useless.
- Enable MAC Address filtering to keep track of all home network MAC devices connecting to your router.
- Assign STATIC IP addresses to network devices.
- Disable ICMP ping on router.
- Review router or firewall logs to help identify abnormal network connections or traffic to the Internet.
- Use passwords for all accounts.
- Have multiple accounts per family member, using non-administrative accounts for day-to-day activities. Disable the guest account (Control Panel> Administrative Tools> Computer Management> Users).
- Raise awareness about information security to children.

Medium Businesses

- A fairly strong firewall or Unified Threat Management System
- Strong Antivirus software and Internet Security Software.
- For authentication, use strong passwords and change it on a bi-weekly/monthly basis.

- When using a wireless connection, use a robust password.
- Raise awareness about physical security to employees.
- Use an optional network analyzer or network monitor.
- An enlightened administrator or manager.

Large Businesses

- A strong firewall and proxy to keep unwanted people out.
- A strong Antivirus software package and Internet Security Software package.
- For authentication, use strong passwords and change it on a weekly/bi-weekly basis.
- When using a wireless connection, use a robust password.
- Exercise physical security precautions to employees.
- Prepare a network analyzer or network monitor and use it when needed.
- Implement physical security management like closed circuit television for entry areas and restricted zones.
- Security fencing to mark the company's perimeter.
- Fire extinguishers for fire-sensitive areas like server rooms and security rooms.
- Security guards can help to maximize security.

School

- An adjustable firewall and proxy to allow authorized users access from the outside and inside.
- Strong Antivirus software and Internet Security Software packages.
- Wireless connections that lead to firewalls.
- Children's Internet Protection Act compliance.
- Supervision of network to guarantee updates and changes based on popular site usage.
- Constant supervision by teachers, librarians, and administrators to guarantee protection against attacks by both internet and sneakernet sources.

Large Government

- A strong firewall and proxy to keep unwanted people out.
- Strong antivirus software and Internet Security Software suites.
- Strong encryption.
- Whitelist authorized wireless connection, block all else.
- All network hardware is in secure zones.
- All host should be on a private network that is invisible from the outside.
- Put web servers in a DMZ, or a firewall from the outside and from the inside.
- Security fencing to mark perimeter and set wireless range to this.

SEPARATION OF PROTECTION AND SECURITY

In computer sciences the separation of protection and security is a design choice. Wulf et al. identified protection as a mechanism and security as a policy, therefore making the protection-security distinction a particular case of the separation of mechanism and policy principle.

Overview

The adoption of this distinction in a computer architecture, usually means that protection is provided as a fault tolerance mechanism by hardware/firmware and kernel, whereas the operating system and applications implement their security policies. In this design, security policies rely therefore on the protection mechanisms and on additional cryptography techniques. The major hardware approach for security or protection is the use of hierarchical protection domains. Prominent example of this approach is ring architecture with "supervisor mode" and "user mode"). Such approach adopts a policy already at the lower levels (hardware/firmware/kernel), restricting the rest of the system to rely on it. Therefore, the choice to distinguish between protection and security in the overall architecture design implies rejection of the hierarchical approach in favour of another one, the capability-based addressing.

Design Models with the Separation

The models with the protection and security separation are: access matrix, UCLA Data Secure Unix, take-grant and filter.

Design Models Without the Separation

The models without such separation are: high-water mark, Bell–LaPadula (original and revisited), information flow, strong dependency and constraints.

CYBER SECURITY AND CRITICAL INFRASTRUCTURE PROTECTION IN INDIA

Cyber Security of India is an essential part of National ICT Policy and Strategy of India. Despite some very good suggestions and critical evaluations, the Government of India (GOI) has not considered it necessary to take some action in this regard. There has been repetitive wake up calls given to the GOI but it seems the GOI is in indefinite sleep.

On the other hand, the International Community is stressing really hard to make cyber security an essential part of their day to day lives. Dartmouth's Institute for Information Infrastructure Protection (I3P) has recently provided its cyber security research recommendations.

They are in the form of a set of recommendations for advancing research in cyber security that can be implemented in the next five to 10 years. The report recognises four areas of need that emerged during the forum:

(1) A coordinated and collaborative approach is needed.
(2) Metrics and assessment tools must be developed.
(3) An effective legal and policy framework for security must be created.
(4) The human dimension of security must be addressed.

It may be a coincidence that similar suggestions were provided by Mr. Praveen Dalal, Managing Partner of Perry4Law to the Government of India. He has also provided the Indian Policies and Strategies for Critical ICT Infrastructure Protection and Management in India. The stress upon Legal Enablement of ICT

Systems in India is very important to make Cyber Law of India strong and effective. There are lot of Problems through which the present Cyber Law of India is passing through. A good account of the same can be found at this nice piece of work.

The problem still remains the same. In India we don't have a dedicated resource that is taking care of Techno-Legal Laws of India in a holistic manner. Of course, we have a Cyber Law Database of India.

We also have a Techno-Legal ICT Regulations Database in India. These two resources are tracing back the history of cyber law in India. However, we need a resource that can trace both history of cyber law in India as well as its current position and the prospective future of the same. The task is very difficult but it has been successfully achieved by Mr. Praveen Dalal, Managing Partner of Perry4Law. He has successfully come out with a "Dedicated Resource" on cyber law in India.

The same is titled "Legal Enablement Of ICT Systems in India" and is the exclusive, most comprehensive and holistic web resource in India dealing with Techno-Legal ICT Laws and Regulations in India. All the cyber law observers can now access information about cyber law in India and the changes that are proposed or actually made from time to time. The resource is very futuristic and promising in nature and it would be good idea if the Government of India (GOI) consults the same while making, amending or reformulating techno-legal laws in India.

One of the important aspects of this resource is that it is the exclusive resource that is providing a "Constitutional Analysis" of the present as well as proposed techno-legal laws in India. Therefore all of the "Civil Liberty Crusaders" keep a close eye upon this resource for issues like Privacy Rights, Life and Liberty, Right to Speech and Expressions, etc.

For instance, surveillance has become a controversial issue since the Information Technology (Amendment) Bill, 2008 (Bill, 2008) has been proposed. Surprisingly some people are justifying these wide and unregulated powers as justified under the garb of security that does not exists at all in India. There is only one answer to the pro surveillance argument and it is a Benjamin

Franklin quote: Those who would give up essential liberty to purchase a little temporary safety deserve neither liberty nor safety.

E-Surveillance should not be a substitute for cyber security and cyber forensics capabilities. Privacy Rights must be respected and followed in both letter and spirit in India. He Bill, 2008 has seriously compromised these Fundamental Rights. So friends, wake up and be a vigilant and legally aware citizens. We will keep on spreading the "Cyber Law Awareness" in India so that we may have an informed citizenry.

ONLINE CYBER STALKING VS. TRADITIONAL OFFLINE STALKING

To some extent, cyber stalking is fundamentally an extension of traditional stalking in which the offender utilizes a high-tech modus operandi to committing the crime. With cyber stalking becoming a growing criminological concern in contemporary society, the offender's behaviours and actions need to be examined in greater depth. Bocij (2005) was one of the very first researchers to study the prevalence and impact of cyber stalking. Cyber stalking behaviours are similar to traditional stalking behaviours in many respects; however, cyber stalking, at least from a criminological and legal perspective, represents an entirely new form of deviant, criminal behaviour. For one, both offender types, traditional and online, resort to tactics and behaviours that are primarily intended to harass, and in some cases, threaten or intimidate the victim (Petrocelli 2005). As mentioned, traditional stalkers and cyber stalkers will frequently react aggressively when confronted, scorned, rejected, or belittled by a victim (Bocij 2005). The research information suggests that cyber stalkers are demographically more in line with the stereotypical white–collar criminal as opposed to the street level criminal offender. The overwhelming majority of cyber stalker offenders are middle to upper class Caucasian males with stable employment and firmly established ties to the community.

Conversely, the research literature also suggests that many cyber stalkers have a prior criminal record, a history of substance abuse, or a personality disorder that directly or partly contributes to, and increases the likelihood of such antisocial behaviours. Although this may be true in some cases, there is very little conclusive evidence to support this claim in all cases. The figures cited throughout this report are purely speculative based on limited empirical evidence in that the actual numbers or percentages can never be known since most crimes, especially cyber stalking crimes, go unreported or undetected, thereby contributing to the so-called dark figure of crime. In addition, scientific information in relation to cyber stalking is still in its infancy and is therefore, anecdotal. The evidence collected thus far suggests that offender suffers from a personality disorder that may range from an abnormally high level of paranoia to delusional behaviours and thoughts that can consume the offender.

As repeatedly mentioned, many of the behaviours displayed by cyber stalkers resemble that of traditional stalkers; however, there are many notable differences that clearly distinguish the former from the latter. One of the most striking similarities is that both offender types are motivated by an insatiable desire and need to have power, control, and influence over the victim (Reno 1999). If left unattended, these actions could conceivably escalate to a potentially volatile physical confrontation between the offender and the victim even though many, including those in law enforcement, perceive cyber stalking to be relatively harmless (Reno 1999).

Traditional stalking behaviours are fairly predictable in that the offender will often follow the victim home, to work, or even to school, thereby making it somewhat effortless for investigators to track, apprehend, arrest, and subsequently prosecute the offender. Further, many stalkers resort to leaving harassing written messages at the victim's home or place of employment and in some cases, the offender will make threatening phone calls that are intended to provoke fear and intimidation in the victim, all of which can often be traced back to the perpetrator with relative ease (Reno 1999). As stated, the aforementioned crimes typically leave a physical trail of evidence behind that will undoubtedly be used to assemble a criminal case against the offender. Another noteworthy comparison between the stalker and the cyber stalker is the distinctively high probability that both offender types had a prior intimate relationship, whether real or perceived, with the victim; however the cyber stalker is more inclined to choose his or her victims at random. According to Reno (1999), nearly 50% of all cyber stalking incidents involved complete strangers who were initially contacted in some perceivably innocent manner via the Internet.

In fact, there has been a considerable increase in the number of stranger cases, particularly with cyber stalkers (Reno 1999). The Internet grants cyber stalkers access to a vast amount of personal information with relative ease (Reno 1999). Information that was once considered private and confidential a few decades ago can easily be accessed through a variety of brokerage websites that cater specifically to individuals innocently searching for friends or loved ones (Reno 1999). Some of these websites are free, but the large majority will charge a small service fee in exchange for a person's name, phone number, address, social security number, date of birth and other confidential identifying information (Reno 1999). The majority of these brokerage sites were established to help people find friends and loved ones of the past, but like anything else, is subject to abuse by those who want to use the service for diabolical reasons.

For example, on July 29, 1999, 21-year old Liam Youens of New Hampshire contacted Docusearch, an Internet-based investigation and information service, and requested information, specifically the date of birth of Amy Lynn Boyer, a 20-year old woman whom Youens had been obsessed with ever since the two attended high school together (Electronic Privacy Information Centre 2006). Shortly after receiving the birth dates for several Amy Boyer's, none of which was the Amy Lynn Boyer sought by Youens, Youens, once again, contacted Docusearch for a second time to request Boyer's social security number and employment information, for which Youens was charged a measly $45 (Electronic Privacy Information Centre 2006).

On September 8, 1999, Docusearch managed to obtain Boyer's employment information and address by having a subcontractor, Michelle Gambino, place a "pretext" call to Boyer (Electronic

Privacy Information Centre 2006). Pretexting is the practice of collecting information about a person using false pretenses in which the caller often claims to be someone "official" calling in regard to some proclaimed legitimate purpose (Electronic Privacy Information Centre 2006). In this particular case, Gambino "pretended" to be affiliated with Boyer's insurance company in order to attain employment verification information concerning Boyer's workplace address, all of which under the false pretense of facilitating the delivery of a fictitious overpayment refund (Electronic Privacy Information Centre 2006). The investigation later revealed that Youens paid Docusearch $109 for this information. On October 15, 1999, Youens, armed with a handgun and a map to Boyer's place of employment, drove to the dentist's office in Nashua, New Hampshire where Boyer worked and fatally shot her – 11 times – as she left work, before turning the gun on himself in a senseless act that was quickly ruled a murder-suicide.

To make matters worse, the investigation into Boyer's murder discovered that Youens had constructed and maintained a website titled, *Amy Boyer,* for nearly two years prior to the murder, which contained explicit details of how he had stalked her for years, how he felt about her, and more alarmingly, how he planned to kill her. On the website, Youens explained how he had fallen in love with Boyer in the eighth grade, how she had rejected him in high school, and in response to the rejection, a detailed chronicle of why and how she must die (Spencer). An excerpt from the webpage reads, "*When she gets in, I'll drive up to the car blocking her in, window to window, then I'll shoot her with my Glock,*" which is tragically the way it occurred on October 15, 1999. How could Youens' rambling messages regarding his intentions to kill Amy Boyer go unnoticed? The existing laws, as will be seen, are virtually meaningless when the cyber stalkers are across states lines, especially when threats are only implied.

In response to Boyer's death, her mother and stepfather (*Helen and Tim Remsburg*) filed a wrongful death suit against Docusearch and the investigators that the agency subcontracted with to obtain Boyer's personal information (Electronic Privacy Information Centre 2006). The suit claimed an invasion of privacy through intrusion upon seclusion; invasion of privacy through commercial appropriation of private information; violation of the Fair Credit Reporting Act; and violation of the New Hampshire Consumer Protection Act (Electronic Privacy Information Centre). The Electronic Information Privacy Centre filed an amicus brief on behalf of the Remsburg's arguing that Docusearch should be held liable under all the aforementioned claims.

In addition to the people-search websites via Google and other popular search engines, the Internet is host to a number of sites that specifically promote retaliation and revenge, which is, in essence, a cyber stalker's dream (Bocij 2005). For instance, cyber stalkers who wish to send anonymous letters or emails can do so through the "payback" website at www.thepayback.com, a site that purposely conceals and protects the sender's name and personal information (Bocij 2005). There are also a number of radical extremist sites, including the Avenger's page, a site that encourages visitors to seek revenge and, in some instances, incite violence (Bocij 2005).

Case in point, a Pennsylvania State Trooper was recently arrested for posting five nude photographs of his former wife on a bondage and sadomasochistic website apparently in order to seek revenge for a failed marriage. According to Christine Pittaro (2007), the Crime Victim/Witness Advocate for the District Attorney's Office of Northampton County, Pennsylvania, Heller had worked as a trooper for approximately 14 years – up until the date of his arrest.

In addition to creating a profile in his wife's name and posting the nude photographs, Heller also posted his wife's occupation as a schoolteacher and date of birth on the bondage website. A forensic examination of Heller's laptop computer revealed that the laptop had been used to post five of the 18 nude photographs of his ex-wife that were taken when the two were initially married.

The forensic examination, which was performed by State Trooper Paul Iannace, determined that Heller, posing as his ex-wife, posted explicit messages on the website-soliciting viewers to contact her to engage in violent sexual acts (2007). This particular cyber stalking offense was unearthed after one of the website's visitors decided to contact Heller's ex-wife at her place of employment. Heller subsequently pleaded guilty to harassment for placing the images on the bondage site and agreed to quit the Pennsylvania State Police in light of the criminal charges lodged against him. According to Assistant District Attorney Patricia Broscious of Northampton County, Pennsylvania, such cases of cyber stalking are difficult to prosecute based on the manner in which many of the statutes are currently written.

One obvious difference between traditional stalking and cyber stalking is the geographic proximity between the offender and the victim. In a traditional stalking case, the offender and victim often live or work within relatively close proximity of one another whereas cyber stalkers could literally be harassing the victim from the house across the street or from a coffee shop in another state, or even another country for that matter (Reno 1999). One of the many advantages that cyber stalkers have over the traditional stalker is that these offenders typically have a high level of computer proficiency and aptitude, essential skills that allow the stalker to take crucial steps toward avoiding detection (Hutton & Haantz 2003). As stated, the anonymity of the Internet allows the cyber stalker to easily conceal one's identity through a variety of inexpensive and simple tactics. For instance, cyber stalkers can connect to several different Internet service providers, thereby creating a number of screen names, which will make it nearly impossible to track the origin of the emails (Reno 1999).

As mentioned, there is rarely any physical contact between the cyber stalker and the victim, therefore, most police officers minimize the seriousness of such harassment and simply dismiss the victim's fears as nuisance complaints (Reno 1999). However, cyber stalking can be just as threatening and as frightening as being followed and watched by a traditional stalker in one's neighbourhood (Reno 1999). Cyber stalking behaviours like those of sexual offenders like the peeping Tom voyeur may simply be a prelude to other dangerous disturbed behaviours, some of which may end in violence. The level of dangerousness is elevated further if the offender has a criminal record, a history of substance abuse, or a psychological disorder, which predisposes the offender to violence (Bocij 2005).

Even though most stalkers act alone, the Internet has made it much easier for cyber stalkers to conspire and encourage third parties to harass victims in chat rooms, discussion boards, and within Internet public forums (Reno 1999). In fact, researchers have coined the term, stalking by proxy, to describe the process in which cyber stalkers encourage others such as family members and friends to aid in harassing the victim. Some cyber stalkers have even been known to hire private investigators to follow and report on the victim's daily activities and whereabouts Private investigators can also be used to obtain additional personal information on the victim that may not be readily available on the Internet as in the case of Amy Lynn Boyer.

11

Cyber Defamation in Cyber Space

The Internet is a cheap, fast means of international communication of text, sound or image. In other words, an information resource without political or content boundaries; limited only by the extent to which the information providers are willing to disclose their materials and the fruits of their own writing and research. In the present day, web sites displaying information of all kinds are proliferating. These sites are established and controlled by Internet Service Providers (ISPs) or, sometimes, by the company's information technology department.

These sites can be accessed through suitable search engines, which will trace and display information to suit the requirements of the searcher. However, not many of the companies are aware of the risks attached with the hosting of a Web site. Who would be held liable, for instance, if an employee clandestinely posts racist, sexist, or defamatory allegations about a competitor on the company's official web site?

It is to be remembered that a number of features unique to the internet distinguishes it from any other medium. These features have led to the current re-examination of existing laws relating to defamation, to allow for their possible evolution and ultimately their application in cyberspace. A key feature of the internet is its highly interactive nature. The ease with which users of the internet can access information and communicate with each other has engendered in its users a false sense of freedom in their communications. Accessibility is another feature of the internet, which distinguishes it from traditional print or broadcast media. The relatively low cost of connecting to the internet and even of establishing one's own website means that the opportunity for defamation has increased exponentially. Now, on the internet everyone can be a publisher and can be sued as a publisher.

Another key feature of the internet is that users do not have to reveal their true identity in order to send e-mail or post messages on bulletin boards. Users are able to communicate and make such postings anonymously or under assumed names. This feature, coupled with the ability to access the internet in privacy and seclusion of one's own home or office and the interactive, responsive nature of communications on the internet, has resulted in users being far less inhibited about the contents of their messages resulting in cyber space becoming excessively prone to defamation.

Defamation can be understood as the intentional infringement of another person's right to his good name. It is the wrongful and intentional publication of words or behaviour concerning another person, which has the effect of injuring that person's status, good name, or reputation in society. Libel is written defamation and slander is oral defamation. The primary difference is that in libel, damages are presumed, whereas in slander actions, unless the slander falls into a certain category, called slander per se, the plaintiff must prove actual or quantifiable damages.

A person's good name can only be damaged if maligning statements are made to someone other than that person; that is, the defamatory statement must be disclosed to a third person, thereby satisfying the requirement of publication. When determining whether or not defamation has taken place, the only issue to consider is whether a person of ordinary intelligence in society would believe that the words would indeed injure the person's reputation.

Thus the law of defamation places a heavy burden on the defendant. All that a plaintiff has to prove, in a defamation action, is the publication of defamatory matter. The onus then lies on the defendant to prove innocence. Once again, most people are unaware of this burden.

In essence, the law on defamation attempts to create a workable balance between two equally important human rights: The right to an unimpaired reputation and the right to freedom of expression.

In a cyber society, both these interests are increasingly important. Protection of reputation is arguably even more important in a highly technological society, since one may not even encounter an individual or organization other than through the medium of the internet.

The elements of a defamation action can be summarized as follows:

- The plaintiff must prove publication of the defamatory statement;
- The plaintiff must prove that the defamation refers to the plaintiff; and
- The plaintiff must prove that the statement is defamatory.

Upon proof of publication, the law makes several presumptions in favour of the plaintiff:

- That the statement is false;
- That it was published with malice; and
- That in the case of libel or slander per se, the plaintiff has suffered damage.

Defences that can be raised against such a defamation action are as follows:

- Truth.
- Fair comment: The defendant is allowed to comment on facts truly stated, as long as the comment is fair and the defendant is not motivated by actual malice.
- Privilege: On certain occasions, the courts have held that policy and convenience require that a person should be free from responsibility for the publication of defamatory words. These occasions constitute privileges. Privilege may be absolute, such as statements in the House of Commons or the Courts. It may be qualified, in that it may be lost if the publication is unnecessarily wide or made with malice.

Innocent dissemination: This last defence is potentially very important in cyber libel.

If a defendant proves that his statements were true and in public interest, then his conduct is regarded as lawful. In addition, if the defendant can show that he had no intention to defame (the plaintiff), then he could avoid liability.

This paper seeks to throw light on the law relating to cyber defamation and to suggest a legal framework to handle such situations, which is inevitable, especially in the light of the present IT boom in India.

CYBER DEFAMATION: A SOCIO-ECONOMIC OFFENCE

Cyber law encompasses cyber crimes, electronic commerce, freedom of expression, intellectual property rights, jurisdiction issues and choice of law, and privacy rights. Cyber crimes involve activities like credit card fraud, unauthorized access to computer systems, child pornography, software piracy and cyber stalking. Freedom of expression includes defamation, obscenity issues and censorship. Jurisdiction issues focuses on who makes and enforces the rules governing cyber space.

The definition of what constitutes a crime in cyber space is still being developed. In the past, the states and federal government defined cyber crime activities to include the destruction or theft of computer data and programs. More recently the definition has expanded to include activities such as forgery, illegal gambling, cyber stalking, cyber defamation etc.

There are several areas on the internet where there is a real risk of liability for defamation. The fact that a user is "alone" with his computer and distanced from other users creates a sense of intimacy. There is no spoken/telephonic conversation or dictated correspondence that would normally instill some caution. In addition, the notion that the internet is a "free-for-all" cyberspace where there are no limits or boundaries results in a user's sense of social norms and propriety generally getting blurred.

The Web results in an instant global publication of information at a very low cost. Information, which would not normally have been revealed prior to the dawning of the internet, can now be unearthed by practically anyone. Intranets are intended to be exclusively used by a company. However, information from an intranet can be easily downloaded and forwarded by e-mail or otherwise to third parties. Information posted to a bulletin board can be accessed by anyone. This means that anyone can place defamatory allegations on the bulletin board. E-mail users generally tend to treat their correspondence as a kind of conversation rather than a written interaction. Users forget that e-mails are stored and can be retrieved as hard copies and that their contents then cannot be disputed. One message can be circulated to literally hundreds of people. As a defamatory allegation need only be disclosed to one person for publication to be proved, every time e-mail is forwarded to another person, it is published again and an additional cause of action for defamation arises.

The scope of every firm having a cyber presence to liability for defamation is global. Internet sites can be accessed in most countries throughout the world; huge amounts of data can be transmitted simultaneously to several different destinations; and e-mail can be forwarded to an indefinite number of recipients without the original author having any control over the transmission.

While a legal action based on defamation is usually aimed at stopping the defamatory allegations, the harm in most cases has already been done. Consequently, the most important relief claimed in a defamatory action is damages. The amount of damages granted will depend on the nature of the defamation sought and the extent of publication.

Furthermore, a defamation claim can be instituted in any jurisdiction in which a cause of action arises. In theory then, a potential defendant to a defamation suit could be sued in respect of a particular defamatory statement in a number of different countries with which it has no connection under any number of different laws with which it is totally unfamiliar. Indeed, a potential plaintiff can choose to litigate in whichever country has the most favourable laws. Theoretically, every time a third party accesses a defamatory posting on the Internet, publication has occurred.

The global nature of the Internet also raises some interesting procedural questions for the libel lawyer. In traditional libel law there are three different types of defamatory statements:

(i) The first is a statement that is defamatory on its face and which is obviously defamatory.

(ii) The second is a statement, which contains false innuendo. False innuendo is a defamatory statement that has an inferential meaning, therefore only persons with the necessary contextual knowledge appreciate that the statement is defamatory. Since statements on the internet are published globally, their inferential meanings may vary depending on the geographic or cultural location of the reader or the newsgroups or the Usenet group involved.

(iii) The third category is legal innuendo. While not defamatory on their face, these statements are defamatory when viewed together with extrinsic circumstances. Once again, contextual knowledge may render a statement defamatory in one jurisdiction but not in another.

Cyber defamation need not necessarily be directed against an individual victim, but it could be harmful to the whole society. No doubt, at times, it could be directed against an individual ('victim'), but the criminal act is potentially capable of harming a large number of persons and that is the principal object behind punishing it.

In short it is an offence, which affects the health or material welfare of the community as a whole and not merely of the individual victim. Similarly it is also an offence, which affects the country's economy and not merely the wealth of an individual victim, since defamation of a corporate house could even adversely affect its share value.

Two very significant aspects of such a social and economic offence are:

(i) the gravity of the harm caused to society; and

(ii) the nature of the offence.

The gravity of the harm is not easily apparent, but is nevertheless, undeniable. The nature of the offence is peculiar, in the sense that they are planned and executed in secrecy by shrewd and dexterous persons with sophisticated means. The public welfare is gravity affected; but detection is unusually difficult.

Cases of cyber defamation do not fit neatly in the accepted categories of crimes. They represent harm of greater magnitude than the traditional crimes and of a nature different from them. Unlike the traditional crimes, they are not in the shape of positive aggressions or invasions. They may not result in direct or immediate injury; nevertheless, they create a danger, which the law must seek to minimise. Hence if legislation applicable to such offences, as a matter of policy, departs from legislation applicable to ordinary crimes in respect of the traditional requirements as to mens rea and the other substantive matters as well as on points of procedure, the departure would be justified.

Position in Other Countries

Defamation laws vary from country to country and in countries such as the Canada, Australia and the United States, it can vary from province to province and state to state. Therefore, plaintiffs may have the luxury of "forum shopping" or choosing the jurisdiction with the laws most favourable to him/her.

Position in US

In the United States, about 75% of defamation lawsuits are filed in state courts, and the remaining 25% in federal courts. A comprehensive discussion of what is and is not libel or slander is difficult, because each state's definition differs. Some states lump slander and libel together into the same set of laws. Some states have criminal libel laws on the books, though these are old laws, which are infrequently prosecuted. Most defendants in libel lawsuits are newspapers, which are involved in about twice as many lawsuits as are TV stations. Most plaintiffs are corporations, business people, entertainers and other public figures, and inmates. Most states do not allow defamation lawsuits to be filed if the allegedly defamed person is already deceased. None of the states allow the plaintiff to be a group of people.

In the various states, whether by case law or actual legislation, there are generally several "privileges" that can get a libel case dismissed without proceeding to trial. These include the allegedly defamatory statement being one of opinion rather than fact; or being "fair comment and criticism", as it is important to society that everyone be able to comment on matters of public interest. If a defamation lawsuit actually gets to trial, truth is an affirmative defense. Further, if the allegedly defamatory statement is not actually capable of being defamatory, i.e., an insulting statement that does not harm someone's reputation is prima facie not libelous.

New York Times Company v. Sullivan was a U.S. Supreme Court case which established the actual malice standard before press reports could be considered to be defamation and libel; and hence allowed free reporting of the civil rights campaigns in the southern United States. It is one of the key decisions supporting the freedom of the press. The actual malice standard requires that the publisher knows the statement is false or acts in reckless disregard of the truth.

The decision established that for a plaintiff to win a libel ruling against a newspaper, "actual malice" or "reckless negligence" must be proved on the part of the paper if the statement in question is about a public official or public figure. In the case of a private figure, the plaintiff must merely prove negligence.

Prior to the enactment of the Telecommunications Act of 1996, the position in US with regard to cyber defamation was such that the Courts applied the common law definition of "publisher," which held liable anyone who exercised a substantial degree of editorial control over the distributed product. This definition distinguished between a distributor, such as a newsstand or a library, and a publisher, such as a newspaper or book author. Distributors were not to be held liable for the information they disseminated, while those who reviewed content before publication would be held liable. Courts generally analyzed ISP liability under the same standards applied to newspapers and other media.

Data Security

Data security is the means of ensuring that data is kept safe from corruption and that access to it is suitably controlled. Thus data security helps to ensure privacy. It also helps in protecting personal data.

DATA SECURITY TECHNOLOGIES

Disk Encryption

Disk encryption refers to encryption technology that encrypts data on a hard disk drive. Disk encryption typically takes form in either software or hardware. Disk encryption is often referred to as on-the-fly encryption ("OTFE") or transparent encryption.

Hardware Based Mechanisms for Protecting Data

Software based security solutions encrypt the data to prevent data from being stolen. However, a malicious programme or a hacker may corrupt the data in order to make it unrecoverable or unusable. Similarly, encrypted operating systems can be corrupted by a malicious programme or a hacker, making the system unusable.

Hardware-based security solutions can prevent read and write access to data and hence offers very strong protection against tampering and unauthorized access. Hardware based or assisted computer security offers an alternative to software-only computer security. Security tokens such as those using PKCS#11 may be more secure due to the physical access required in order to be compromised. Access is enabled only when the token is connected and correct PIN is entered. However, dongles can be used by anyone who can gain physical access to it. Newer technologies in hardware based security solves this problem offering fool proof security for data.

Working of Hardware based security: A hardware device allows a user to login, logout and to set different privilege levels by doing manual actions. The device uses biometric technology to prevent malicious users from logging in, logging out, and changing privilege levels. The current state of a user of the device is read by controllers in peripheral devices such as harddisks. Illegal access by a malicious user or a malicious programme is interrupted based on the current state of a user by harddisk and DVD controllers making illegal access to data impossible. Hardware based access control is more secure than protection provided by the operating systems as operating systems are vulnerable to malicious attacks by viruses and hackers. The data on harddisks can be corrupted after a malicious access is obtained. With hardware based protection, software cannot manipulate the user privilege levels, it is impossible for a hacker or a malicious programme to gain access to secure data protected by hardware or perform unauthorized privileged operations. The hardware protects the operating system image and file system privileges from being tampered. Therefore, a completely secure system can be created using a combination of hardware based security and secure system administration policies.

Backups

Backups are used to ensure data which is lost can be recovered

Data Masking

Data Masking of structured data is the process of obscuring (masking) specific data within a database table or cell to ensure that data security is maintained and sensitive information is not exposed to unauthorized personnel. This may include masking the data from users (for example so banking customer representatives can only see the last 4 digits of a customers national identity number), developers (who need real production data to test new software releases but should not be able to see sensitive financial data), outsourcing vendors, etc.

Data Erasure

Data erasure is a method of software-based overwriting that completely destroys all electronic data residing on a hard drive or other digital media to ensure that no sensitive data is leaked when an asset is retired or reused.

INTERNATIONAL LAWS AND STANDARDS

International Laws

In the UK, the Data Protection Act is used to ensure that personal data is accessible to those whom it concerns, and provides redress to individuals if there are inaccuracies. This is particularly important to ensure individuals are treated fairly, for example for credit checking purposes. The Data Protection Act states that only individuals and companies with legitimate and lawful reasons can process personal information and cannot be shared.

International Standards

The International Standard ISO/IEC 17799 covers data security under the topic of information security, and one of its cardinal principles is that all stored information, i.e. data, should be owned so that it is clear whose responsibility it is to protect and control access to that data. The Trusted Computing Group is an organization that helps standardize computing security technologies.

Database Model

A *'database model'* is the theoretical foundation of a database and fundamentally determines in which manner data can be stored, organized and manipulated in a database system. It thereby defines the infrastructure offered by a particular database system. The most popular example of a database model is the relational model.

A database model is a theory or specification describing how a database is structured and used. Several such models have been suggested. Common models include:

- Hierarchical model
- Network model
- Relational model
- Entity-relationship
- Object-relational model
- Object model.

A data model is not just a way of structuring data: it also defines a set of operations that can be performed on the data. The relational model, for example, defines operations such as select, project, and join. Although these operations may not be explicit in a particular query language, they provide the foundation on which a query language is built.

MODELS

Various techniques are used to model data structure. Most database systems are built around one particular data model, although it is increasingly common for products to offer support for more than one model. For any one logical model various physical implementations may be possible, and most products will offer the user some level of control in tuning the physical implementation, since the choices that are made have a significant effect on performance. An example of this is the relational model: all serious implementations of the relational model allow the creation of indexes which provide fast access to rows in a table if the values of certain columns are known.

Flat Model

The flat (or table) model consists of a single, two-dimensional array of data elements, where all members of a given column are assumed to be similar values, and all members of a row are assumed to be related to one another. For instance, columns for name and password that might be used as a part of a system security database. Each row would have the specific password associated with an individual user. Columns of the table often have a type associated with them, defining them as character data, date or time information, integers, or floating point numbers. This may not strictly qualify as a data model, as defined above.

Hierarchical Model

In a hierarchical model, data is organized into a tree-like structure, implying a single upward link in each record to describe the nesting, and a sort field to keep the records in a particular order in each same-level list. Hierarchical structures were widely used in the early mainframe database management systems, such as the Information Management System (IMS) by IBM, and now describe the structure of XML documents. This structure allows one 1:N relationship between two types of data. This structure is very efficient to describe many relationships in the real world; recipes, table of contents, ordering of paragraphs/verses, any nested and sorted information. However, the hierarchical structure is inefficient for certain database operations when a full path (as opposed to upward link and sort field) is not also included for each record. Parent–child relationship: Child may only have one parent but a parent can have multiple children. Parents and children are tied together by links called "pointers". A parent will have a list of pointers to each of their children.

Network Model

The network model (defined by the CODASYL specification) organizes data using two fundamental constructs, called *records* and *sets*. Records contain fields (which may be organized hierarchically, as in the programming language COBOL). Sets (not to be confused with mathematical sets) define one-to-many relationships between records: one owner, many members. A record may be an owner in any number of sets, and a member in any number of sets.

The network model is a variation on the hierarchical model, to the extent that it is built on the concept of multiple branches (lower-level structures) emanating from one or more nodes (higher-level structures), while the model differs from the hierarchical model in that branches can be connected to multiple nodes. The network model is able to represent redundancy in data more efficiently than in the hierarchical model.

The operations of the network model are navigational in style: a programme maintains a current position, and navigates from one record to another by following the relationships in which the record participates. Records can also be located by supplying key values. Although it is not an essential feature of the model, network databases generally implement the set relationships by means of pointers that directly address the location of a record on disk. This gives excellent retrieval performance, at the expense of operations such as database loading and reorganization. Most object databases use the navigational concept to provide fast navigation across networks of objects, generally using object identifiers as "smart" pointers to related objects. Objectivity/DB, for instance, implements named 1:1, 1:many, many:1 and many:many named relationships that can cross databases. Many object databases also support SQL, combining the strengths of both models.

Relational Model

The relational model was introduced by E.F. Codd in 1970 as a way to make database management systems more independent of any particular application. It is a mathematical model defined in terms of predicate logic and set theory. The products that are generally referred to as relational databases in fact implement a model that is only an approximation to the mathematical model defined by Codd. Three key terms are used extensively in relational database models: *relations, attributes,* and *domains*. A relation is a table with columns and rows. The named columns of the relation are called attributes, and the domain is the set of values the attributes are allowed to take.

The basic data structure of the relational model is the table, where information about a particular entity (say, an employee) is represented in rows (also called tuples) and columns. Thus, the "relation" in "relational database" refers to the various tables in the database; a relation is a set of tuples. The columns enumerate the various attributes of the entity (the employee's name, address or phone number, for example), and a row is an actual instance of the entity (a specific employee) that is represented by the relation. As a result, each tuple of the employee table represents various attributes of a single employee.

All relations (and, thus, tables) in a relational database have to adhere to some basic rules to qualify as relations. First, the ordering of columns is immaterial in a table. Second, there can't be identical tuples or rows in a table. And third, each tuple will contain a single value for each of its attributes.

A relational database contains multiple tables, each similar to the one in the "flat" database model. One of the strengths of the relational model is that, in principle, any value occurring in two different records (belonging to the same table or to different tables), implies a relationship among those two records.

Yet, in order to enforce explicit integrity constraints, relationships between records in tables can also be defined explicitly, by identifying or non-identifying parent-child relationships characterized by assigning cardinality (1:1, (0)1:M, M:M). Tables can also have a designated single attribute or a set of attributes that can act as a "key", which can be used to uniquely identify each tuple in the table. A key that can be used to uniquely identify a row in a table is called a primary key. Keys are commonly used to join or combine data from two or more tables. For example, an *Employee* table may contain a column named *Location* which contains a value that matches the key of a *Location* table. Keys are also critical in the creation of indexes, which facilitate fast retrieval of data from large tables.

Any column can be a key, or multiple columns can be grouped together into a compound key. It is not necessary to define all the keys in advance; a column can be used as a key even if it was not originally intended to be one.

A key that has an external, real-world meaning (such as a person's name, a book's ISBN, or a car's serial number) is sometimes called a "natural" key. If no natural key is suitable (think of the many people named *Brown*), an arbitrary or surrogate key can be assigned (such as by giving employees ID numbers).

In practice, most databases have both generated and natural keys, because generated keys can be used internally to create links between rows that cannot break, while natural keys can be used, less reliably, for searches and for integration with other databases. (For example, records in two independently developed databases could be matched up by social security number, except when the social security numbers are incorrect, missing, or have changed.)

Dimensional Model

The dimensional model is a specialized adaptation of the relational model used to represent data in data warehouses in a way that data can be easily summarized using OLAP queries. In the dimensional model, a database consists of a single large table of facts that are described using dimensions and measures.

A dimension provides the context of a fact (such as who participated, when and where it happened, and its type) and is used in queries to group related facts together. Dimensions tend to be discrete and are often hierarchical; for example, the location might include the building, state, and country. A measure is a quantity describing the fact, such as revenue. It's important that measures can be meaningfully aggregated - for example, the revenue from different locations can be added together. In an OLAP query, dimensions are chosen and the facts are grouped and added together to create a summary. The dimensional model is often implemented on top of the relational model using a star schema, consisting of one table containing the facts and surrounding tables containing the dimensions.

Particularly complicated dimensions might be represented using multiple tables, resulting in a snowflake schema. A data warehouse can contain multiple star schemas that share dimension tables, allowing them to be used together. Coming up with a standard set of dimensions is an important part of dimensional modeling.

Objectional Database Models

In recent years, the object-oriented paradigm has been applied to database technology, creating a new programming model known as object databases. These databases attempt to bring the database world and the application programming world closer together, in particular by ensuring that the database uses the same type system as the application programme.

This aims to avoid the overhead (sometimes referred to as the *impedance mismatch*) of converting information between its representation in the database (for example as rows in tables) and its representation in the application programme (typically as objects).

At the same time, object databases attempt to introduce the key ideas of object programming, such as encapsulation and polymorphism, into the world of databases. A variety of these ways have been tried for storing objects in a database. Some products have approached the problem from the application programming end, by making the objects manipulated by the programme persistent.

This also typically requires the addition of some kind of query language, since conventional programming languages do not have the ability to find objects based on their information content. Others have attacked the problem from the database end, by defining an object-oriented data model for the database, and defining a database programming language that allows full programming capabilities as well as traditional query facilities.

Object databases suffered because of a lack of standardization: although standards were defined by ODMG, they were never implemented well enough to ensure interoperability between products.

Nevertheless, object databases have been used successfully in many applications: usually specialized applications such as engineering databases or molecular biology databases rather than mainstream commercial data processing. However, object database ideas were picked up by the relational vendors and influenced extensions made to these products and indeed to the SQL language.

12

Data Theft in Cyber Space: Issues and Laws

The rapid development of Information technology poses new challenges before the law. These challenges are not confined to any single traditional legal category but arise in, for example, Criminal Law, Intellectual Property Law, Contract and Tort. One such challenge is the growing menace of "Data Theft". It is the term used when any information in the form of data is illegally copied or taken from a business or other individual without his knowledge or consent.

DATA AS A VALUABLE ASSET

Data is a valuable asset in this modern era of Information Technology (IT). Data is an important raw-material for Call Centers and I.T. Companies. Data has also become an important tool and weapon for Corporates to capture larger market shares. Due to the importance of Data in this new era, its security has become a major issue with the I.T. industry. The piracy of data is a threat, faced by the I.T. players, who spend millions to compile or buy data from the market. Their profits depend upon the security of the Data.

Issues

The major issue regarding Data Theft is its International character, for example Systems may be accessed in USA, the data manipulated in China and the consequences felt in India. The result of this ability is that different sovereignties, jurisdictions, laws and rules will come into play which again is an issue in itself. Further, collection of evidence in such circumstances become another issue as investigation in three different countries, all of whom may not be in talking terms, is almost impossible and poor technical know-how of our cops adds to the woes. Also, the lack of coordination between different investigating agencies and a not-so-sure extradition process is another head ache. However the biggest of all these issues is the lack of specific laws in the country dealing with this crime, so even if the culprit is caught he can easily get away by picking and choosing any of the of various loopholes in our law.

Does India have Sufficient Laws?

The problem of data theft which has emerged as one of the major cyber crimes worldwide has attracted little attention of law makers in India. Unlike U.K which has The Data Protection Act, 1984 there is no specific legislation in India to tackle this problem, though India boasts of its Information Technology Act, 2000 to address the ever growing menace of cyber crimes, including data theft. The truth is that our IT Act, 2000 is not well equipped to tackle such crimes. The various provisions of the IT Act, 2000 which deal with the problem to some extent are briefly discussed below.

Section 43:- This section provides protection against destruction and unauthorized access of the computer system by imposing heavy penalty up to one crore. The unauthorized downloading, extraction and copying of data are also covered under this section. Clause 'C' of this section imposes penalty for unauthorized introduction of computer viruses of contaminants. Clause 'G' provides penalties for assisting the unauthorized access.

Section 65:- This section provides for computer source code. If anyone knowingly or intentionally conceals, destroys, alters or causes another to do as such shall have to suffer imprisonment of up to 3 years or fine up to 2 lakh rupees. Thus protection has been provided against tampering of computer source documents.

Section 66:- Protection against hacking has been provided under this section. As per this section, hacking is defined as any act with an intention to cause wrongful loss or damage to any person or with the knowledge that wrongful loss or damage will be caused to any person and information residing in a computer resource must be either destroyed, deleted, altered or its value and utility get diminished. This section imposes the penalty of imprisonment of up to three years or fine up to two lakh rupees or both on the hacker.

Section 70:- This section provides protection to the data stored in the protected system. Protected systems are those computers, computer system or computer network to which the appropriate government, by issuing gazette information in the official gazette, declared it as a protected system. Any access or attempt to secure access of that system in contravention of the provision of this section will make the person accessed liable for punishment of imprisonment which may extend to ten years and shall also be liable to fine.

Section 72:- This section provides protection against breach of confidentiality and privacy of the data. As per this, any person upon whom powers have been conferred under IT Act and allied rules to secure access to any electronic record, book, register, correspondence, information document of other material discloses it to any other person, shall be punished with imprisonment which may extend to two years or with fine which may extend to one lakh rupees or both.

Can Data Theft be Covered under IPC?

Section 378 of the Indian Penal Code, 1860 defines 'Theft' as follows:-

Theft – Whoever, intending to take dishonestly any movable property out of the possession of any person without that person's consent, moves that property in order to such taking, is said to commit theft.

Section 22 of I.P.C., 1860 defines "movable property" as follows:-

"The words "movable property" are intended to include corporeal property of every description, except land and things attached to the earth or permanently fastened to anything which is attached to the earth."

Since Section 378 I.P.C., only refers to "Movable Property" i.e. Corporeal Property, and Data by itself is intangible, it is not covered under the definition of "Theft". However, if Data is stored in a medium (CD, Floppy etc.) and such medium is stolen, it would be covered under the definition of 'Theft', since the medium is a movable property. But, if Data is transmitted electronically, i.e., in intangible form, it would not specifically constitute theft under the IPC.

"Data", in its intangible form, can at best be put at par with electricity. The question whether electricity could be stolen, arose before the Hon'ble Supreme Court in the case "Avtar Singh vs. State of Punjab" (AIR 1965 SC 666). Answering the question, the Supreme Court held that electricity is not a movable property, hence, is not covered under the definition of 'Theft' under Section 378 IPC. However, since Section 39 of the Electricity Act extended Section 378 IPC to apply to electricity, so it so became specifically covered within the meaning of "Theft". It is therefore imperative that a provision like in the Electricity Act be inserted in the IT Act, 2000 to extend the application of section 378 IPC to data theft specifically.

What do we need and why do we need?

It is imperative in today's world that an emerging IT super power like India has a comprehensive legislation to protect its booming IT and BPO Industries (worst affected industries) against such crimes. Though the IT Act may appear sufficient in this regard but it is not comprehensive enough to tackle the minute technological intricacies involved in such a crime which leaves loopholes in the law and the culprits get away easily. Since this problem is not confined to one nation and has international dimensions, India must look forward to be a signatory to any international convention or treaty in this regard. Also it high time that our national police organizations are trained to deal with such crimes.

IPR And Enforcement Mechanism: Problem And Prospects

"Determine that things can and shall be done and then we shall find the way" - *Abraham Lincoln*

The objective of IPR is to give the greatest good to greatest number. In other words this approach states that these rights induce people to behave in the ways that increase socially valuable goods and services and distribute these goods and services in the fashion that maximizes the net profit that people reap from them. The distinctive characteristics of most intellectual products are that they are easily replicated eg.Copyright and this can be easily done when a person is working in digital environment. Digital environment is intrinsically different from print and mass media. The digital environment can be characterized as ephemeral and ethereal. In the words of Benkler," There are three attributes of information society:

1. Plasticity
2. Transmissibility
3. Processibility.

The plasticity, transmissibility and processibility are unique to digital environment. These characteristics are the product of electric impulses of binary language of 0's and 1's.At best, they are symbols and therefore intangibles. These symbols are converted in human readable forms and also know no borders. Written and printed texts, sounds, speech and pictures can be reduced to 0's and 1's and once reduced they become signals and hence vulnerable to mutations by the use for multimedia, become capable of being combined, separated or manipulated in any or all forms of expressions in ways which were never thought of. However it is not the intangibility alone which is problematic because Common Law incorporates incorporeal rights. The problem is intangibility plus plasticibility, transmissibility and processibility which require law and legal institutions for remapping of the contours of digital environment.

The digital environment offers a wide range of possibilities to all stake holders. In particular, the technical development has moved the internet increasingly from a centralized structure where the users utilizes those contents offered by website to one where more powerful devices with cheaper connectivity and faster transmission speeds, offer consumers access to richer online contents. The advent of broadband promised ubiquitous access to all types of intellectual property in a manner previously not possible. This permits not only a greater dissemination of such Intellectual Property, but also stimulates consumer demands for the services that enabled access. The problem arises just after the contents take the digital form and are put on internet. There are some inherent weaknesses associated with the management of digital rights as the same being prone to violation by use of technology itself. There have been several efforts to overcome the problem and find a way for the efficient management and the protection of digital rights. It has rightly been recognized that digital rights neither be protected nor be enforced unless solution for the problem is sought in the technology itself.

As with the ever developing technological advancement the number of people using internet services is increasing so is the malpractices to negate the interests of IPR and to reproduce the contents available thereon. The most common act of violation is observed as piracy, which has not earlier been specifically defined in the Copyright Act 1957 or in any other legislation dealing in Intellectual Property Rights. Even IT Act, 2000 does not provide specific provision dealing with piracy.

This paper is an attempt to analyze the Intellectual Property violation with special reference to digital rights management. Copyright and its related rights are essential to human creativity, by giving creators incentives in the form of recognition and fair economic rewards. Under this system of rights, creators are assured that their works can be disseminated without fear of unauthorized copying or piracy. This in turn helps increased access to the work and further enhances enjoyment of culture, knowledge and entertainment all over the world. It is recognized worldwide that copyright piracy is a serious crime which not only adversely affects the creative potential of society by denying the creators their legitimate dues, but also causes economic losses to all those who had invested their money in bringing out copyrighted material in various forms for use by the end users.

With advancement in technology new techniques have been developed to control the internet piracy on copyrighted contents. Digital Rights Management is an impressive attempt amongst such techniques. DRM is primarily a process of insertion of particulars of the intellectual property into it. And, therefore it is an aid to curb the piracy practices.

Digital Rights and Information Management is usually construed as protection of copyright and controlling internet piracy but our submission identifies DRM as a technology used to identify, describe, distribute and trading of contents and regulation and enforcement policies on digital media. Information stored on electronic form is cheaper, easy to store, retrieve and speedier to communicate. These advantages of Web have attracted many people and easy access to information on the website may result in conflict with their copyright interests.

Globalization has forced the copyright issues to forefront because large number of copyright products is traded internationally. But the challenge imposed by the development and growth of the internet to the existing copyright laws is immense. There are several issues to be discussed:

1. What is copyrighted on contents available on Internet?
2. How should one decide where the copyright infringement has taken place?
3. Who should be held liable for copyright infringement and how?
4. How the balance is to be achieved in protecting the works of the author and the usage and awareness of works of such authors?
5. How does the DRM help in the copyright protection and enforcement?

THE INDIAN CYBERSPACE

The National Informatics Centre (NIC) was set up as early as 1975 with the goal of providing IT solutions to the government. Between 1986 and 1988, three NWs were set up: INDONET, connecting the IBM mainframe installations that made up India's computer infrastructure; NICNET (the NIC Network), being a nationwide very small aperture terminal (VSAT) NW for public sector organisations as well as to connect the central government with the state governments and district administrations; and the

Education and Research Network (ERNET), to serve the academic and research communities.

Policies such as the New Internet Policy of 1998 paved the way for multiple Internet service providers (ISPs) and saw the Internet user base grow from 1.4 million in 1999 to over 15 million by 2003. Though the rate of growth has slowed subsequently, with Internet users now approximately numbering 100 million, exponential growth is again expected as Internet access increasingly shifts to mobile phones and tablets, with the government making a determined push to increase broadband penetration from its present level of about 6%.

The target for broadband is 160 million households by 2016 under the National Broadband Plan. Despite the low numbers in relation to the population, Indians have been active users of the Internet across various segments. The two top e-mail providers, Gmail and Yahoo, had over 34 million users registered from India.

Similar figures have also been seen in the social networking arena, which is the most recent entrant to the cyber platform. India currently has the fastest growing user base for Facebook and Twitter, the two top social networking sites. An indication of the rapid pace of adaptation to the Internet in India is that Indian Railways, India's top e-commerce retailer, saw its online sales go up from 19 million tickets in 2008 to 44 million in 2009, with a value of Rs. 3800 crore ($875 million).

Even though the Indian government was a late convert to computerisation, there has been an increasing thrust on e-governance, seen as a cost-effective way of taking public services to the masses across the country. Critical sectors such as Defence, Energy, Finance, Space, Telecommunications, Transport, Land Records, Public Essential Services and Utilities, Law Enforcement and Security all increasingly depend on NWs to relay data, for communication purposes and for commercial transactions. The National e-governance Programme (NeGP) is one of the most ambitious in the world and seeks to provide more than 1200 governmental services online.

Looking to the future, the Cisco Visual Networking Index estimates that India's Internet traffic will grow nine-fold between now and 2015, topping out at 13.2 Exabytes in 2015, from 1.6 Exabytes in 2010. That will be the equivalent of the data contained in 374,372 DVDs being carried every hour through these NWs.

In terms of contribution to the economy, the ICT sector has grown at an annual compounded rate of 33% over the last decade. The contribution of the IT-ITeS industry to GDP increased from 5.2% in 2006-7 to 6.4% in 2010-11. Much of the activities of the IT/BPO sector, which was responsible for putting India on the services export map, would not have been possible but for the cost-efficiencies provided through the expansion of global data NWs.

The government has ambitious plans to raise cyber connectivity. There has been a boom in e-commerce, and many activities related to e-governance are now being carried out over the Internet.

As we grow more dependent on the Internet for our daily activities, we also become more vulnerable to any disruptions caused in and through cyberspace. The rapidity with which this sector has grown has meant that governments and private companies are still trying to figure out both the scope and meaning of security in cyberspace and apportioning responsibility. As in other countries, much of the infrastructure related to cyberspace is with the private sector, which also provides many of the critical services, ranging from banking, to electricity to running airports and other key transportation infrastructure.

Taking telecommunications as a case in point, CII in India comprises around 150 Internet and telecom service providers, offering Internet, mobile and wireless connectivity to a user base of nearly 800 million. A major portion of data communication is facilitated by submarine cables.

India has landing points for major submarine cable systems which are minimally protected. A preview of what could happen by way of these cables being disabled took place in 2008 when a series of outages and cable cuts in undersea cables running through the Suez Canal, in the Persian Gulf and Malaysia caused massive communications disruptions to India and West Asia.

Other sectors that could be subject to serious threats include the financial sector, which has largely transferred operations online.

Stock exchanges in the United States and Hong Kong have reportedly been subject to cyber attacks. The electricity grid is also vulnerable with the inevitable move towards a smart grid, given the economic and efficiency factors. The protection of critical infrastructure is a complex task requiring forethought, planning, strong laws, technologies, PPP and resources. For all these reasons it needs to be given top priority by the government. The country cannot afford to wait indefinitely for a robust policy to protect this critical infrastructure.

Need for a Comprehensive Cyber Security Policy

As in most countries around the world, the cyber security scenario in India is one of relative chaos and a sense of insecurity arising out of the periodic reports of cyber espionage, cyberterrorism, cyber warfare and cyber crime. The complexity of the issue has resulted in a virtual paralysis. Legal and law enforcement mechanisms have not shifted gears fast enough to grapple with growing cyber crime. Periodic newspaper reports indicate that a wide variety of offensive measures are being contemplated by various agencies, but that is all. The lack of a coherent cyber security policy will seriously interfere with India's national security and economic development.

It is essential that more attention at the highest levels is paid to ensuring that cyber-related vulnerabilities that can impact on critical sectors are identified and removed. A coherent and comprehensive cyber security policy will have several major elements, including accurate conceptualisation of cyberspace threats; building of robust cyberspace through a variety of measures, including technical, legal, diplomatic, international cooperation; creation of adequate organisational structures; strengthening of PPPs; HR development; and implementation of best practices and guidelines. The list is only illustrative. India's approach to cyber security has so far been ad hoc and piecemeal. A number of organisations have been created but their precise roles have not been defined nor synergy has been created among them. As it transcends a vast domain, this falls within the charter of the NSCS.

However, there appears to be no institutional structure for implementation of policies. Neither the private sector nor government has been able to build information systems that can be described as reasonably robust. There has not been enough thinking on the implications of cyber warfare.

Meanwhile, many countries are seriously engaged in attending to their cyber security doctrines and strategies. The US, Russia, UK, France, Australia, Germany, New Zealand, South Korea, China, Brazil, South Africa, Denmark, Sweden, EU, Singapore, Malaysia–the list is long and growing–are actively engaged in ensuring a safe and secure cyber environment for their citizens. The international community is also engaged in a variety of discussions. NATO has taken the task of creating cyber security institutions in member countries. A group of governmental experts (GGE), set up by the UN Secretary General, gave a report in 2010 on "developments in the field of ICT in the context of international security". The report noted that there was increasing evidence that states were developing ICTs as "instruments of warfare and intelligence, and for political purposes". To confront challenges in cyberspace, the GGE recommended cooperation among likeminded partners, among states, between states, and between states and civil society and the private sectors.

The draft cyber security policy document put out by the DIT for public discussion is an important step but it is essentially a departmental effort, not taking a whole of-government approach. DIT does not have jurisdiction over departments. The document lists a number of major stakeholders, including: (1) National Information Board (NIB); (2) National Crisis Management Committee (NCMC); (3) NSCS; (4) Ministry of Home Affairs (MHA); (5) Ministry of Defence; (6) DIT; (7) DoT; (8) National Cyber Response Centre (NCRC); (9) CERT-In; (10) National Information Infrastructure Protection Centre (NIIPC); (11) National Disaster Management Authority (NDMA); (12) Standardisation, Testing and Quality Certification (STQC) Directorate; and (13) sectoral CERTs. However, only CERT-In is mandated under the IT Amendment Act, 2008 to serve as the national agency in charge of cyber security. The Act also provided for a national nodal agency for protection of CII but it is not clear whether such an organisation exists other than on paper; NDMA and some others play only a peripheral role; and many of the sectoral CERTs are yet to come up. In the meantime, real oversight over cyber security may be said to be distributed amongst the Ministries of Communication and Technology, Home Affairs and Defence, and the office of the NSA.

COUNTERING THREATS THROUGH CYBERSPACE

In the United States, surveillance has been at the heart of changes in traditional defence, as well as attempts to counter so-called "asymmetric" security threats. Guided by the principle that "what can be seen can be hit," battlefield surveillance was at the heart of the U.S., "revolution in military affairs" during the 1970s, 1980s, and 1990s. Two asymmetric threats in particular have caught the imaginations of those within the United States who have worked consistently to increase government surveillance capabilities: the threats of terrorism and cyber attack.

The idea that information-age conflict in general, and the fight against terrorism in particular, constitute a global "battle for hearts and minds" has been popular among U.S., defence and security professionals for at least a decade. Various observers have worried about terrorist use of the Internet as a tool for fundraising, organising, recruiting, and propaganda. It is in this spirit that Arquilla has urged the U.S., government to remove terrorist web sites from the Internet. Likewise, it is in this spirit that groups of self-organised, online volunteers engage in various types of online activities in support of the U.S., "war on terrorism," including intelligence gathering and counter-propaganda activities.

The work of Shannen Rossmiller and her group Phoenix Global Information Systems is the most notable example of intelligence-focused, volunteer cyber-counterterrorism. In response to the terrorist attacks of September 11, 2001, Rossmiller, a municipal judge from a small town in Montana, began trolling jihadist web sites to learn more about those who had attacked the United States and what they might be planning next. In January 2003, Rossmiller joined forces with at least six other individuals whom she met in the online discussion forum. They created a web site and began calling themselves 7-Seas Global Intelligence.

Members of 7-Seas live in the United States, Canada, Australia, and Singapore and include an economist, a physicist, a computer systems engineer, a corporate security consultant, and a private investigator. Rossmiller and members of 7-Seas have used a number of techniques to gather intelligence about terrorists online. These have included creating multiple false personas complete with pictures and detailed life histories. To appear as convincing as possible to her targets, Rossmiller has learned Arabic, studied the Quran, and read Arabic literature. They also employ translation software, tools to map the IP addresses of the online jihadists with whom they interact, software to mask their own IP addresses and make it appear that they are located in the Middle East or South Asia, and even spyware that is remotely installed on the computers of some of those that they investigate.

While their initial goal was to predict future terrorist attacks, they soon shifted to gathering and analysing information from terrorist web sites, forums, and chat rooms, and then turning that information over to authorities. Rossmiller's efforts in particular have contributed to two high-profile arrests of would-be terrorists, including the 2004 case of Specialist Ryan Anderson, a Washington state National Guardsman who attempted to sell classified information about vulnerabilities of U.S., weapons systems to an al-Qa'ida member that he met online.

That al-Qa'ida member was actually Rossmiller. Anderson is now in prison serving five consecutive life sentences, the harshest penalty yet dealt to an American in the war on terrorism. In another case, and again posing online as a member of al- Qa'ida, Rossmiller uncovered a plot by Pennsylvania resident and al-Qa'ida sympathiser, Michael Reynolds, to blow up several gas pipelines and oil refineries in the United States. Reynolds was convicted and is now serving fifty seven years in prison. Rossmiller is reported to have provided information to U.S., law enforcement or intelligence in as many as 240 other cases, leading to the detention of dozens of suspects worldwide and even some arrests and deportations of terrorism suspects from the United States.

For all the success that Rossmiller and 7-Seas has had, there remains a great deal of ambivalence, ambiguity, and tension in their relationship with authorities. On the one hand, the volunteers are motivated in part by calls by authorities to be vigilant. They believe authorities' claims about the seriousness of the threat of terrorism and want to help. One the other hand, they are also motivated by feelings that the government is either unable or unwilling to counter extremists' use of the Internet. Similarly, while Rossmiller has received a great deal of praise and assistance from authorities—the FBI has compensated her for her expenses, provided her with Arabic translation services, and provided her with security, a former Secretary of Commerce has said that she deserves a medal, she has been consulted by the Defence Intelligence Agency, and she has been an invited speaker at an FBI cyber security conference—these agencies have also sometimes expressed concern or doubt about her work and the work of others like her.

For her part, Rossmiller has at times complained that her work is being undervalued by authorities and has been clear to assert her independence from the state. But for all the tensions between authorities and volunteers, and for all that Rossmiller and 7-Seas have tried to distance themselves from the authorities, they nonetheless seek both approval and profit from the authorities. Both 7-Seas and later Phoenix Global Intelligence Systems have sought government contracts and intelligence and security consulting work for government clients.

In 2009, Rossmiller announced at an FBI-sponsored cyber security conference that she had formed a company and was seeking a partnership with a defence contractor to offer cyber-intelligence training and services to the government. She has been encouraged to do so by former CIA Director, James Woolsey. In the end, there are real reasons for tension and for concern. Both sides are right. The authorities likely cannot monitor and analyse that much Web content, making the work of the volunteers indispensable.

However, the volunteers do not have the ability to physically arrest suspects or materially disrupt terrorist planning or operations in any significant way, making the capabilities of the state indispensable in achieving their goals. Additionally, there are clear difficulties in making the relationship work. Sometimes authorities and volunteers can work at cross purposes. If authorities rely too much on volunteers, or if the role of volunteers becomes formally institutionalised, then their main value can be compromised. Finally, Michael Reynolds' defence strategy—i.e., claiming that he too was just trying to catch terrorists online like Rossmiller—also points to some of the potential difficulties in this new relationship between producers and consumers of security online.

COUNTERING THREATS TO CYBER SPACE

Other groups have worked to counter threats to cyber space. This includes efforts to investigate and analyse cyber attack incidents such as denial of service attacks and targeted use of malware. Founded in August 2008 by former intelligence analyst Jeffrey Carr, Project Grey Goose was an experiment in online, volunteer, open source intelligence (OSINT) aimed at investigating possible Russian government involvement in the large-scale cyber attacks that hit the country of Georgia during the Russian military invasion earlier that month. On August 22, 2008, Carr used his blog to announce the project and to put out a call for volunteers.

The final cadre of twelve that was listed in the group's October 2008 report was comprised primarily of current and former members of the intelligence community, academic researchers, and defence and security professionals. Contributors to a second Grey Goose report released in early 2009 largely fit the same demographic profile. The group has described their OSINT methodology as relying on "data mining" and "machine translation" of "foreign language forums and social media sites," technical analysis of "serverlevel data," "an examination of geopolitical events occurring around the time of the cyber attacks," and "a review of the Nation State's military doctrine related to Information Warfare." They believe that the open source nature of their work is a distinct advantage, allowing them to work more quickly and with greater participation from international volunteers.

The two Grey Goose reports have had a substantial impact on shaping perceptions of Russia's involvement in the 2008 Georgia cyber attacks, as well as shaping public debate about the threat of cyber war. Members and supporters of Project Grey Goose even believe that data that they turned over to authorities may have prevented some cyber attacks, as well caused the Kremlin "to reduce its support of various [hacker] groups". Jeffrey Carr has become a sought-after expert on issues of cyber war, resulting in his publication of the book *Inside Cyber Warfare* for O'Reilly Media in 2009. Carr's book is now on the Commander's recommended reading list for members of U.S., Strategic Command, the parent organisation of the newly-formed U.S., Cyber Command.

Once again, the case of Project Grey Goose indicates the ambivalence and ambiguities that often exist between producers and consumers of security. Like Rossmiller and others, Carr has argued that bureaucratic inefficiencies often prevent government from effectively countering "terrorism in cyber space". One of those limitations, he argues, is that state actors do not yet understand the power of either the Internet, open sources of information, or collaborative processes of knowledge production.

Thus, governments have proven ill-equipped for countering terrorists online or meeting the challenge of cyber attacks. He sees Project Grey Goose as exemplary of the value of applying the open source software development model to intelligence work and hopes that "it will prove that we do not have to wait for official channels to adopt innovative solutions". Carr and his supporters identify Project Grey Goose as an example of what they call a "security trust network" (STN). Michael Sinkowitch, an executive at Fujitsu Australia who specialises in national security and intelligence, has defined STNs as "expert affiliations of interested organisations and individuals that can investigate and mitigate cyber crime threats".

Alexander Klimburg, a fellow at the Austrian Institute for International Affairs and a contributor to Carr's 2009 book, defines them as the liberal, democratic, Western antithesis to Russian and Chinese "patriotic hackers." Where "patriotic hackers" are seen as beholden to or controlled by the state and composed of malicious actors with a dubious moral code, STNs are defined as free to "choose when and if" to support a government, as trustworthy and credible partners for government, and as "shar[ing] a common moral code" based in "doing the right thing" and "operating within the remits of the law". Carr, Sinkowitsch, and Klimburg all see STNs like Project Grey Goose as examples of the security-producing "informal groups and volunteer networks" that Klimburg speaks about in the epigraph to this chapter.

In the realm of cyber security in particular, Klimburg has claimed that most work is already being done by STNs and business with "government bringing up the rear". He has claimed that STNs are particularly good at addressing the "attribution problem" in cyber security—i.e., figuring out the origin of a cyber attack, which is "a notoriously difficult task". Sinkowitsch has gone so far as to claim that cyber security STNs are able to "defeat, or at the very least limit the damage of, these adversaries [i.e., cyber attackers of various sorts]". But like the other cases of convergence security examined here, STNs too are ultimately dependent upon their relationship to the state.

Even Sinkowitsch admits that "There is not much they [STNs] can do about stopping the threats". Though STNs are theoretically free to choose when and if they work with the state, in practice having an impact requires working with the state. Since, the original call for volunteers for Project Grey Goose, Carr has solicited volunteers for a project he calls "Grey Balloons," which is an open-ended project to create a standing pool of volunteers that are ready and able to help the U.S., intelligence community with whatever challenges it might face. Grey Balloons is a reflection of Carr's "hope that a bridge could be established connecting intelligence community professionals with independent volunteers with the necessary expertise". Finally, as in the case of Rossmiller and cyber-counterterrorism, there is profit to be made in assisting the state.

In 2009, Project Grey Goose became Grey Logic, "a consultancy and information services provider to governments". It is perhaps unsurprising then that Sinkowitsch and Klimburg have encouraged Western governments to promote and support the formation of

STNs as a necessary component of their national cyber security strategies. Finally, there are real reasons for concern when it comes to STNs. When questioned about the legal status of STNs and whether their work borders on vigilantism, Sinkowitsch claimed that there is no legal problem with what STNs do because they rely on information that is freely available on the Web; they are merely collecting and analysing it in a different, more effective way.

But recent scandals over advertiser use of social media content, as well as the case of a defence contractor mining and analysing social media content to smear supporters of WikiLeaks and political opponents of the U.S., Chamber of Commerce, indicate that there are legitimate privacy and legal concerns when volunteers begin doing their own online intelligence work on behalf of the state or powerful corporate interests.

PATROLLING NATIONAL BORDERS IN CYBERSPACE

Online, volunteer cyber-surveillance efforts have also been used to aid in the production of more traditional forms of security, such as defending territorial integrity by patrolling national borders. Since, 9/11, the debate over immigration from the global South has been increasingly linked to the "War on Terror." Part of this linkage can be found in the actions and discourse of what are collectively called "Minutemen" groups. Minutemen groups are most known for their use of physical presence on the U.S.-Mexico border, especially in 2005, a presence spurred by organisers who wanted to draw attention to what they perceived to be the government's lack of intervention in illegal immigration.

Although the Minutemen are not a government agency, their border-watching efforts were meant to supplement—and not replace —the physical intervention of the U.S., Border Patrol; thus the Minutemen appropriated part of the state's power of surveillance without impinging on the state's monopoly on the use of force. In addition, Minutemen groups have also deployed "Cyber Minutemen," extending surveillance onto the Web. Using a mix of fibre-optic fencing, Web cameras, motion detectors, infrared sensors, and even aircraft, various Minutemen groups have posted images and live streams to a variety of Web sites.

This use of relatively inexpensive surveillance and Web technology is touted by Cyber Minutemen as a viable, high-tech, modern way for citizens to succeed where the state has ostensibly failed in stemming the flow of immigrants across the Mexican border. Jim Wood, founder of the nowdefunct Border Fence Project, argues that citizen groups are more efficient and cost-effective than state efforts to secure the border. "The bottom line is this," he argues in a letter to supporters, "Despite bureaucratic refusals, delays and boondoggles, we civilians on the border can build a national Border Fence without them, repairing the old and erecting the new... Therefore, we as American citizens and patriots must stand up and do this ourselves."

Part of the efficiency arises from the use of distributed volunteers across the Web; volunteers from as far away as Australia have reportedly spotted illegal border crossings. In this case, the convergence of state aims and privately deployed technologies echoes previous, new media "crowdsourcing" efforts such as Wikipedia and the NASA Clickworkers project. As in the other convergence security cases, Cyber Minutemen have enjoyed some support from the state, as well as from Internet entrepreneurs. Texas governor Rick Perry, the Texas Border Sheriff's Coalition, and private landowners joined Internet company BlueServo in a "publicprivate partnership" to distribute live feeds of the border to Web volunteers. This public-private partnership is a for-profit endeavor. BlueServo claims, "Because www.BlueServo.net is an internet social network, in the future, BlueServo anticipates that high volume of traffic to its web site will generate advertising revenue to defray the operations cost of the Virtual Community Watch to the Texas Border Sheriff's Coalition." Thus, in keeping with convergence media business practices, BlueServo intends to meld the Cyber Minutemen desire to secure the border with the political economy of attention found in other Web 2.0 sites such as Facebook and YouTube. This entrepreneurial form of convergence border security has also been proposed by the Heritage Foundation.

However, as with other convergence security groups, the Minutemen have had ambivalent, ambiguous, and tense relationships with the state. Although Texas Governor Perry and California Governor Arnold Schwarzenegger publicly endorsed the movement, George W. Bush referred to them as "vigilantes". The Department of Homeland Security rejected a proposal to formally integrate volunteer citizen patrols into the Border Patrol.

For their part, the Minutemen groups have not sought integration with the state. Rather, they have largely called for an increased police or military presence at the border; they tend to frame their activity as drawing attention to the perceived problem of illegal immigration, drug trafficking, and terrorism. In the main, the Minuteman movement has been strict with members about the use of violence; thus the Minutemen have been careful not to infringe on the state's monopoly on violence for fear of political and legal repercussions.

A large Minuteman group, the Minutemen Civil Defence Corps (MCDC), disbanded in 2010 not long after a leader in that organisation called for a "locked and loaded"—i.e., publicly armed—patrol of the border. The "locked and loaded" muster was intended as a show of arms rather than an explicit call to violence. However, the proposed muster led to an enthusiastic response among members that the MCDC leadership interpreted as potentially violent, stoking fears within the organisation that the MCDC would not be able to prevent members from using weapons on alleged illegal border crossers, thus echoing Bush's earlier fears of vigilantism. The leaders of the MCDC did not want to cross the border between civil society groups and state-sponsored military groups.

Ultimately, in the case of the Minutemen, their proposed virtual surveillance of the border was accepted by the state far easier than their proposed, *embodied* patrol of the border. While the MCDC disbanded in light of the potential use of force by members, BlueServo and its Web camera network remains active to this day. State officials who decry potential vigilantism at the border tend to ignore or tolerate the use of Web-based surveillance. Most state officials who want increased border security eschew Minutemen-style groups and opt instead for state-sanctioned groups such as the U.S., Border Patrol, the National Guard, or new bureaucratic formations such as the Department of Homeland Security.

INTERNATIONAL LAW ON DATA EXCLUSIVITY

The Pharmaceutical companies are demanding data exclusivity law by resorting to Article 39(3) of TRIPS. Article 39(3) of the TRIPS states that that "Members when requiring, as a condition of approving the marketing of pharmaceutical or of agricultural chemical products which utilize new chemical entities, the submission of undisclosed test or data, the origination of which involves a considerable effort, shall protect such data against unfair commercial use.

In addition, Members shall protect such data against disclosure, except where necessary to protect the public, or unless steps are taken to ensure that data are protected against unfair commercial use "But it should be remembered that Article 39(3) does not talk about "Data Exclusivity" but only about "unfair commercial use" and it is this phrase that is interpreted by Multi-national companies as containing "Data Exclusivity" provision and thus demanding data exclusivity law.

Case against Data Exclusivity Law

The demand for data exclusivity law has come under intense debate all over the world. Many generic drug manufacturers and public interest groups are against such data exclusivity law. Their main contention is that if such data exclusivity law is introduced in India, the Drug Controller of India (DCI), which is regulatory authority, will be barred from relying on test data, submitted by pharmaceutical giants, in granting marketing approval to generic medicines. Instead, it will ask the generic drug manufacturer to undertake its own clinical trials and submit test data to controller of drugs to assess the quality, efficacy and safety of the generic version of the drugs. Sine clinical trial is a very complex and time consuming process and demand huge investment in Research and Development, the generic companies usually lack the financial infrastructural capabilities to undertake such task and even if they undertake such task, it will led to significant increase in the price of such generic drugs because generic companies by using test data of innovator companies save significant expenditure cost which is reflected in their affordable pricing system and thus paves the way for easy accessibility of life saving drugs to common people.

Moreover, the long gestation period undertaken by generic companies in conducting clinical trials will delay the process of arrival of life saving drugs at affordable price in the market by a number of years and would amount to monopolization of the pharmaceutical giants. It is also said that since Indian drug companies export significant amount of life saving drugs to other developing and least developed countries, any significant rise in the pricing of such drugs or delay in the introduction of generic version of such drugs in the market would significantly affect the population in and out of the country. The argument against data exclusivity law is that it will have detrimental impact on public health. The absence of cheaper generics will put many life saving drugs out of the reach of patients suffering from deadliest diseases such as HIV/AIDS, diabetes, cancer and Alzheimer disease.

Secondly, It is argued that clinical trial process involves ethical questions, as the proposed drugs have to be tested on animals and then on the human beings, usually on volunteer patients, in order to determine its efficacy, quality and safety. If data exclusivity law is enacted, then generic drugs manufacturers have to undertake clinical trials for getting the marketing approval of the generic version of the same medicine and it will led to duplicative testing and it would also amount to unnecessary and possible human injury associated with clinical trial process. It is unethical to conduct clinical trials on the drugs, which have already proven effective. And it is also important to obviate social and economic costs of repetitive animal and human testing. Hence, data exclusivity law can be challenged on moral and ethical grounds also.

Thirdly, it is also argued that TRIPS agreement and specifically Article 39(3) does not at all refer to data exclusivity. It only talks about "unfair commercial use". The pharmaceutical giants are misinterpreting Article 39(3) and construing "unfair commercial use" as "data exclusivity" with the sole purpose of monopolizing pharmaceutical business all over the world and maximizing their revenue with utter disregard for accessibility of medicines for the poor.

Since it is very much clear that the term "unfair commercial use" appearing in Article 39(3) does not obligate implementation of data exclusivity law, the opponent is of the opinion that if such law is implemented it would amount to go beyond TRIPS agreement, in the light of the fact that Indian Government have also made clear that it is under no obligation to implement data exclusivity law under TRIPS Agreement. If such law is implemented it would amount to succumbing to the pressure of Multi-National companies and developed world and thus increasing the health care cost in the third world. The opponent points out that India is one of the largest global suppliers of the low-cost generic medicines and without access to it million of people in third world countries will lose access to such medicines.

Thus in Indian context, the issue acquires global importance since India is one of the top 10 pharmaceutical products of the world and is also the major supplier of such drugs to third world. Any exclusivity right which hampers the growth expectation of the India's pharmaceutical industry will have world wide ramification and would obstruct accessibility of life savings drugs to third world. Today 6.5 million people around the world urgently require HIV treatment and only 1.3 million are receiving therapy. The patenting regulation such as data exclusivity will severely restrict access to AIDS therapy globally.

To support their viewpoint, the opponent of data protection law points out how such measures in other countries is already preventing drug regulatory authorities from granting approval to generic medicines thus seriously delaying access to affordable generic version of medicines. For example, in Guatemala, in February 2004, Atazanvira drug used in HIV treatment, priced at US$ 10,000 per person per year, received data protection for five years under the law passed by the Guatemala government. However more generic version of Atazanavir cannot enter the Guatemalan market until 2009 as drug regulatory authorities have to provide data exclusivity protection to test data related to Atazanavir. As a result drug accessibility in the form of generic version of Atazanavir is severely restricted.

Fourthly, it is argued that data exclusivity law would led to ever greening of patent. The innovator companies will make minor modification of their drugs and will get it protected under data exclusivity law. Data exclusivity will encourage investment in modifying existing drugs rather than inventing new one. While patent would not cover data protection due to ever greening concept, data exclusivity is seen as new form of intellectual property right to effectively extend patent life. The Indian pharmaceutical alliance (IPA) argues that if data exclusivity law is implemented in India, and if data exclusivity allowed, say for five years, and a patented drug is introduced in the 17th year of the 20th year patent life, it could effectively extend the patent to seventeen plus five equaling 22 years and thus crossing the limit of patent protection of 20 years.

Fifthly, the greatest disadvantage of data exclusivity is that it could prevent the registration of generic version of medicines even where innovator drugs lack patentability. For example, when a pharmaceutical product does not meet the standard of patentability or when no patents are granted, the test data could still comes under "Data exclusivity" purview. Hence, pharmaceutical giants will get protection of both patented as well as non-patented products and it would amount to double protection. Thus, even when any patent, Multi-National Pharmaceutical companies do not protect a medicine are assured minimum period of monopoly in countries having law on data exclusivity.

Sixthly, one of the other disadvantages of implementing data exclusivity law is that it can defeat the provision of Compulsory Licensing. The Indian Patent Act under Section 84 contains law on Compulsory Licensing which can be enforced under certain conditions such as when patented drug is available in insufficient quantity or when the price is out of the reach of common people or in order to remedy anti-competition practice and in circumstance of extreme urgency or emergency. But if data exclusivity law protects such data, then the grant of Compulsory Licensing will be of no use to generic companies, as data exclusivity law will act as a barrier to marketing approval of generic version of patented drugs thus defeating the whole philosophy behind Compulsory Licensing.

Case for Data Exclusivity

The proponent for data exclusivity put forward the argument that test data, which are submitted to the drug regulatory authorities to assess the quality, efficacy and safety of the drug, are the result of huge and risky investment made by the innovator companies. According to Mr Hitesh Gajaria,partner, KPMG, "It takes around 8-10 years of intensive clinical research and trials and investment between $800 million to $1.2 billion to bring a new drug to the market". If such data are made available to the generic companies, it means that huge investment in Research and Development(R & D) made by the innovator companies to launch new drugs are unprotected. Echoing the same view, Mr Ranjit Sahani,vice-chairman and MD of Novartis points out that Research and Development is a high risk business.

He says that it takes around 15 years to bring out a new molecule and a whole lot of data to provide the safety and efficacy and toxicology data which is proprietary to the company It is extremely unfair to allow the third party commercial exploitation of such data which are obtained after huge investment of time and money. The proponents also points out that Article 39.3 of TRIPS talks about "unfair commercial use" and any commercial use of such data by generic companies without prior consent of the innovator companies would amount to "unfair commercial use" and thus violating India's obligation under TRIPS. Further where Substantial cost and expenditure is incurred by originator companies in the form of huge investment in R & D and clinical trials, it would be unfair and unjust to deprive him of legitimate and reasonable profits by allowing the generic companies to avoid the cost of undertaking similar procedure and coming out with the generic version of patented drugs without incurring expenditure on investment. This would amount to acting in manner contrary to prudent commercial practice.

Secondly, if such data are protected, it would encourage pharmaceutical giants to make massive investment in R & D which is complex, time consuming and most importantly very expensive. Such huge investment in R & D is beyond the scope of the domestic manufacturers and even outside the financial limit of the third world countries. Thus data exclusivity will act as a incentive for such companies to make more risky and huge investment in drugs and medicines. The proponents are of the view that developing countries with appropriate data exclusivity law will enjoy better access to more innovative products sooner.

Thirdly, it is being emphasized that since patent protection are not available in all countries, data exclusivity law at national level will encourage and act as an incentive for the innovator companies to launch innovative drugs in those markets and where adequate intellectual property protections are not available. And since it is not easy to launch the new products everyday, new uses are being found for the existing ones. While patent would not cover these because of ever greening concept, data exclusivity law can play a crucial role in protecting the investors interest where new uses are made of the existing products or where new products in the market lacks the standard of patentability or were denied patent protection.

Fourthly, it is said that data exclusivity law will encourage and boost Foreign Direct Investment (FDI) in the country by Multi-national pharmaceutical giants and it would be good for India's economic development. Concerned over absence of data exclusivity law in the country, multinational pharmaceutical companies are of the view that India could lose out on foreign investment in the pharma sector as protection of test data was the key to company decision on location of clinical trials. India's technological and research and development will expand with resultant economic benefits if the data exclusivity law is implemented in the country.

Fifthly, the proponents also argue that enactment of data exclusivity will encourage brain- gain as Indian scientists will return home to pursue innovation in their own country and will gain increased access to clinical trials in the country and hence Indian scientists will acquire global competitiveness and world class expertise in clinical trials in their own country.

Sixthly, one important argument advanced in favour of data exclusivity law is that, if implemented, India may be excluded from the list of "Priority Watch List" of United States Trade Representative (USTR) under special 301 of the U.S Trade Act of 1974.The Priority Watch List is the list of all those countries that failed to provide and adequate level of Intellectual Property (IP) protection or market access to U.S manufacturer that failed to provide an adequate level of IP protection. Special 301 is an important part of the U.S Trade Law that requires the USTR to identify countries that deny adequate protection for intellectual property rights or that deny fair equitable market access for the U.S companies and/or persons who rely on IP protection. Inclusion of India in the Priority Watch List is not good for country's economic development as it hampers the prospects of better trade relation with U.S and the prime reason for India's inclusion in the list is the absence of data exclusivity law in the country. Once India will implement such law, it will lead to significant expansion of India's trade relation with U.S.A.

Seventhly, the proponents argue that all the fears created regarding accessibility of the drugs with the implementation of data exclusivity law are baseless. They point out that when Patent Act was amended in 2005 as required by TRIPS Agreement, hue and cry were made by generic drug manufacturers and health activists that it will led to catastrophe in pricing, availability or access to essential medicines in India or in developing countries importing life saving drugs from India. Such arguments advanced against 2005 amendment proved to be baseless with no evidence of such increased inaccessibility or price rise of essential medicines in the country. Instead they point out that inclusion of data exclusivity law in the country will accelerate access to new medicine therapies and will encourage the companies to innovate new drugs in the exporting market which will improve the quality of health care in the country.

Bibliography

Ahuja, Vijay: *Network and Internet Security*. Academic Press, Inc.: Boston, 1996.

Amoroso, E. : *Fundamentals of Computer Security Technology*, Prentice Hall, Englewood Cliffs, 1994.

Augastine, Paul T : *Combating Cyber Crime,* Crescent Pub, Delhi, 2007.

BloomBecker, Buck: *Spectacular Computer Crimes*. Dow Jones-Irwin: Homewood, IL, 1990.

Brenner, Susan W. : *Cybercrime : Criminal Threats from Cyberspace,* Pentagon Press, Delhi, 2012.

Clausewitz, C. V. : *Principles of War,* Minneola, New York, Dover Publication, 2003.

Daniel J.: *Bandits on the Information Superhighway*. O'Reilly & Associates, Inc.: Sebastopol, 1996.

David Post : *The Rise of Law in Cyberspace,* 48 Stan, L. Rev. 1367, 1996.

Dery, Mark. *Escape Velocity: Cyberculture at the End of the Century* . Grove Press, 1997.

Dudeja, V. D. : *Crimes in Cyber Space-Scams and Frauds: Issues and Remedies,* Commonwealth, Delhi, 2003.

Elia Zureik: *Computers, Surveillance, And Privacy*. University of Minnesota Press, 1996

Erbschloe, Michael: *Information Warfare : How to Survive Cyber Attack.* New York: Osborne/ McGraw-Hill, 2001.

Frederick B.: *Protection and Security on the Information Superhighway*. John Wiley & Sons, Inc.: New York, 1995.

Froomkin, Michael : *The Essential Role of Trusted Third Parties in Electronic Commerce,* 75 Ore. L. Rev. 49, 1996.

Gast, A. P. : *The impact of Restricting Information Access on Science and Technology* Retrieved October 1, 2008.

Godwin, Mike: *Cyber Rights: Defending Free Speech in the Digital Age*. Times Books, 1998

Gupta, A., & Laliberte, S. : *Security by Example Defend I.T.* New York, Addison Wesley, 2004.

Hahn, Harley: *Harley Hahn's Internet InSecurity*. Prentice Hall: Upper Saddle River, 2002.

Harish, Chander : *Cyber Laws and It Protection*, PHI Learning, Delhi, 2012.

Hoffman, Bruce: *Inside Terrorism and Internet Crime*, New York: Columbia University Press, 1998.

Joel Moses: *The Computer Age, A Twenty-Year View.*Cambridge, MA, The MIT Press, 1979.

Karanjit Siyan: *Internet Firewalls and Network Security*. New Riders Publishing: Indianapolis, 1996.

Keane J.: *Democracy and Cyber Crimes*, London, Verso, 1988.

Laquer, Walter: *Terrorism Attack from Computer Hacking*, Oxford: Oxford University Press, 1999.

McMahon, David: *Cyber Threat: Internet Security for Home and Business*. Warwick Publishing Inc.: Toronto, 2000.

Nagia, Rajan : *The Transnational Dimension of Cyber Crime and Terrorism*, Cyber Tech, Delhi, 2010.

Peter T.: *Manager's Guide to Internet Security*. CSI: San Francisco, 1994.

Posen, B.R.: *The Sources of Cyber Crime*, Ithaca, 1984, Cornell Univ. Press.

Richard Klau. *Law Law Law on the Internet: The Best Legal Web Sites and More*. Chicago, IL.: American Bar Association, 1998.

Rizvi, Askari : *Nuclear Terrorism and South Asia*, Albuquerque, NM: Sandia National Laboratories, February 2003.

Robert L.: *Software Creativity*, Prentice Hall PTR, 1995.

Rosen, P.: *Policy of Cyber Laws*, Ithaca, Cornell University Press, 1996.

Schroeer, Dietrich: *Science, Technology, and the Cyber Crimes*, Ontario: John Wiley & Sons, 1984.

Scott M.: *Managing IP Networks with Cisco Routers*. O'Reilly & Associates, Inc.: Sebastopol, 1997.

Sharma, Vakul : *Handbook of Cyber Laws*, Macmillan Publishers India, Delhi, 2002.

Singh, Y.K. : *Cyber Crime and Law*, Shree, Delhi, 2005.

Taylor, Paul: *Hackers: Crime in the Digital Sublime* . Routledge, 1999

Uday O. and Vijay K. Gurbani: *Internet & TCP/IP Network Security*. McGraw-Hill: New York, 1996.

Verton, D. : *Black Ice: The invisible Threat of Cyber-terrorism*, New York: McGraw-Hill/Osborne, 2003.

William Aspray: *Computer, A History of the Information Machine*, New York, Basic Books, 1996.

Wilson, C. : *Information Operations and Cyberwar, Capabilities and related Policy Issues*, In C. R. Service, Congressional Research Service, The Library of Congress, 2006.

Zanini, M.: *Countering the New Terrorism*, Santa Monica, CA: RAND, 1999.

Index

I

L

M

N

O

P

S